Intensive Exposure Experiences in Second Language Learning

SECOND LANGUAGE ACQUISITION
Series Editor: Professor David Singleton, *Trinity College, Dublin, Ireland*

This series brings together titles dealing with a variety of aspects of language acquisition and processing in situations where a language or languages other than the native language is involved. Second language is thus interpreted in its broadest possible sense. The volumes included in the series all offer in their different ways, on the one hand, exposition and discussion of empirical findings and, on the other, some degree of theoretical reflection. In this latter connection, no particular theoretical stance is privileged in the series; nor is any relevant perspective – sociolinguistic, psycholinguistic, neurolinguistic, etc. – deemed out of place. The intended readership of the series includes final-year undergraduates working on second language acquisition projects, postgraduate students involved in second language acquisition research, and researchers and teachers in general whose interests include a second language acquisition component.

Full details of all the books in this series and of all our other publications can be found on http://www.multilingual-matters.com, or by writing to Multilingual Matters, St Nicholas House, 31–34 High Street, Bristol BS1 2AW, UK.

Intensive Exposure Experiences in Second Language Learning

Edited by
Carmen Muñoz

MULTILINGUAL MATTERS
Bristol • Buffalo • Toronto

Library of Congress Cataloging in Publication Data
Intensive Exposure Experiences in Second Language Learning/Edited by Carmen Muñoz.
Second Language Acquisition: 65
Includes bibliographical references and index.
1. Immersion method (Language teaching) 2. Language and languages—Study and teaching. 3. Second language acquisition—Study and teaching. 4. Education, Bilingual. I. Muñoz, Carmen.
P53.44.I58 2012
418.0071–dc23 2012022009

British Library Cataloguing in Publication Data
A catalogue entry for this book is available from the British Library.

ISBN-13: 978-1-84769-805-6 (hbk)
ISBN-13: 978-1-84769-804-9 (pbk)

Multilingual Matters
UK: St Nicholas House, 31–34 High Street, Bristol BS1 2AW, UK.
USA: UTP, 2250 Military Road, Tonawanda, NY 14150, USA.
Canada: UTP, 5201 Dufferin Street, North York, Ontario M3H 5T8, Canada.

Copyright © 2012 Carmen Muñoz and the authors of individual chapters.

All rights reserved. No part of this work may be reproduced in any form or by any means without permission in writing from the publisher.

The policy of Multilingual Matters/Channel View Publications is to use papers that are natural, renewable and recyclable products, made from wood grown in sustainable forests. In the manufacturing process of our books, and to further support our policy, preference is given to printers that have FSC and PEFC Chain of Custody certification. The FSC and/or PEFC logos will appear on those books where full certification has been granted to the printer concerned.

Typeset by Techset Composition Ltd., Salisbury, UK.

Contents

Contributors		vii
Acknowledgements		xi
Introduction		xiii

Part 1: Theoretical Underpinnings of Intensive Learning

1. Is Intensive Learning Effective? Reflecting on the Results from Cognitive Psychology and the Second Language Acquisition Literature — *Raquel Serrano* — 3

Part 2: Intensive Instruction

2. Intensive L2 Instruction in Canada: Why not Immersion? — *Patsy M. Lightbown* — 25

3. Closing the Gap: Intensity and Proficiency — *Laura Collins and Joanna White* — 45

4. When Comprehensible Input is not Comprehensive Input: A Multi-dimensional Analysis of Instructional Input in Intensive English as a Foreign Language — *Laura Collins, Joanna White, Pavel Trofimovich, Walcir Cardoso and Marlise Horst* — 66

5. What Language is Promoted in Intensive Programs? Analyzing Language Generated from Oral Assessment Tasks — *Joanna White and Carolyn E. Turner* — 88

6. Time and Amount of L2 Contact Inside and Outside the School – Insights from the European Schools — *Alex Housen* — 111

Part 3: Learners' Perceptions and Intensive Exposure

7 The Significance of Intensive Exposure as a Turning Point in Learners' Histories 141
   Carmen Muñoz

8 Change or Stability in Learners' Perceptions as a Result of Study Abroad 161
   Elsa Tragant

Part 4: Naturalistic Immersion

9 The Impact of Study Abroad and Age on Second Language Accuracy Development 193
   Àngels Llanes

10 Oral and Written Development in Formal Instruction and Study Abroad: Differential Effects of Learning Context 213
   Carmen Pérez-Vidal, Maria Juan-Garau, Joan C. Mora and Margalida Valls-Ferrer

11 Differences in L2 Segmental Perception: The Effects of Age and L2 Learning Experience 234
   Romana Kopečková

Index 256

Contributors

Walcir Cardoso (PhD, McGill University) is an associate professor of applied linguistics at Concordia University (Montreal, Canada). He conducts research on the second language acquisition of phonology, morphosyntax and vocabulary, and the effects of computer technology (e.g. clickers, text-to-speech synthesizers, automatic speech recognition) on L2 learning.

Laura Collins is an associate professor of applied linguistics in the Department of Education at Concordia University in Montreal and co-editor of the Canadian Modern Language Review. Her research interests include the relationship between pedagogical practices and language learning outcomes, cross-linguistic influence and the acquisition of tense and aspect.

Marlise Horst is an associate professor in applied linguistics at Concordia University in Montreal. Her recent research explores second language vocabulary acquisition from a corpus-informed perspective. She is also interested in the effects of instruction designed to raise learners' cross-linguistic language awareness.

Alex Housen (MA, UCLA; PhD, University of Brussels) is professor of English and applied linguistics at the Vrije Universiteit Brussel. His research interests include second language acquisition, (second) language teaching, bilingualism and bilingual education.

Maria Juan-Garau is associate professor in English applied linguistics at the University of the Balearic Islands, Spain. Her research has focused on bilingualism and second language acquisition. She is currently interested in the influence of learning context on the acquisition of English as an additional language, with special attention to content-and-language-integrated learning and study abroad settings.

Romana Kopečková holds a PhD in Applied Linguistics from Trinity College Dublin and has published on age-related differences in second language speech learning. Her current research examines cross-linguistic influence in third or additional language phonological acquisition. She has collaborated on a multi-disciplinary research project 'Second Language Acquisition and Native Language Maintenance in the Polish Diaspora in Ireland and France', funded by the Irish Research Council for the Humanities and Social Sciences.

Patsy Martin Lightbown is Distinguished Professor Emeritus (Applied Linguistics), Concordia University in Montreal, Canada. With Nina Spada, she co-authored *How Languages are Learned* (Oxford University Press), an introduction to second language acquisition research for teachers, now in its fourth edition. For more than 25 years her research focused on language acquisition in Quebec classrooms. She now lives and works in the USA, continuing to work with teachers and teacher trainers through conferences and professional development courses.

Àngels Llanes received her PhD on Applied Linguistics at Universitat de Barcelona and is currently a lecturer at the English and Linguistics Department at Universitat de Lleida, Spain. Her research mostly focuses on the role of age and learning context (study abroad, study at home and summer camps) on L2 development. Her current research interests also include the effects of individual differences, time distribution (intensity), task type, and content and language integrated learning on L2 outcomes.

Joan Carles Mora is a lecturer in English phonetics, language and linguistics in the University of Barcelona, Spain. His current research interests include L2 phonological acquisition, bilingual and L2 speech perception and production, perceptual dimensions of L2 speech, and individual differences in L2 pronunciation development.

Carmen Muñoz is a professor in English and applied linguistics in the Department of English Studies at the University of Barcelona, Spain. Her research interests include the effects of age and input on the acquisition of a foreign language, as well as the role of aptitude and individual differences. A special focus of her recent research is foreign language learning by young learners.

Carmen Pérez-Vidal is an associate professor of English in the Department of Translation and Linguistic Sciences at the Universitat Pompeu Fabra, in Barcelona, Spain. Her research focuses on language progress in different contexts of acquisition, including study abroad and European content and language integrated programmes, bilingualism and the development of oral and written competence.

Raquel Serrano is an assistant professor in the Department of English Studies at the University of Barcelona, Spain. Her research interests include the effect of learning context and time distribution on the acquisition of English as a foreign language, the role of explicit classroom instruction in the acquisition of explicit/implicit knowledge, and bilingualism.

Elsa Tragant holds an MEd in TESOL (Teachers College, Columbia University) and a PhD in English philology at the University of Barcelona, where she is associate professor. She currently teaches English as a foreign language teaching and research methods courses. Her current interests are language learning strategies, L2 motivation and classroom research. She has conducted research both in foreign language and in study abroad contexts.

Pavel Trofimovich is an associate professor of applied linguistics in the Department of Education at Concordia University, in Montreal, Canada. His research focuses on cognitive aspects of second language processing, second language phonology, sociolinguistic aspects of second language acquisition and the teaching of second language pronunciation.

Carolyn E. Turner is associate professor of second language education in the Department of Integrated Studies in Education at McGill University. Her research examines language testing/assessment in educational settings and in healthcare contexts concerning access for linguistic minorities. She is presently Immediate Past President of the International Language Testing Association and Senior Associate Editor of *Language Assessment Quarterly*.

Margalida Valls-Ferrer is a lecturer in the Department of English Studies at the University of Barcelona, Spain. Her research focuses on second language phonology, in particular the acquisition of suprasegmental phenomena by L2 learners, and second language acquisition in different learning contexts.

Joanna White is an associate professor in the Department of Education at Concordia University in Montreal. In her research and in her teaching, she is interested in the relationship among programme design, pedagogical practices and learning outcomes. Specific areas of research include form-focused instruction, the cross-linguistic awareness of teachers and students, oral proficiency development, vocabulary learning and teaching, and programme comparisons.

Acknowledgements

This book is the outcome of intensive cross-fertilizations. It owes its existence to the common interests of colleagues from different research sites, and as such it is a celebration and a meeting point. Above all I am grateful to the inspiring work of all the contributors and their commitment to this collective volume. I would like to especially thank Patsy Lightbown for her contribution, since her pioneer research in intensive classes has been crucial for the present and future of intensive instruction.

I would also like to express my gratitude to the GRAL research group, who provide the daily support and motivation for enjoyment of research, and especially to Àngels Llanes and Raquel Serrano, who were a source of continuous encouragement for this task. Sincere thanks are also due to David Singleton, who gave this project all of his support.

I wish also to express my appreciation for the financial support provided by the Spanish MICINN (through grant FFI2010-21478), the AGAUR (through grant SGR137) and the ICREA Acadèmia programme.

Introduction

The role of intensive exposure to the target language (TL) in second language acquisition has not frequently been addressed as an issue in and of itself. However, intensive exposure is a critical distinctive characteristic in the comparison of the learning processes and outcomes in different learning contexts: naturalistic and foreign language instruction; stay abroad and at home; and extensive and intensive instruction programmes.

Here as elsewhere dichotomous divisions are convenient but simplifying labels. Take the case of foreign language instruction, which encompasses very diverse teaching–learning situations with different degrees of focus on, for example, the explicit learning of grammar rules or the learners' use of the TL in real tasks. The conception of language learning that underlies these choices or the characteristics of the educational system in which teaching takes place will define the amount and type of input to which learners are exposed in a continuum that is also influenced by the use of the TL outside the classroom (in both the immediate surroundings and the community context; see Housen, this volume; Muñoz & Lindgren, 2011). Likewise, learning through immersion in the TL community does not result in homogeneous outcomes, one of the causes being the large differences in opportunities for input and interaction as well as the choices learners make in relation to contact with fellow native speakers of their first language (L1) or native speakers of the second language (L2). In that respect, age of immigration and related socio-psychological factors appear to be determinant factors. On the one hand, the compulsory schooling of younger arrivals and the intense contact with peers that it affords most frequently result in a language dominance switch, from the L1 to the L2. In contrast, older arrivals may be more motivated to maintain their more fully formed linguistic–cultural identity through contact with native speakers of their L1, and are less prone to switching their language dominance (see, among others, Jia & Aaronson, 2003). Another case in point is the very high inter-individual variability in language gains that participants in study abroad programmes present, which seems to be in consonance with learners' orientations towards the TL and TL speakers (e.g. Kinginger, 2008). These orientations may ultimately determine the amount and quality of language contact in which learners engage and their learning outcomes.

Notwithstanding the diversity found across foreign language (FL) teaching situations, traditional classrooms are commonly considered limited in their provision of input and possibilities of contact with the TL (see White & Turner, this volume). One specific consequence of this input limitation is an alleged ceiling effect for learning, which may be assumed to be lower or higher in relation to the relative difficulty of the TL (i.e. its distance from the L1 or the individual's language repertoire). Breaking through this ceiling into the more advanced level proficiencies may be difficult if learners are not provided with immersion learning experiences (Rifkin, 2005). In fact, the perception of a ceiling in their FL progress may push learners to provide themselves with intensive input experiences (see Muñoz, this volume). Another consequence of an input-limited learning setting may be that the time pressure that results from it enhances individual differences, as Collins and White (this volume) suggest.

In contrast, an immersion setting has the potential to provide the large amount of practice that is necessary for language automatization processes to take place, such as the gradual reduction of reaction time or error rate (see Llanes, this volume). In skill theory, declarative knowledge is said to become procedural knowledge through initial practice. This initial practice may be afforded by the classroom, but for procedural knowledge to become automatized, much more input and practice with this input are necessary than a typical classroom offers (DeKeyser, 2007). The large amount of input that is provided by an immersion experience also leads naturally to implicit learning, which is argued to be advantageous for complex structures that are difficult to learn explicitly (e.g. Robinson, 1996). Another type of learning that is facilitated when learners are exposed to massive amounts of input is incidental learning, which may play a major role in lexical learning. This ties in with usage-based theories for which input frequency is the key determinant of language acquisition (e.g. Ellis, 2002).

However, TL improvement during immersion experiences is not homogeneous, as observed above. In addition to the variability in the quality and the quantity of interaction that learners experience, individual internal factors play a significant role. One such factor seems to be initial proficiency level. From the perspective of skill theory, DeKeyser (2007) argues that, to obtain optimal benefits from a stay abroad, students need to be in possession of sufficient procedural knowledge that can then become automatic through practice in the immersion setting. This may explain the apparent continuity effect observed by Pérez-Vidal *et al.* (this volume) that highlights the value of previous FL instruction for students who experience a stay abroad.

The issue of the optimum initial proficiency level for intensive learning experiences has educational relevance for both study abroad programmes and intensive instruction programmes. Serrano (2011, this volume) reports on a study in which learners with lower initial L2 proficiency level benefit more from intensive instruction than students with higher proficiency level. Collins and White (this volume) demonstrate that the amount and concentration of instructional time allow beginner-level learners to make rapid progress over the course of a few months. The relative benefits of intensity for different proficiency levels is one of the questions that further research should answer. A related question is the most effective time distribution (e.g. concentrating all time into a single sustained intensive experience vs a series of spaced intensives) for immediate L2 learning and long-term retention (see Collins & White, 2011; Serrano, this volume).

Whereas this and other important questions have not yet been answered, research findings have accumulated showing the linguistic and attitudinal benefits of intensive instruction, and how it may be a valuable alternative to a 'drip-feed' early start approach (see Lightbown, this volume). Furthermore, research is now revealing some of the limitations of intensive classes, and pointing out the need to pay attention to the occurrence of certain target forms in the input (see Collins *et al.*, this volume). Likewise, research on L2 learning in the European Schools system highlights the importance of form-focused instruction at some stage of schooling to help students acquire the less accessible aspects of the TL and ensure lexical precision and grammatical accuracy (see Housen, this volume).

This Book

The chapters in this volume investigate L2 learning in different contexts with intensive TL exposure: longer- and shorter-term naturalistic immersion (in an immigration or a study-abroad situation), intensive instruction and informal intensive environments in FL settings.

The first chapter, by Raquel Serrano, reflects on the results obtained by different studies on the effect of time distribution on learning and tries to account for the different tendencies suggested by research within the cognitive psychology literature and the second language acquisition literature. In general, time concentration has been shown to be negative for learning and retention in psychology experiments. In contrast, the revision of studies in second language acquisition suggests a certain benefit of concentrating the hours of instruction instead of spreading them over long periods of time. The chapter highlights the difficulties in establishing a comparison between the studies in the two research fields because of methodological differences and differences in the type of learning under examination.

The next four chapters look at intensive programmes in Quebec from different and complementary angles. Intensive classes in Quebec have become a privileged setting for classroom research on L2 learning because – as Laura Collins and her colleagues note in the introduction of Chapter 4 – in the space of a few months the progress made in language development is substantial, the reason being directly related to the time on the task, including both its distribution and its quality. In Chapter 2 Patsy Lightbown, a key contributor to research in intensive instruction, sets the ground for the following three chapters. She begins by relating the origins of intensive English instruction in the 1970s to the success of French immersion programmes, which inspired the efforts of French-speaking parents in Quebec to look for ways to help their children learn English. She describes the characteristics of the two approaches, remarking that the major difference between them was that immersion included content-based instruction while intensive English focused on the teaching of the language itself. She goes on to relate how the latter also met with success and, as a result, the intensive approach was adapted for the teaching of French in other Canadian provinces in the 1990s. In addition to describing and comparing Canadian approaches to teaching English and French intensively and through immersion, the chapter discusses the potential for applications of these approaches outside of Canada.

In the next chapter, Laura Collins and Joanna White examine the effects of intensive instruction on different aspects of proficiency over time. The research question of this longitudinal study was whether the differences in L2 knowledge at the outset would be maintained throughout the intensive experience, or whether the removal of the time-pressure factor, which characterizes drip-feed access, would enable the lower proficiency students to catch up to their peers. The results showed that, midway through their intensive programme, the lower-level students were already closing the gap, and by the end they demonstrated similar levels of knowledge of English on many of the tasks. The findings suggest that intensive L2 instruction may mitigate the role of individual factors (such as aptitude) on classroom learning at beginner level.

Whereas Chapter 3 shows the benefits of intensive instruction, Chapter 4 shows some of its limitations. In this chapter, Laura Collins, Joanna White, Pavel Trofimovich, Walcir Cardoso and Marlise Horst examine the distribution and the characteristics of two forms known to present learning challenges for francophone students of English: the simple past and the possessive determiners *his/her*. The analysis of a corpus consisting of transcriptions of video recordings of three teachers' input to 11- to 12-year-old francophone learners at four intervals of 400 hours shows that the target forms are rare in the aural input, occur in restricted lexical contexts and have low perceptual salience. A qualitative analysis of the pedagogical input reveals that text-based input and events that include the teachers as participants provide richer exposure to the target forms. In sum, the study signals that intensity alone is not sufficient and highlights the need for attention to target forms in the input that are challenging for second language learners.

The next chapter, by Joanna White and Carolyn E. Turner, looks at the nature of the language promoted in intensive programmes, specifically language generated from oral assessment tasks. The study forms part of the Oral Proficiency Project that was planned to build a profile of the oral proficiency of students at the end of five months of intensive exposure, as well as to compare the oral performance ability of students in intensive English as a Second Language with that of students in regular English as a Second Language programmes at the end of elementary school. The chapter discusses the two-phase explanatory sequential mixed methods design of the study. It begins by reporting the results of the first, quantitative phase, which showed that the gain scores for students in grade 6 in intensive classes were significantly greater than for those in regular classes at the end of the year. It then goes on to present the qualitative phase results with a wealth of discourse examples from three oral tasks performed by students in intensive and regular classes.

Chapter 6, by Alex Housen, focuses on a different instructed learning context, that of the European Schools, which also provides higher intensity of exposure to the target language than typical FL instruction settings. The two empirical studies that are presented focus on how the outcomes of the L2 learning process, in the various contexts within the European Schools system and by various groups of European Schools pupils, are affected by the interplay between curricular factors and contextual, extracurricular factors. The results suggest that pupils in these multilingual schools reach global levels of L2 proficiency that are comparable to those attained in other models of bilingual education, although they also highlight an extensive range of variation in rate and outcomes that seems to depend on factors such as L1 background and the status and availability of the TL both within the schools and in their wider context.

The next two chapters provide the reader with analyses of learners' perceptions in relation to intensive exposure experiences. Chapter 7, by Carmen Muñoz, explores the significance that intensive exposure experiences have for learners through the analysis of their responses to a question in an oral interview concerning a turning point in their learning trajectory. The analysis reveals that in most cases turning points are identified in intensive exposure settings, especially in stays abroad but also at home, both in formal settings and in informal immersion environments created by learners themselves. The chapter also analyses the themes that emerge in participants' responses: agency, practice, language improvement and linguistic assimilation are illustrated with learners' accounts and linked to the different contexts in which they appear more frequently. These qualitative findings complement previous results that showed the significance of input for instructed learners in a quantitative manner, specifically through significant correlations between a number of input measures and language test scores.

In the next chapter, Elsa Tragant examines learners' perceptions in order to investigate the impact of an intensive experience abroad as reported by students in an Erasmus exchange programme. Her study focuses on the changes in learners' perceptions concerning their beliefs about the L2 and themselves as language learners, their attitudes towards L2 speakers and orientations towards L2 learning, as well as their linguistic and non-linguistic development. Data were collected through questionnaires, field notes and a research log. Results show that students are able to perceive some type of linguistic development and that they experience some interpersonal, intrapersonal and intercultural development over time. The discussion considers the conditions that might bring about more changes in participants' perceptions over a stay abroad, and suggests that the intensity of the experience seems to be a central mediator of students' self-development.

The next two chapters investigate learners' language gains by means of study abroad (SA) experiences and compare them with gains obtained in instructed language learning settings or at home (AH). In Chapter 9 Àngels Llanes sets out to determine to what extent learning context (SA and AH) and age (children and adults) affect L2 oral and written accuracy as measured by type and frequency of errors. Following a pre/post- design, the analysis shows that the SA context is more effective than the AH context, which can be explained by the role of input and interaction. The analysis also reveals that adults experienced significantly greater gains than children in absolute terms, but that SA children experienced greater significant gains than SA adults when these groups were compared with the AH groups. A third finding is that the SA context helps learners to reduce lexical errors more than other types of errors, whereas the AH context does not seem to benefit the reduction of any specific type of error. The study suggests that the intensity and quality of input and the type of learning mechanisms employed could be mediated by participants' age and learning context.

The next chapter, by Carmen Pérez-Vidal, Maria Juan-Garau, Joan C. Mora and Margalida Valls-Ferrer, focuses on linguistic progress in both written and oral skills as a differential effect of practice in two learning contexts, an SA and a foreign instruction context. The study follows a group of L2 learners over the span of 14 months, encompassing an SA context of acquisition preceded by a foreign instruction context. The analysis shows that the SA context seems to have a higher impact on both oral and written skills than the foreign instruction context. The results also show that in both learning contexts progress is steady in the domain of accuracy, but that fluency and complexity differ, with oral lexical complexity improving at home and written lexical complexity abroad. These findings seem to suggest that the two learning contexts complement each other, and/or that there can be knowledge transfer from one learning context to another.

In the last chapter, Romana Kopečková sets out to evaluate the role of cross-language phonetic similarity perception and L2 experience on L2 perception abilities of child, teenage and adult L2 learners. The results indicate that the interaction between the L1 and L2 sound systems at the time of L2 acquisition may create at least one source of differences in L2 speech learning between age groups. The results also show that a three-year-long naturalistic experience of learning the TL benefits all learners in terms of their L2 perceptual abilities, although child and teenage naturalistic L2 learners seem to be advantaged in a qualitatively different manner. The chapter remarks that it may not be possible to disentangle the relative strength of the influence of each of these factors on L2 speech learning, owing to the fact that age is a macro-variable associated with a number of other underlying variables, one of the most prominent ones being phonetically relevant L2 input.

The book is addressed to applied linguists, second language researchers, academics and graduate university students majoring in second language studies, psycholinguistics and/or bilingualism. It is also for the use of teachers, language teacher educators and language education policy-makers; hopefully the book will engage them in searching for innovative ways to increase the quantity and quality of learners' input.

References

Collins, L. and White, J. (2011) An intensive look at intensity and language learning. *TESOL Quarterly* 45, 106–133.

DeKeyser, R. (2007) Study abroad as foreign language practice. In R. DeKeyser (ed.) *Practice in a Second Language: Perspectives from Applied Linguistics and Cognitive Psychology* (pp. 208–226). New York: Cambridge University Press.

Ellis, N. (2002) Frequency effects in language acquisition: A review with implications for theories of implicit and explicit language acquisition. *Studies in Second Language Acquisition* 24, 143–188.

Jia, G. and Aaronson, D. (2003) A longitudinal study of Chinese children and adolescents learning English in the United States. *Applied Psycholinguistics* 24, 131–161.

Kinginger, C. (2008) *Language Learning in Study Abroad: Case Histories of Americans in France*. Modern Language Journal Monograph Series, 1.

Muñoz, C. and Lindgren, E. (2011) Out-of-school factors – the home. In J. Enever (ed.) *ELLiE, Early Language Learning in Europe* (pp. 103–122). London: British Council.

Rifkin, B. (2005) A ceiling effect in traditional classroom foreign language instruction: Data from Russian. *The Modern Language Journal* 89 (1), 3–18.

Robinson, P. (1996) Learning simple and complex second language rules under implicit, incidental, rule-search, and instructed conditions. *Studies in Second Language Acquisition* 18 (1), 27–67.

Serrano, R. (2011) The time factor in EFL classroom practice. *Language Learning* 61, 117–143.

Part 1
Theoretical Underpinnings of Intensive Learning

1 Is Intensive Learning Effective? Reflecting on the Results from Cognitive Psychology and the Second Language Acquisition Literature

Raquel Serrano

The Spacing Effect in the Cognitive Psychology Literature

Introduction

The main objective of this chapter is to consider the effect of time distribution of instructional hours on second language learning. In order to understand this effect better it is crucial to know how time distribution affects learning in general. That is why a brief review of some of the most relevant articles in the cognitive psychology literature will be presented. Cognitive psychologists have demonstrated that spacing the time devoted to learning is more beneficial than concentrating it in short periods of time. This phenomenon is known as the spacing effect. In contrast, in the second language acquisition literature, intensive (or concentrated) courses have been shown to be highly effective for students' language development. This chapter shows that the apparently contradictory results can be explained if we consider the characteristics of the experiments in cognitive psychology discussed in this section. Additionally, some accounts of the spacing effect (especially the 'study-phase retrieval'), or the fact that the spacing effect often disappears at short retention intervals (see below), can easily explain the findings from the second language acquisition literature.

In the cognitive psychology literature it has been demonstrated that repeated practice strengthens the memory representation of an item or structure (Pavlik & Anderson, 2005). Similarly, a large amount of empirical evidence suggests that an item is better recalled and learned when it is repeated in spaced sequences (with other intervening items or long time lapses between the repetitions) than in massed presentations, in which repetitions appear subsequently or within short time lapses. This phenomenon is well known in the literature as the *spacing effect*. As explained in the following paragraphs, the spacing effect has been found mostly in verbal learning (involving words in the participants' first language, non-words and foreign language words), but experiments have also been conducted that examine the effect of time distribution on learning to solve mathematical problems, recognizing faces or identifying advertisements.

Spacing effect in verbal learning

Verbal learning tasks are probably the most common tasks used in studies investigating the spacing effect (Delaney & Knowles, 2005; Dempster, 1988; Elmes *et al.*, 1983; Greene, 1989; Ross & Landauer, 1978; Seabrook *et al.*, 2005; Toppino *et al.*, 2002). Participants see lists of words on a computer screen that they have to recall (either in cued-memory tasks, for which retrieval cues are provided, or in free recall tasks) in one or several tests at different time intervals. For example, Greene (1989) included a list of 96 common words, the repetitions of which appeared separated by 0, 1, 2, 4, 8 or 16 intervening words. The spacing effect was significant in both free- and cued-recall tasks.

Toppino *et al.* (2002) examined recall of items that belonged to three different sets: words that were presented once; words that were repeated three times in massed repetitions (one presentation after the other); and words that were repeated in spaced sequences (separated by three or four intervening words). As in the previous case, spaced items were recalled significantly more accurately than massed items. Significant differences were also obtained between items presented once and repeated items in favor of the latter.

Spacing effect in foreign language vocabulary learning

Experiments analyzing foreign language vocabulary learning (Bahrick, 1979; Bahrick & Phelps, 1987; Bloom & Shuell, 1981; Pavlik & Anderson, 2005; Rohrer & Pashler, 2007) tend to suggest that spacing training sessions is beneficial for long-term retention, even though immediate recall tends to be comparable for spaced and massed items. Bloom and Shuell (1981) performed a classroom experiment including 28 high-school students who received distributed foreign vocabulary practice (one 1 minute unit a day on three successive days) and 28 who received massed practice (three 10 minute units on one day). An immediate test demonstrated that the performance of the two groups was identical; however, a delayed post-test four days later showed that the distributed practice led to significantly better retention.

Pavlik and Anderson (2005) included 104 Japanese–English pairs that were presented to a group of 40 participants, who were then tested with 2, 14 or 98 intervening presentations in one session. Retention was then examined after one day ($N = 20$) or seven days ($N = 20$). The results show that, in the first session, the greater the spacing between presentation and trial, the worse participants' performance was. Nevertheless, in session 2 (after seven days), wider spacing resulted in less forgetting (as reflected in the performance in the initial trial in session 2 as compared with the final trial in session 1). Regarding the two retention intervals considered, participants forgot less at the one-day retention interval than at the seven-day interval.

Bahrick and Hall (2005) analyzed the learning of 40 Swahili–English word-pairs by 41 undergraduate students who followed four training sessions under different schedules: massed (all sessions in one day); one-day between-session interval; and 14-day between-session interval. The participants were tested at the end of each session and 14 days after the last session (session 5). The results of the analyses show that the participants performed similarly at the end of the first session; however, in sessions 2–4 the massed group and the one-day group performed significantly better than the participants assigned to the 14-day interval, suggesting forgetting between training sessions for the more spaced schedule. Nevertheless, when all participants were tested 14 days after their last session, it was found that both the one-day interval and the 14-day interval group significantly outperformed the massed group, indicating that massed practice is detrimental to long-term retention.

Other experiments examining the spacing effect: Solving problems, face recognition and identification of advertisements

Even though most experiments examining the spacing effect deal with word learning, others have analyzed different practice schedules for teaching participants to solve mathematical problems. Rohrer and Taylor (2006) report on an experiment in which 116 undergraduate students were taught how to solve a specific type of mathematical problem under two schedules: massed (10 problems in one day) and distributed (5 problems/day with a seven-day interval). Retention was examined after one week and after four weeks. The results of the analyses show that there was no difference in the performance of students undergoing massed and distributed practice after one week; however, those following a spaced schedule scored significantly higher at a four-week retention interval.

Mammarella *et al.* (2002) examined face recognition, considering the lags between repetitions (zero, two and four intervening items) of 84 unfamiliar faces. Eighteen students were shown 84 faces and 84 'non-faces' (manipulated faces with, for example, only two eyes in the middle of the face and no nose or mouth) for 4 seconds. Participants had to decide whether the picture they saw on their computer screen was a face or a non-face. As expected, participants were faster when the repetitions occurred at shorter lags. After this task, participants underwent an unexpected recognition memory task in which they had to decide whether the faces they saw (only real faces were considered) had been included in the previous task. In this case, the faces that had been presented in spaced sequences were recalled better than those in massed sequences. Another variable that was examined in this study was pose: sometimes the same faces were presented in a different pose during the study session. An interesting finding of the study was that the spacing effect disappeared when different poses were presented.

Appleton-Knapp *et al.* (2005) examined how spacing and repetition type among other factors affected the identification of printed advertisements. In one of the experiments included in their study, 74 undergraduates were exposed to 48 different advertisement sequences in two 12-page booklets. The adverts were repeated after zero, two or four intervening advertisements. Some repetitions were exact, while others were modified. Participants had 10 seconds to study each advertisement and then performed a cued-recall test. The results show that spaced items were more accurately recalled than massed. Nevertheless, there was an interaction effect between type of repetition and spacing, indicating that at short retention intervals modified repetitions helped retrieval, while at longer lags, exact repetitions were better remembered.

Summary

In general, then, most experiments in the cognitive psychology literature demonstrate that, when subsequent presentations of the same item appear either (1) among other intervening items or (2) in widely-spaced sessions, the item is more easily remembered in test trials (immediate, and especially delayed) than an item repeated in a massed schedule (in which repetitions appear subsequently or with few intervening items, or in sessions with short intervals). The spacing considered in previous experiments can range from a few seconds or minutes when the presentation and testing take place in a single session (Appleton-Knapp *et al.*, 2005; Greene, 1989; Mammarella *et al.*, 2002; Toppino *et al.*, 2002), to days or weeks in the case of experiments that include several training sessions (Bahrick, 1979; Bahrick & Hall, 2005; Bloom & Shuell, 1981; Rohrer & Taylor, 2006). It should be noted that there is no objective characterization of how many intervening items should appear for a sequence to be considered spaced or massed, nor is there a specific session interval that would make learning massed or distributed. In general, comparisons are established between different time distributions, some being more concentrated than others. Generally, the more spaced the intervals between repetitions of the same item or between learning sessions, the more accurately participants tend to remember what they have learned.

The spacing effect is one of the most robust effects found in the cognitive psychology literature (Demptser, 1988). The following verse by the psychologist Ulric Neisser, quoted by Bjork (1988), is highly illustrative in terms of the belief about the superiority of distributed over massed practice:

You can get a good deal from rehearsal
If it just has the proper dispersal.
You would just be an ass
To do it *en masse*:
your remembering would turn out much worsal.[1]

Why is learning enhanced when repetitions occur in spaced or distributed intervals rather than in massed sequences?

Proposed answers to this question fall into the following groups: (1) encoding variability theories; (2) deficient-processing theories; and (3) study-phase retrieval accounts. Lately, though, many researchers have used a combination of different theories to account for the spacing effect (Raaijmakers, 2003; Riches *et al.*, 2005; Russo & Mammarella, 2002; Verkoeijen *et al.*, 2005). Moreover, some mathematical models have been proposed to account for the spacing effect, such as those provided by Raaijmakers (2003) or Pavlik and Anderson (2005).

Encoding variability theories

According to encoding variability theories, the more spaced two items are, the more likely it is that they will be encoded differently in the participant's mind (Glenberg, 1979; Melton, 1970; Johnston & Uhl, 1976). This variability in memory representation, which is facilitated by the different contexts in which spaced items appear, provides more retrieval cues. Consequently, remembering is favored in spaced distributions more so than in massed, for which the context of the first and the second presentation is the same, encouraging a similar encoding.

Deficient processing theories

Deficient processing theories suggest that the reason spaced items are better recalled than massed is that they are more deeply processed. When participants are exposed to two items simultaneously or within a short period of time, they do not devote as much attention to these items as when they are presented with sufficient spacing. When the memory trace is too accessible, processing is deficient and so is learning (Challis, 1993; Greeno, 1970; Hintzman, 1976; Jacoby, 1978). In the words of Cuddy and Jacoby's (1982: 465), 'If the trace of a prior presentation is too readily accessible when an item is repeated, few of the operations originally required to encode that item will be repeated and the result will be an impoverished trace of the later presentation'.

In spaced sequences, the first presentation (P1) is not easily accessible at the time of the second presentation (P2), and full processing of P2 is thus necessary (Cuddy & Jacoby, 1982; Dellarosa & Bourne, 1985; Dempster, 1988; Glover & Corkill, 1987; Jacoby, 1978). This processing facilitates learning and retention. In the case of massed presentations, P1 is too accessible when P2 appears; as a consequence, less processing is involved (and also less attention on the participant's part), which explains why massed items are not as efficiently recalled.

Apart from spacing, there are other factors that can hinder accessibility and will thus encourage processing. One is paraphrased rather than verbatim repetitions in massed presentations. Glover and Corkill (1987) report that the remembering of brief lectures in massed paraphrased repetitions is much better than in massed verbatim repetitions. Moreover, massed paraphrased repetitions can be remembered equally as well as spaced paraphrased repetitions.

Another study that supports this effect is that of Mammarella *et al.* (2002), reported in the previous section. When faces were presented in different poses, the spacing effect disappeared, suggesting that making P1 less accessible at the time of P2 in massed presentations can reduce the spacing effect. Similar results were obtained in their Experiment 5, which included 96 non-words repeated twice at lag 0 or 6 in the same or different font: there was a large spacing effect when the non-words were repeated in the same font. Additionally, for spaced items, there was no difference between non-words presented in the same or different font. Nevertheless, for massed presentations this difference was significant, favoring non-words in different fonts.

In conclusion, as Dellarosa and Bourne (1985: 533) suggest, 'Anything that increases the probability of a repetition receiving full processing, or conversely, anything that decreases the probability of the item being recognized as a repetition, should improve memorability of the item'. Conversely, when accessibility of P1 is not simply hindered but made impossible owing to very long lags between P1 and P2, contrary effects can be obtained. If the trace of P1 is no longer in the participant's memory, P2 will not be able to strengthen that trace (Verkoeijen *et al.*, 2005) and the repeated presentations may simply count as two separate items.

Apart from the accessibility of P1 at the time of P2, another factor that influences the spacing effect is the complexity of the to-be-learned material. In their meta-analysis of studies on the effect of time distribution, Donovan and Radosevich (1999) observed that the spacing effect is less common in complex tasks than in simple tasks.

Study-phase retrieval theories

According to study-phase retrieval theories, retrieving P1 at the time of P2 determines recall (Appleton *et al.*, 2005; Russo *et al.*, 2002; Thios & D'Agostino, 1976; Toppino & Bloom, 2002; Toppino *et al.*, 2002). Some studies have demonstrated empirically that, when participants are asked to retrieve P1 when P2 appears, they recall the item more accurately than when they are simply presented with the items without any need for retrieval (Thios & D'Agostino, 1976).

According to Toppino and Bloom (2002: 443), 'The point of maximum performance would be expected to occur at higher or lower levels of spacing depending on whether conditions were more or less favorable for successful study-phase retrieval'. Similarly, Bahrick and Phelps (1987: 349) claim that 'The optimum interval is likely to be the longest interval that avoids retrieval failures'.

Verkoeijen *et al.* (2005) combine study-phase retrieval accounts of the spacing effect with contextual variability accounts. These authors suggest that spacing is beneficial because the contextual change between P1 and P2 provides more retrieval cues, following contextual variability theories. However, according to study-phase retrieval, P1 must be retrieved at the time of P2: if the spacing between the two is too large, such retrieval might be impossible, and as a consequence such wide spacing would not be beneficial for later recall. Verkoeijen *et al.* (2005) suggest that spacing the presentations of two items will initially improve memory, until P1 and P2 are so widely spaced that P1 is not retrieved at P2.

These three theories provide different explanations for the spacing effect; nevertheless, they do not offer clear accounts as to why the spacing effect is not so obvious at short retention intervals (as reported, for example, in the studies by Bahrick and Hall, 2005 or Rohrer and Taylor, 2006 reviewed above). The next section aims to provide an answer to that question. The topic of retention intervals will be very relevant later on in the discussion of the second language acquisition literature.

Why does the spacing effect often disappear at short retention intervals?

One commonly reported finding related to the spacing effect is that, while distributed items are recalled better at long retention intervals, this advantage is not often apparent at immediate testing (Bahrick & Hall, 2005; Bloom & Shuell, 1981; Pavlik & Anderson, 2005; Rohrer & Taylor, 2006). According to Pavlik (2005) and Pavlik and Anderson (2005), massed items are recalled better at immediate testing because the presentations are temporarily increased in activation owing to recency effects. However, since those items are not encoded in long-term memory (the activation of P1 is too high when P2 occurs, which prevents long-term encoding), they are not recalled as well when the retention interval increases. This contrasts with spaced items, the learning of which is slower but long-lasting.

The determining effect of the intersession interval (ISI) – which is the time between the learning sessions – and the retention interval (RI) – which refers to the time between the last learning session and the testing session – on the results of spacing effect experiments is emphasized by Rohrer and Pashler (2007). These authors suggest that there is an interaction between intersession and retention intervals. Depending on how massed or spaced the learning sessions have been, there will be an optimal retention interval. To support their claim, Rohrer and Pashler (2007) report on two studies that had different optimal ISIs depending on the RI. In one study (Swahili–English word pairs), the ISIs varied from 5 minutes to 14 days, and the one-day ISI was found to be the most favorable considering an RI of 10 days. The second study (learning names for objects) considered an RI of six months and found that the one-month ISI was the one leading to the best recall among the several ISIs analyzed, ranging from 5 minutes to six months. These studies show that it is not always the case that more spaced sessions lead to more retention, but it greatly depends on when learning is tested.

Summary: The spacing effect in cognitive psychology

In summary, according to the studies reported in this brief review of the literature on the spacing effect, learning in spaced or distributed sequences is in general more effective than concentrating such learning in massed presentations. Several explanations have been proposed within the cognitive psychology field for this finding, some emphasizing the fact that more diverse contexts in the case of spaced items help retrieval. Other explanations focus on the fact that, in massed sequences, there is less processing of the items because the repetitions are too close. Nevertheless, it must be emphasized that more spacing is not necessarily better under all circumstances, and that there is a limit to the effectiveness of spacing between repetitions. Some factors that also interact with time distribution are the following: (1) paraphrased vs verbatim repetitions (lack of spacing effects in the case of the former); (2) complexity of the material (spacing effects minimized for more complex items and structures); (3) possibility of retrieval of the first presentation (when spacing is too wide, retrieval of P1 is not possible and thus massed distributions are comparably more beneficial for learning); and (4) the retention interval (sometimes at short retention intervals, massed items are better recalled).

Time Distribution and Language Learning

Repetitions and frequent exposure to linguistic items or structures are crucial to second language acquisition (and first language acquisition), especially for the automatization of language skills (Ellis, 2002; DeKeyser, 2007; Segalowitz, 2010; Segalowitz & Hulstijn, 2005). What is not so clear is whether this 'input repetition' (Segalowitz, 2010) should ideally be spaced or concentrated. In this section, some of the literature analyzing time distribution in language learning will be reviewed. First, key experimental studies that follow the cognitive psychology framework will be presented. Then, a sample of studies on time distribution in second language (L2) acquisition will be reviewed and analyzed. As will be seen, this second set of studies cannot be considered experimental but rather exploratory.

Experimental studies

First language acquisition

Although most studies on the spacing effect include adult participants learning lists of words, some researchers have used this framework to analyze first language acquisition of vocabulary (Childers & Tomasello, 2002) and grammar (Ambridge et al., 2006). Childers and Tomasello (2002) examined how 36 two-year-olds learned new vocabulary under different schedules. Some of these schedules were considered massed: Massed 4 (four exposures in one day) and Massed 8 (eight exposures in one day). Within the spaced schedule, two different types were examined: Widely Spaced (one exposure per day during four days; three-day interval) and Spaced (one exposure per day; four consecutive days). Other schedules were considered a compromise between massed and spaced: Clumped 4 (two exposures on one day, two exposures on another day; three-day interval) and Clumped 8 (two exposures on one day, four exposures on one day, two exposures on one day; three-day interval). The results of this study reveal significant differences between the massed and the spaced conditions in favor of the latter, even in cases in which there were fewer repetitions (four repetitions on different days led to better recall than eight repetitions on one day).

Ambridge et al. (2006) analyzed the acquisition of the past tense object-cleft construction in English (*It was the [OBJECT] that the [SUBJECT] [VERBed]* as in *It was the cup that the frog took*). The participants in this study included 36 children aged 3:6–4:6 and 36 children aged 4:10–5:10. Different schedules were considered: Massed (10 trials in one session), Distributed-Pairs Condition (two trials/day; five consecutive days) and Distributed (one trial/day; 10 days). The results suggest that the children learned the target construction more effectively in the two distributed conditions than in the massed condition. Consequently, the results of these experiments examining first language acquisition are in line with those previously analyzed regarding the spacing effect in the cognitive psychology literature.

Second language acquisition

In terms of second language acquisition, Bird (2010) also used the cognitive psychology framework to analyze whether longer intervals between learning sessions would help learning and retention of tense contrasts in English as an L2. The author considered two groups of adult participants ($N = 19$ each), who were taught the difference in use between simple past and present perfect (contrast 1), and present perfect and past perfect (contrast 2). They all had five 30-minute sessions, with ISIs of three days (massed) or 15 days (distributed) for each of the contrasts: one group had short ISI for contrast 1 and long ISI for contrast 2, while the other group had short ISI for contrast 2 and long ISI for contrast 1. Learning was checked at RIs of seven and 60 days through two grammaticality judgment tests. All the students (regardless of the ISIs they were assigned) showed a significant improvement from the pretest to the seven-day retention test, with no difference between the massed and the distributed groups. At the 60-day retention test, though, the participants in the distributed group were significantly more advanced: they performed similarly at both RIs, whereas the massed learners performed significantly worse after 60 days.

The studies reviewed in this section can be considered experimental, even if some took place in classroom contexts. There is a focus on particular words or particular structures, and not on skill acquisition. In the next section, various studies will be reviewed that analyze the development of general language proficiency with a prominent focus on skills rather than items.

Time distribution and second language acquisition: Contrasting L2 program types

In the second language acquisition (SLA) field there are several research studies that have examined the effect of time distribution on language learning by examining language gains in different program types, some of them offering concentrated L2 instruction (intensive courses) and others more spaced or distributed scheduling (regular L2 classes). This research consists of classroom-based exploratory studies, which contrast with the more controlled experimental settings from the cognitive psychology literature. The first set of studies that will be reviewed refers to the Canadian context (intensive English for French-speaking children) and the second concerns adults (Spanish–Catalan bilingual learners of English). At the end of this section, the findings from all of these studies will be discussed.

Intensive English in Canada

The context in which most research has been conducted on intensity in language learning is Quebec, Canada, where intensive English courses have been promoted as a preferable alternative to regular 'drip-feed' (Stern, 1985) courses for francophone children. These 'drip-feed' courses (1–2 hours of instruction through elementary school and 2.5 hours in secondary school) have not succeeded in promoting high levels of L2 proficiency in Canada

(Spada & Lightbown, 1989) or in other contexts in which students learn English over long periods of time (starting when they are 5 or even younger until they are 18): English proficiency after school is below expectations (see also Muñoz, 2006). Intensive English in Quebec has increased in popularity since it was first introduced in the 1980s owing to its success, although the regular limited exposure program is still the most common. The popularity of intensive English in this context has also had an impact on the teaching of French in other Canadian provinces, where intensive French programs are now being offered as an alternative to French immersion (Germain & Netten, 2005; Netten & Germain, 2004). Intensive English courses are typically offered in grade 5 or 6 and consist of approximately 400 hours of language instruction (not content), which can be distributed over one academic year (8 hours/week), over one semester (18–20 hours/week) or through a series of 'mini-intensives' across the 10-month school year (see review of Collins & White, 2011 below). The research in intensive English has reported highly positive results, both for language learning itself and for attitudes and motivation towards language learning.

Spada and Lightbown (1989) conducted a large-scale study including approximately 1000 learners, which was one of the first to examine the effect of intensive English instruction in Quebec. The authors compared students in grade 5 and 6 taking intensive English classes in eight different school boards with, on the one hand, students in the same grade receiving regular instruction and, on the other hand, students who had received a similar number of hours of instruction but were older (grade 11). The performance of the students in intensive English was significantly more advanced than that of the learners in the other two groups in all language tests. Moreover, after receiving intensive instruction, the students were more motivated to learn English and practice it outside of class.

White and Turner (2005) compared the oral production skills of students receiving regular instruction ($N = 73$) and intensive instruction ($N = 79$) through a series of tasks (Audio-Pal, Info-Gap and Story Retell). The results of the statistical analyses of the students' performance in all three tasks suggest a significant advantage for the students in the intensive course.

Although the study by White and Turner (2005) was necessary in the Canadian context to show how effective intensive English was, these researchers did not aim to isolate the role of time concentration alone, as there was also time increase in the case of the intensive program. Collins *et al.* (1999) and Collins and White (2011) focused more on the role of time distribution and examined the performance of learners in intensive English only. These studies compared different types of intensive programs that offered roughly the same number of hours. It is important that total time across programs is held constant when the goal is to investigate the effect of time distribution on L2 learning.

Collins et al. (1999) examined three types of intensive English programs, which included around 400 hours of English instruction spread over 10 months (*distributed*, $N = 236$), five months (*massed*, $N = 324$), or five months plus out-of-class exposure (*massed plus*, $N = 149$). In order to compare students' performance across programs, three different types of instruments were used: a yes/no vocabulary recognition test; a test developed by the MEQ emphasizing listening comprehension (and some reading); and a written narrative. The results of the statistical analyses showed some significant advantages in favor of the learners in the two massed programs (and especially in the massed plus program). However, there were two intervening variables that made it difficult to have a clear picture of the relative benefits of the different distributions of intensive time. Owing to the way the school year was organized, students in the massed programs ended up with more total hours of instruction (approximately 100 hours more). Moreover, in the massed program the enrollment criteria were stricter than in the other two programs; consequently, the student population in the three programs might not have been entirely comparable.

The role of time distribution in intensive English courses was further examined by Collins and White (2011). Two different intensive programs (400 hours of instruction) were analyzed: *concentrated* ($N = 137$) and *distributed* ($N = 107$). In the former, which is equivalent to the *massed* program in Collins et al. (1999), the students received concentrated English instruction in the second semester after having completed their French curriculum in the first semester. In the distributed program, the 400 hours of instruction were distributed over the whole academic year in the form of 'mini-intensives': the students received blocks of full days of English alternating with blocks of full days of French. The authors were interested in the effect of time distribution after different numbers of hours of instruction, since most research in intensity tends to look at end-of-program results only, and not progress across time. The instructional time intervals were 100 hours (Time 1), 200 hours (Time 2), 300 hours (Time 3) and 400 hours (Time 4). Additionally, a pretest was included to control for initial proficiency (for more details on the design of this study see Collins & White, this volume). The results of the statistical analyses comparing the two types of programs (concentrated vs distributed) showed comparable performance across most of the measures over time, with any differences observed in favor of learners in the more concentrated program.

Collins and White (2011) suggest that these results do not necessarily mean that concentrating all the hours of intensive English in one semester is more effective than distributing them in 'mini-intensives'. First of all, the effect sizes of group differences tended to be small. Moreover, certain differences in the teaching approach used in the two program types could explain some results. Finally, during Time 4 the students in the distributed program were busy preparing for their French exams, which the students in the concentrated program had already taken in the first semester. After considering all these factors, Collins and White (2011) claim that both program types are effective models to promote the learning of English.

Intensive English for adults

In the case of adult learners, Serrano and Muñoz (2007) and Serrano (2011) analyzed the English language development of Spanish–Catalan bilinguals in different program types in Barcelona, Spain. Serrano and Muñoz (2007) compared the linguistic gains demonstrated by a total of 76 learners in three different types of programs that offered the same number of hours of English instruction (110). The *extensive* program ($N = 22$) offered 4 hours/week, the *semi-intensive* ($N = 33$) offered 10 hours/week, and the *intensive* ($N = 21$) consisted of 25 hours/week of English instruction. The learners performed a pretest towards the beginning of the course and a post-test towards the end that included the same tasks: listening comprehension, sentence conversion, cloze and reading comprehension. The results of the between-groups statistical analyses comparing the three program types found no statistically significant differences. Nevertheless, when within-group comparisons were performed, it was observed that learners in the two intensive programs made significant gains in all tasks, while those in the extensive course did so only in the cloze test. The authors interpret this finding as a positive effect of time concentration for L2 learning.

Serrano (2011) compared learners of different proficiency levels in *regular* (110 hours/10 months; 4 hours/week) and *intensive* courses (110 hours/month; 25 hours/week). In this study there were 87 participants at the intermediate proficiency level (49 regular; 38 intensive) and 65 at the advanced (34 regular; 31 intensive). The design was pretest/post-test and included the same tasks at both times: an achievement test, an oral narrative and a written descriptive essay. The results of the statistical analyses indicate that, for learners at the intermediate proficiency level, time concentration seemed to be advantageous. At the advanced level, however, no differences were registered between the learners in the two program types. These results were interpreted as evidence of a positive effect of concentrating L2 instruction at the intermediate level.

General findings regarding intensive L2 learning

As shown here, most studies in the SLA literature examine learning at the end of the different program types and do not generally include longitudinal measures taken throughout the intensive experience or retention intervals between learning and testing. One of the few studies analyzing the long-term effects of intensive instruction is Lightbown and Spada (1991). The authors compared the performance of two groups of students in grade 11: one group had done intensive English in grade 5 or 6 ($N = 30$), and the other had only received regular instruction ($N = 30$). The authors found that intensive English learners had more contact with the English language outside of school (as the students reported in a questionnaire), as well as greater fluency and accuracy in a series of oral tasks.

In general, research conducted on time distribution and SLA suggests a certain benefit of concentrating the hours of instruction instead of spreading them over long periods of time. This benefit is clearer when the comparison includes intensive programs that offer more hours of instruction than regular 'drip-feed' programs. However, in this comparison we cannot know whether it is time increase or time concentration (or both) that is causing the effect. When the number of hours of instruction is controlled for, concentrated instruction offers fewer clear-cut advantages, but some do appear. In the study by Collins *et al.* (1999) such advantages could be due to other factors that mediated the results (the students in the intensive course ended up having a few more hours of instruction, plus they might have been initially better learners as the enrollment criteria were stricter). In Collins and White (2011), the advantages for the more concentrated program type could also be explained by external factors (more listening practice – and possibly verb practice – and better timing for testing). In the case of the studies by Serrano and Muñoz (2007) and Serrano (2011), the advantages reported for the more concentrated program types do not occur for all the tasks and measures considered or all the proficiency levels under examination, but when there are differences, they favor the intensive program.

Even though the Canadian and the Spanish results are highly similar (few differences between learners in different program types, but favoring more concentrated programs), there are many differences in the two contexts. Apart from the age factor (children vs adults), an important difference between the Canadian and the Spanish studies lies in the number of hours of instruction under consideration. The intensive programs in Canada examined by Collins *et al.* (1999) and Collins and White (2011) consist of 400 hours of exposure, while the Spanish programs include only 110. Also, the comparison group in Canada is an intensive program, while the comparison group in Spain is a regular, 'drip-feed' program. Despite the differences between the two contexts, however, there are many commonalities in the results, which confirms the tendency of intensive instruction to have positive effects on L2 learning.

There are many questions, however, that still remain unanswered with respect to time distribution and L2 learning: (1) how many hours per week or per session qualify a program as 'intensive'; (2) is it more effective to concentrate hours of instruction per session and have longer days of exposure to the L2 followed by non-exposure (as in the 'mini-intensives' included in Collins & White, 2011), or to have fewer hours and more continuous exposure (i.e. 2 hours/day everyday during 10 months; as in the 'distributed' analyzed by Collins *et al.*, 1999); and (3) what is more effective for long-term retention, concentrating L2 instruction or spreading it over longer time periods?

Contrasting the Studies in Cognitive Psychology and SLA

It seems that most studies in the SLA field have suggested certain advantages for intensive instruction. Moreover, no study so far has shown negative effects of time concentration, as is the case for most research in the cognitive psychology literature. Why are the general conclusions about time distribution so different in the two fields?

First of all, in the cognitive psychology experiments, participants generally must memorize words, non-words, foreign words, and so on, and repetitions of the items tend to be exact. On the other hand, L2 learning in classroom settings does not generally involve rote learning (at least in more contemporary programs). Moreover, repetitions of items and structures are not exact and do not occur one after the other (or with few intervening items) in intensive instruction, as in some experiments in cognitive psychology. Indeed, it is easy to lose concentration and motivation when memorizing material through concentrated repetitions, which could be one reason why whatever needs to be learned is deficiently processed, as shown in the cognitive psychology experiments (Challis, 1993; Greeno, 1970; Hintzman, 1976; Jacoby, 1978). This type of scenario, however, does not correspond to the L2 classes considered in the studies here, where rote learning is not encouraged. It has also been shown in the cognitive psychology literature that, when experiments include *paraphrased* rather than verbatim repetitions of the items to be learned (which would be normally the case in L2 classes, except for the very exceptional vocabulary-only tasks), often no advantages are found for distributed learning (Appleton-Knapp et al., 2005; Glover & Corkill, 1987; Mammarella et al., 2002).

Another important difference between the cognitive psychology and the SLA studies lies in testing. The tests that are used by cognitive psychologists usually tap the declarative memory of words, faces, and so on (Bahrik & Hall, 2005; Pavlik & Anderson, 2005). These tests would correspond to what has been referred to as 'discrete point tests' (Hulstijn, 2010), as they only assess one particular type of knowledge. On the other hand, the tests that are normally used in the SLA literature that examines time distribution can be considered 'integrative tests', as different types of knowledge and skills are required to complete them. In fact, even if Childers and Tomasello (2002) and Ambridge et al. (2006) were examining language acquisition (L1 in this case), they focused on vocabulary and a particular grammatical structure, which might explain why spacing effects were found. Similarly, Bird (2010) focuses on three grammatical structures, and the test administered to check learning could also be considered a discrete point test. In contrast, integrative tests (as the ones used in the SLA literature) can be considered more complex, and, as Donovan and Radosevich (1999) suggest, the spacing effect is less significant in complex tasks (see Collins & White, 2011 for further discussion of this point).

In a similar vein, DeKeyser (2007) differentiates between practice of components (e.g. specific vocabulary or grammatical structures) and practice of skills (listening, reading, writing and speaking). It could certainly be the case that spaced practice of *components* is better than massed practice (as reflected in the results of the cognitive psychology experiments, which usually assess this type of practice). However, massed or intensive practice of *skills* might still be efficient, as shown in the SLA literature.

One important factor not normally considered in the studies analyzing time distribution in SLA is retention. Most studies investigating different L2 program types perform tests immediately after the course finishes (or is about to finish) for all program types. This retention interval is indeed quite short, and at such short retention intervals there are also studies in the cognitive psychology literature that have reported benefits for massed distribution (Bahrick & Hall, 2005; Bird, 2010; Bloom & Shuell, 1981; Pavlik & Anderson, 2005; Rohrer & Taylor, 2006). Short RIs lead to recency effects, which could certainly explain why some L2 learners in intensive courses perform better. For example, in Serrano (2011) the intermediate learners in the intensive course under analysis demonstrated more gains in an achievement test than those in the regular program at a short RI (at the end of their respective courses). The learners in the intensive program type had done the pretest only a few weeks before (while it was months before for the other group). Moreover, the students following intensive instruction could also retrieve the structures, items, etc., they had learned during their course more easily because such learning was more recent. The fact that the learners in the advanced group did not benefit from the same conditions still remains to be explained. Therefore, RIs should be considered in studies examining time distribution, as they seem to mediate its effect (Rohrer & Pashler, 2007). Indeed, there are few studies analyzing time distribution in L2 learning that examine long-term retention, and it could be that learners in massed programs showing more language gains at the end of the course (Collins *et al.*, 1999; Collins & White, 2011; Serrano, 2011; Serrano & Muñoz, 2007) might not maintain those gains after a long time lapse. Bird (2010) demonstrates that performances on a language test at a short and a long RI are different, and that, while no differences between concentrated and distributed learning existed at a short RI, at a long RI learning in spaced sequences seemed more beneficial.

The findings from the cognitive psychology and SLA literature could also be reconciled if we consider study-phase retrieval theories of the spacing effect. According to these theories, for a repetition of an item to be beneficial, the first presentation of the item needs to be retrieved. If the spacing between the two presentations is too wide (in some distributed conditions), retrieval will not occur, and the second presentation will not serve as a repetition (Bahrick & Phelps, 1987; Toppino & Bloom, 2002; Verkoeijen *et al.*, 2005).

It could be the case in some studies comparing intensive and non-intensive instruction that the spacing between sessions in regular courses is too wide, and when items, structures, patterns, etc., reappear after a long interval the students no longer recall the first presentations.

General Summary

The purpose of this chapter was to establish a comparison between the studies performed in cognitive psychology and those in SLA concerning the effect of time distribution on learning. Many variables differ between the two fields (instruments, designs, procedures, type of learning examined, etc.), which make a direct comparison of findings difficult. It would greatly enrich the SLA field to perform more controlled experiments and analyze retention, following the cognitive psychology model, so that the effect of time distribution could be more effectively assessed from a theoretical perspective. For practical purposes, it is less useful to perform classroom experiments that only assess the learning of a particular structure or vocabulary list (discrete point tests), as the results from such experiments would be difficult to extrapolate to effectiveness of intensive programs for language learning in general, which is a skill. A study that combines both types of analyses (a controlled one for particular items or structures, or 'components', and another focused on skills) would shed more light on the effect of time distribution for different types of L2 learning. Indeed, more research is necessary in this area, as it could be a crucial aspect to consider in program design when the objective is to maximize L2 learning and, hopefully, retention.

Acknowledgments

This research was supported by grants FFI2010-18006 and SGR137. I would like to thank Carmen Muñoz and Laura Collins for their insightful comments.

Note

(1) I thank Norman Segalowitz for bringing this limerick to the attention of applied linguists.

References

Ambridge, B., Theakston, A.L., Lieven, E.V.M. and Tomasello, M. (2006) The distributed learning effect for children's acquisition of an abstract syntactic construction. *Cognitive Development* 21, 174–193.
Appleton-Knapp, S.L., Bjork, R.A. and Wickens, T.D. (2005) Examining the spacing effect in advertising: Encoding variability, retrieval processes, and their interaction. *The Journal of Consumer Research* 32, 266–276.
Bahrick, H.P. (1979) Maintenance of knowledge: Questions about memory we forgot to ask. *Journal of Experimental Psychology* 108, 296–308.

Bahrick, H.P. and Hall, L.K. (2005) The importance of retrieval failures to long-term retention: A metacognitive explanation of the spacing effect. *Journal of Memory and Language* 52, 566–577.

Bahrick, H.P. and Phelps, E. (1987) Retention of Spanish vocabulary over 8 years. *Journal of Experimental Psychology: Learning, Memory, and Cognition* 13, 344–349.

Bird, S. (2010) Effects of distributed practice on the acquisition of second language English syntax. *Applied Psycholinguistics* 31, 635–650.

Bjork, R.A. (1988) Retrieval practice and the maintenance of knowledge. In M.M. Gruneberg, P.E. Morris and R.S. Sykes (eds) *Practical Aspects of Memory: Current Research and Issues* (pp. 396–401). Chichester: Wiley.

Bloom, K.C. and Shuell, T.J. (1981) Effects of massed and distributed practice on the learning and retention of second-language vocabulary. *Journal of Educational Research* 74, 245–248.

Challis, B.H. (1993) Spacing effects on cued-memory tests depend on level of processing. *Journal of Experimental Psychology, Learning, Memory, and Cognition* 19, 389–396.

Childers, J.B. and Tomasello, M. (2002) Two-year olds learn novel nouns, verbs and conventional actions from massed or distributed exposures. *Developmental Psychology* 38, 867–978.

Collins, L. and White, J. (2011) An intensive look at intensity and language learning. *TESOL Quarterly* 45, 106–133.

Collins, L., Halter, R.H., Lightbown, P.M. and Spada, N. (1999) Time and the distribution of time in L2 instruction. *TESOL Quarterly* 33, 655–680.

Cuddy, L.J. and Jacoby, L.J. (1982) When forgetting helps memory: An analysis of repetition effects. *Journal of Verbal Learning and Verbal Behavior* 21, 451–467.

DeKeyser, R.M. (2007) Introduction: Situating the concept of practice. In R.M. DeKeyser (ed.) *Practice in Second Language: Perspectives from Applied Linguistics and Cognitive Psychology* (pp. 1–18). Cambridge: Cambridge University Press.

Delaney, P.F. and Knowles, M.E. (2005) Encoding strategy changes and spacing effects in the free recall of unmixed lists. *Journal of Memory and Language* 52, 120–130.

Dellarosa, D. and Bourne, L.E. (1985) Surface form and the spacing effect. *Memory & Cognition* 13, 529–537.

Dempster, F.N. (1988) The spacing effect: A case study in the failure to apply the results of psychological research. *American Psychologist* 43, 627–634.

Donovan, J.J. and Radosevich, D.J. (1999) A meta-analytic review of the distribution of practice effect: Now you see it, now you don't. *Journal of Applied Psychology* 84, 795–805.

Ellis, N.C. (2002) Frequency effects in language processing. *Studies in Second Language Acquisition* 24, 143–188.

Elmes, D.G., Craig, J.D. and Herdelin, N.J. (1983) What is the role of affect in the spacing effect? *Memory & Cognition* 11, 144–151.

Germain, C. and Netten, J. (2005) Pedagogy and second language learning: Lessons learned from intensive French. *Canadian Journal of Applied Linguistics/Revue canadienne de linguistique appliquée* 8, 183–210.

Glenberg, A.M. (1979) Component-levels theory of the effects of spacing of repetitions on recall and recognition. *Memory & Cognition* 7, 95–112.

Glover, J.A. and Corkill, A.J. (1987) Influence of paraphrased repetitions on the spacing effect. *Journal of Educational Psychology* 79, 198–199.

Greene, R.L. (1989) Spacing effects in memory: Evidence for a two-process account. *Journal of Experimental Psychology, Memory and Cognition* 15, 371–377.

Greeno, J.G. (1970) Conservation of information-processing capacity in paired-associate memorizing. *Journal of Verbal Learning and Verbal Behavior* 9, 581–586.

Hintzman, D.L. (1976) Repetition and memory. In G.H. Bower (ed.) *The Psychology of Learning and Memory* (pp. 47–91). New York: Academic Press.

Hulstijn, J.H. (2010) Measuring second language proficiency. In E. Blom and S. Unsworth (eds) *Experimental Methods in Language Acquisition Research* (pp. 185–199). Amsterdam: John Benjamins.

Jacoby, L.L. (1978) On interpreting the effects of repetition: Solving a problem versus remembering a solution. *Journal of Verbal Learning and Verbal Behavior* 17, 649–667.

Johnston, W. and Uhl, C.N. (1976) The contributions of encoding effort and variability to the spacing effect on free recall. *Journal of Experimental Psychology: Human Learning and Memory* 2, 153–160.

Lightbown, P.M. and Spada, N. (1991) Étude des effets à long terme de l'apprentissage intensif de l'anglais, langue seconde, au primaire. *The Canadian Modern Language Review* 48, 90–117.

Mammarella, N., Russo, R. and Avons, S.E. (2002) Spacing effects in cued-memory tasks for unfamiliar faces and nonwords. *Memory & Cognition* 30, 1238–1251.

Melton, A.W. (1970) The situation with respect to the spacing of repetitions and memory. *Journal of Verbal Learning and Verbal Behavior* 9, 596–606.

Muñoz, C. (ed.) (2006) *Age and the Rate of Foreign Language Learning*. Clevedon: Multilingual Matters.

Netten, J. and Germain, C. (2004) Theoretical and research foundations of Intensive French. *The Canadian Modern Language Review/La Revue canadienne des langues vivantes* 60, 275–294.

Pavlik, P.I. (2005) The microeconomics of learning: Optimizing paired-associate memory. Unpublished PhD dissertation, Carnegie Mellon University, USA.

Pavlik, P.I. and Anderson, J.R. (2005) Practice and forgetting effects on vocabulary memory: An activation-based model of the spacing effect. *Cognitive Science* 29, 559–586.

Raaijmakers, J.G.W. (2003) Spacing and repetition effects in human memory: Application of the SAM model. *Cognitive Science* 27, 431–452.

Riches, N.G., Tomasello, M. and Conti-Ramsden, G. (2005) Verb learning in children with SLI: Frequency and spacing effects. *Journal of Speech, Language, and Hearing Research* 48, 1397–1411.

Rohrer, D. and Pashler, H. (2007) Increasing retention without increasing study time. *Current Directions in Psychological Science* 16, 183–186.

Rohrer, D. and Taylor, K. (2006) The effects of overlearning and distributed practice on the retention of mathematics knowledge. *Applied Cognitive Psychology* 20, 1209–1224.

Ross, B.H. and Landauer, T.K. (1978) Memory for at least one of two items: Test and failure of several theories of spacing effects. *Journal of Verbal Learning and Verbal Behavior* 17, 669–680.

Russo, R. and Mammarella, N. (2002) Spacing effects in recognition memory: When meaning matters. *European Journal of Cognitive Psychology* 14, 49–59.

Russo, R., Mammarella, N. and Avons, S.E. (2002) Toward a unified account of spacing effects in explicit cued-memory tasks. *Journal of Experimental Psychology, Learning, Memory, and Cognition* 28, 819–829.

Seabrook, R., Brown, G.D.A. and Solity, J.E. (2005) Distributed and massed practice: From laboratory to classroom. *Applied Cognitive Psychology* 19, 107–122.

Segalowitz, N. (2010) *The Cognitive Bases of Second Language Fluency*. New York: Routledge.

Segalowitz, N. and Hulstijn, J. (2005) Automaticity in bilingualism and second language learning. In J.F. Kroll and A.M.B. De Groot (eds) *Handbook of Bilingualism: Psycholinguistic Approaches* (pp. 371–388). Oxford: Oxford University Press.

Serrano, R. (2011) The time factor in EFL classroom practice. *Language Learning* 61, 117–143.

Serrano, R. and Muñoz, C. (2007) Same hours different time distribution: Any difference in EFL? *System* 35, 305–321.

Spada, N. and Lightbown, P.M. (1989) Intensive ESL programs in Quebec primary schools. *TESL Canada Journal* 7, 11–32.

Stern, H.H. (1985) The time factor and compact course development. *TESL Canada Journal*, 3, 13–27.

Thios, S.J. and D'Agostino, P.R. (1976) Effects of repetition as a function of study-phase retrieval. *Journal of Verbal Learning and Verbal Behavior* 15, 529–536.

Toppino, T.C. and Bloom, L.C. (2002) The spacing effect, free recall, and two-process theory: A closer look. *Journal of Experimental Psychology: Learning, Memory and Cognition* 28, 437–444.

Toppino, T.C., Hara, Y. and Hackman, J. (2002) The spacing effect in the free recall of homogeneous lists: Present and accounted for. *Memory & Cognition* 30, 601–606.

Verkoeijen, P.P.J.L., Rikers, R.M.J.P. and Schmidt, H.G. (2005) Limitations to the spacing effect: Demonstration of an inverted u-shaped relationship between interrepetition spacing and free recall. *Experimental Psychology* 52, 257–263.

White, J. and Turner, C.E. (2005) Comparing children's oral ability in two ESL programs. *The Canadian Modern Language Review* 61, 491–517.

Part 2
Intensive Instruction

2 Intensive L2 Instruction in Canada: Why not Immersion?

Patsy M. Lightbown

Demographics and Languages in Canada

Outside of Canada, one often encounters people who think that most Canadians are bilingual. This perception arises in part from the fact that Canada has two official languages – French and English. However, for most of Canada's history, English and French communities were largely separate from each other, and relatively few people felt the need to use both languages. The title of Hugh MacLennan's 1945 novel, *Two Solitudes*, was in part a reference to the distance that existed between French-speaking and English-speaking Canadians from the time the nation was established in the 18th century until well into the 20th century.

In the 21st century, the perception of Canada as a nation of individuals who speak more than one language has some foundation. However, even now, in most of the country, individuals who say in response to census questions that they are able to speak both French and English are still a minority. In the 2006 census, Canada's population was reported as 31,241,030. Two-thirds of census respondents said that they knew only English; just over 13% said that they knew only French (the vast majority of these in Quebec); and 17% said they knew both. When asked what language they typically speak *at home*, two-thirds of Canadians said that they 'most often' speak English; 21% said that they most often speak French; and nearly 13% said that they usually speak a language other than French or English, or that they speak one of the official languages and another language. Only 0.3% (94,000 respondents) said that they typically use both French and English at home. Canada's linguistic profile is far more diverse than would be suggested by its image as a country with two languages. Hundreds of thousands of Canadians, including Canada's indigenous population, speak other languages instead of, or in addition to, English and French.

Languages and Education in Quebec

The linguistic profile of the province of Quebec has always been different from that of the other Canadian provinces. The majority – roughly 80% – of Québécois identify themselves as francophone. At the time of MacLennan's *Two Solitudes*, the stereotype of Quebec society was that anglophones rarely learned to speak French fluently, and if they did, it was more likely to be the school-learned variety of French spoken in Europe than the variety spoken in the cities or rural areas of Quebec. In Quebec, anglophones tended to hold greater social and economic power, and francophones learned enough English to do their jobs, supervised by English 'bosses', but the language of their daily lives was French. Some francophones, especially those who aspired to success in business or government, became bilingual, but even in Quebec, most people spoke *either* French or English, not both. In the 1960s and 1970s that pattern began to undergo significant change.

Because of political action taken by the Canadian government in the 1960s, Canada became an officially bilingual country, with French and English having equal status as official languages. From that time forward, federal government services and publications were provided in both French and English. This led to the necessity for many individuals, most notably civil servants, to develop skill in the 'other' official language. It also led parents to pressure local schools to provide instruction that would lead to their children becoming proficient in both languages, arguing from their own experience that the existing programs for teaching French in English-medium schools and English in French-medium schools were not adequate.

The federal government had made both French and English official languages in the 1960s, but in the 1970s Quebec's provincial government introduced new legislation that not only made French the only official language of the provincial government, but also made it the language of the public face of business. French became the language of commercial signs, contracts, legal documents and even communication within large companies. Professionals, from nurses to engineers, had to show proficiency in French in order to be certified to practice their profession. During the early days of these changes, many anglophones moved away from Quebec. For those who stayed, however, the need to know French was very real, and the language skill profile of 21st century Quebec anglophones is very different from that of their predecessors. Indeed, the most recent census information shows that the Canadians who are most likely to have achieved proficiency in both official languages are Quebec's anglophones. In the 2008–2009 Annual Report of the Office of the Commissioner of Official Languages (Government of Canada, Office of the Commissioner of Official Languages, 2009), the extent of this dramatic change in language skill is highlighted:

[in Quebec] more than one-third of Francophones (36%) and two-thirds of Anglophones (69%) ... stated that they speak English and French. Among Anglophones aged 18 to 34, this percentage has increased to nearly 80%. In fact, in the past 40 years, no other Canadian community has increased its ability to speak a second official language as much as the Anglophone communities in Quebec. (p. 46)

How did this change come about? Part of the answer lies in the legislation that required the use of French in many aspects of life and work where it had previously been possible to function mainly or only in English. One of the ways in which anglophones began this process was through French immersion instruction in Quebec's English language schools.

French Immersion in Quebec

In the 1960s, a group of anglophone parents in St Lambert, a suburb of Montreal, saw the benefit of their children acquiring better French skills than they typically got in their English-medium schools. As a result, they considered the possibility of sending the children to a French-medium school for a period of language 'immersion'. Individual families – both francophone and anglophone – had sometimes exercised this home-school language switch option, especially in the elementary grades. However, when the parents proposed to send a whole group of children to a French-medium school, the idea was rejected by the prospective host school, partly based on the fear that the presence of so many anglophone children would cause English to 'spread rapidly among French-speaking children, somewhat like a contagious disease' (Lambert & Tucker, 1972: 4). Eventually, the school board and the parents agreed on a plan to open an experimental French immersion kindergarten class in an English-medium school. The children, all English speakers, would be taught by a French-speaking teacher. In the first experimental class, the kindergarten teacher spoke only French while the children sometimes replied in English. The teacher would provide feedback and encourage – but not require – the children to try again, in French. In the first year, there was only one class, but a new kindergarten class was added in each subsequent year. For each of these classes, instruction was entirely in French for the first two or three years, with English language arts introduced gradually, when students were about eight or nine years old.

One significant aspect of this early experiment was that Wallace Lambert and a team of researchers from McGill University were invited to follow the students, assessing their progress as they received their early schooling, including initial literacy instruction, in a language they were just beginning to learn (see e.g. Lambert & Tucker, 1972). Their reports were widely read and their influence was considerable.

The students who had been enrolled in the first two years of this program were followed throughout their elementary schooling by the McGill University team. The focus of that research included a comparison of the learning outcomes of French immersion students with those of English-speaking peers who received their schooling in English, focusing particularly on their continued development of their English language abilities and their mastery of subject matter that they had been taught in their second language. The findings may be summarized in the following generalizations:

- Students did not fall behind their peers in the development of their English language skills.
- Students did not fall behind their peers in their learning of academic content.
- Although there was some delay in the development of reading ability in English, those delays were overcome within a few years.
- Students did not lose their identity as English-speaking Canadians, but they did develop more positive attitudes toward French Canadians.

The findings of that first study were surprising to some observers who had worried that having to learn through a new language would cause significant problems for these students. In retrospect, it is interesting that the focus of the earliest studies of French immersion was on ensuring that educating students through a second language would not do them harm, that is, making sure that students' development of their English language skills and their subject matter knowledge were not impaired. Such concerns arose in part from the view, particularly widespread in the USA, that bilingualism caused numerous problems, including failure to develop either language to a high level of proficiency, confused identity and poor cognitive development owing to the 'burden' of using more than one language (see Jensen, 1962 for review). Quebec's French immersion research provided evidence against such negative expectations.

French Immersion beyond Quebec

Findings similar to those from the first experimental classes were reported time and again as more and more schools implemented immersion programs. Having begun as a response to a local parental initiative in a suburb of Montreal, French immersion soon spread to every province in Canada and has also been adopted – and adapted – for foreign language instruction throughout the world (Genesee, 1987; Lyster, 2007; Swain & Johnson, 1997). Over time, numerous variations on the original immersion model have been developed. These include programs in which the immersion element is introduced after students have acquired basic literacy in their first language (often at grade 4, or about age nine), programs in which students experience immersion instruction at the end of their elementary schooling (at about age 11), and even some that implement immersion for secondary school students. There are many differences in programs that bear the label 'French immersion', but they are all based on two principles: (1) effective teaching requires adequate time for language learning; and (2) the best context for learning is one in which students have a concrete and immediate need to use the language. With all the variations, programs based on these principles have led to language learning outcomes that are far superior to what has been achieved in classrooms where the language itself is the only subject matter and where the amount of time devoted to language learning is measured in minutes per week rather than hours per day.

For a number of years, the primary focus of evaluations was on students' maintenance of their first language and their success in subject matter learning. As educators became more comfortable with the idea that immersion did not harm students in terms of these fundamental issues, more attention was paid to the French language skills they were developing. A number of studies reported that, even after years of immersion instruction, students continued to speak a variety of French that was marked by errors, especially in morphosyntactic features such as gender agreement and verb tense markings (e.g. Harley & Swain, 1984) but also in some aspects of vocabulary (e.g. Harley & King, 1989) and pragmatic features (e.g. Lyster, 1987). This research led to two more generalizations regarding French immersion:

- Students in French immersion programs develop very good comprehension skills.
- Students who have learned French in immersion programs, with little exposure to French outside school, do not achieve native-like mastery of the grammar, pronunciation and sociopragmatic rules of the language.

French immersion has its critics. Some are harsh, focusing on the errors that some immersion students continue to make in their spoken and written French after several years of content-based exposure to the language (e.g. Billy, 1980). Others are strong supporters of immersion, acknowledging limitations in the French language skills that students develop, but emphasizing the unprecedented degree of bilingualism in a widely implemented school program. The focus of these critics is on ways to improve what is already a far more successful approach to teaching French to anglophone Canadians than any that have come before. Although, as Swain (1988) put it, good content teaching may not always be good language teaching, many researchers and educators in Canada and elsewhere have contributed to making it better (e.g. Genesee, 1987; Lyster, 2007; Tedick et al., 2011), and it continues to be supported as a means by which children from a majority or prestige language background may become bilingual.

Immersion for Minority Language Students?

Inevitably, questions have been raised about whether the success of Canadian French immersion programs for majority language children makes it a valid approach for the education of children from minority groups in Canada and elsewhere, including the USA. As reports of this successful innovation in Canada began to be heard in the USA, some educators who had fought hard for the right to provide bilingual education to minority language children were particularly concerned. Immersion education seemed to go against the notion that children learn better if they receive their earliest education, especially their first literacy instruction, in the language they know best. During the 1960s and 1970s, many American educators and advocates argued that minority language children had the right to education that included their L1. They pointed out that some important characteristics that are typical of French immersion programs are different from those present in classrooms where immigrant and minority language children must learn the local official or majority language (see e.g. Genesee, 1987). Among those characteristics that distinguish French immersion from the education of minority language children are the following:

- Even though instruction is provided through the second language, there is no expectation that students in Canadian French immersion classes will give up or stop developing their primary language.
- Students in immersion classes typically come from the same L1 background, and their teachers acquire the ability to communicate with them, using a level of language that is appropriate for their developing proficiency.
- Although there are now many different models of immersion education, students always receive some of their schooling in their L1.
- Immersion is usually a voluntary program, most often offered to children of educated parents who anticipate benefits for their children and who are able to offer encouragement and support as well as opportunities for continuing development of the L1.
- Immersion programs do not – and are not expected to – result in students' acquisition of native-like skill in their L2. Instead, they achieve high proficiency in comprehension and the ability to make themselves understood in spite of persistent limitations in the accuracy and sophistication of their speaking and writing abilities.

English-only instruction for minority group children is often called 'immersion' and Canadian research is sometimes cited as the basis for implementing it. However, it is clear that such instruction is quite different from immersion based on the Canadian model. Unlike Canadian anglophones in

French immersion, minority language students are expected to achieve full mastery of English within a short time and their L1 may be ignored, gradually withdrawn from the instructional setting or actively discouraged (Cummins, 1992). An approach to instruction for minority language students in the USA that is actually more aligned with the principles of French immersion is the 'dual immersion' approach, to which we will return later in this chapter.

In summary, French immersion, an innovation in education that was inspired by a group of suburban anglophone parents in Quebec, has contributed to the growth of bilingualism among many anglophones in that Canadian province and others. It has spread to schools in many other countries. We turn now to developments in the learning of English by francophone students in Quebec.

Intensive ESL in Quebec

The dramatic increase in the number of young Quebec anglophones who can speak French has not been matched by a comparable increase in bilingualism among young francophones. Before the implementation of Quebec's Charter of the French Language in 1977, educated middle class francophone parents in Quebec sometimes sent their children to an English-medium school for a few years in order to encourage them to acquire good English skills. Peal and Lambert (1962) described the linguistic and academic success of one group of students who represented this educational option. When that option was closed, owing to the Charter's limitations on who could attend English-medium schools, students in French-medium public schools were left with ESL instruction that was offered in the regular program.[1] In principle, that instruction began in late elementary school and was offered at a rate of about 120 minutes a week in elementary school and 150 minutes in high school – a total of less than 700 hours of instruction, spread over six or seven years of schooling. In fact, few schools provided the full number of minutes that the Ministry of Education recommended. Not surprisingly, few students achieved anything approaching fluency if they had no opportunities to learn English outside of school. Furthermore, with the enhanced status and value of French within Quebec, some young people came to question the utility of learning English. Indeed, in the same 2008–2009 Annual Report that described the high level of second language ability among Quebec's young anglophones, the Office of the Commissioner of Official Languages also observed that many francophone students 'lacked motivation to learn English because they viewed the language as being of little use' (Government of Canada, Office of the Commissioner of Official Languages, 2009, p. 46). Many families, however, continued to believe that knowing English was an essential part of the skill set of a well-educated person, recognizing that certain careers and educational options would be closed to students without that ability.

In the early 1970s, the success of French immersion had prompted some francophone parents and educators in Quebec to consider the option of English immersion for their children. The situation in Quebec represented a special case with regard to language policy and planning and the characterization of minority and majority language groups. On the one hand, French speakers were and remain the majority of Quebec's population. Thus, in a sense, francophone children are members of a majority group. However, seen in the Canadian and North American context, francophones may be said to represent a tiny minority group – 6 million French-speakers surrounded by more than 350 million speakers of English. In the 1960s and 1970s, both federal and provincial governments had sought to encourage and protect the role of French, especially outside Quebec, where French speakers really are a tiny minority. Even in Quebec, however, with its 80% francophone population, proposals for educational innovations in which young francophones might be 'immersed' in English were sometimes met with alarm. As we have seen, in 1977 the provincial government, through the Charter of the French Language, restricted access to English language schools and also to subject matter instruction in English, effectively making English immersion illegal in French-language schools.

Even before the publication of the Charter, however, educators began to look for alternatives that would promote the learning of English while ensuring that francophone students would continue to develop their French language knowledge and skill. In a school board outside Montreal, a series of events and observations had led to some innovation in the teaching of both English and French. In that board, which had both French-medium and English-medium schools, educators evaluating their French immersion programs were struck by what they saw as the relative weakness in the language abilities of anglophone children in French immersion classes when compared with those of immigrant students in *classes d'accueil* (welcoming classes). In the latter, children who were newcomers to Quebec were taught French intensively for a year or two, in preparation for their full integration into French-medium instruction alongside French-speaking peers. School board evaluators concluded that the *classes d'accueil* were more effective in promoting proficiency in French than were immersion classes.

On the basis of these findings, the school board began to experiment with intensive French classes for anglophone students in grade 1 (age six years) and also students in grade 6 (age 11 years). Called *le bain linguistique* (language bath), these programs differed from immersion in that there was no teaching of subject matter but rather an intensive focus on learning the language itself for six months, with the other half of the school year was devoted to following the regular curriculum in their first language. The younger group of students had one year of kindergarten in English followed by six months of intensive French in grade 1. Evaluators reported that these students had better oral French skills than students who had done both kindergarten and grade 1 in French immersion. More surprisingly, it was claimed that students who participated in the six-month program at grade 6 were as good as and sometimes better at spoken French than students who had completed six years of immersion (Billy, 1980).

In this same school board, a five-month intensive experiment was also tried in ESL classes for francophone students. Again, the school board reported excellent results. In this case, in fact, a comparison was reported between francophone students at the end of sixth grade who had done five months of intensive ESL and their peers who had attended an English-medium school for six and a half years (from kindergarten through grade 6). Billy (1980) reports that 'les enfants soumis à un apprentissage oral intensif de cinq mois ont un degré de compréhension de la langue seconde égal à celui des enfants francophones inscrits à une école anglaise depuis le début de leur scolarité' (p. 427) [children subjected to five months of intensive oral instruction have a degree of comprehension of the second language equal to that of francophone students attending English schools since the beginning of their education]. No replication of this comparison would be possible in Quebec now since francophone students do not have the option of attending English-medium elementary schools (see discussion below). Without such replication, it is difficult to evaluate or interpret the claims (Lightbown, 1988). Furthermore, it is difficult to obtain documentation about these programs and the evaluation measures that were used. Some of the claims are certainly counterintuitive and may reflect a type of evaluation that emphasized accuracy over fluency.[2] Nevertheless, there was a high degree of satisfaction with the intensive approach, and it was widely implemented throughout the school board as a way to improve the second language proficiency of both anglophone and francophone students.

At around the same time, in another suburb of Montreal, intensive ESL classes were being tried at the grade 5 level. Here too, the school year was divided between a focus on learning English in one half of the school year and a focus on completing the grade level curriculum during the other half. The approach to teaching ESL in this school was strongly influenced by the trend toward communicative language teaching. Rather than engaging in the audio-lingual types of repetition and drill that had been typical of ESL instruction up to that time, students became involved in projects and group activities that were closely structured by their teacher so that, in spite of starting with a very basic knowledge of English, they were able to communicate effectively, if not always accurately, with a rapidly expanding vocabulary (Lightbown & Spada, 1994).

Although English instruction in Quebec's regular programs was normally offered in 30 minute classes two or three times a week, not exceeding the 120 minutes per week that were allocated for English instruction, schools were allowed to implement 'experimental' classes that deviated from this norm. In some schools, the experimental instruction might mean a special science or music program, but others took the opportunity to introduce intensive ESL instruction. Intensive ESL was a response to local demands to improve the quality of instruction in English for francophone students. By the late 1980s, other school boards, especially in Montreal's suburbs, were offering intensive ESL classes, usually at the grade 5 or 6 (age 10–11 years) level.

Whatever the pedagogical approach, students in these intensive classes were getting substantially more exposure to English than students in the regular ESL program, which was based on what Stern (1985) called 'drip feed' instruction. As noted above, most students in Quebec primary schools at that time received less than the recommended 120 minutes of ESL instruction per week. The intensive classes could offer 300–400 hours in just a few months (Spada & Lightbown, 1989).

It was essential that these experimental programs respect the Charter of the French Language, which, as we saw above (see details in footnote 1), made it unlawful for all but a minority of Quebec residents to send their children to the English language schools that served the anglophone population. Further, within the French-language schools, the strict interpretation of the regulations governing the language of instruction in Quebec schools was that nothing could be taught in a language other than French – except a second or foreign language itself. Thus, schools were authorized to teach English or Spanish but not to teach maths or social studies *in* English or Spanish.[3]

This restriction on what could be taught in a language other than French led to some challenges for the teachers in schools that implemented intensive ESL in the early years. Because the intensive English instruction could not be based on 'subject matter' in the way that French immersion was, and because no official curriculum had been written for these experimental classes, teachers were often left to design, develop and manufacture their own materials. They often did this by taking one of the ESL textbooks that had been approved for use in regular ESL classes with their maximum of 120 minutes per week, and expanding on it to create instructional activities to fill 200–300 minutes a day. Furthermore, there were no objectives for students in intensive ESL other than those in place for students in the regular program. Not surprisingly, instructional activities varied greatly across individual schools. Some teachers were exceptionally creative and productive; others found it difficult to come up with enough material to fill the time. Furthermore, the principles of communicative language teaching were, by the mid-1980s, strongly advocated by the Ministère de l'Éducation du Québec, leading some teachers to believe that they should emphasize only communicative interaction rather than engaging students in any systematic study of grammar or vocabulary. In some classes, this view resulted in an emphasis on 'conversational' language that was enjoyable and motivating.

For example, one teacher managed to start from an ESL textbook chapter on 'my home' and expand it from a few vocabulary items and simple phrases to a unit on housing, decorating and real estate that led students to acquire astonishing vocabulary knowledge of construction materials, home design and furniture styles. Other teachers found it difficult to come up with 'communicative' material that did not feel superficial and repetitive. Some teachers seemed to interpret 'no subject matter' to mean that no cognitively challenging content should be introduced, leaving them to fill their time with games and role plays rather than substantive informational topics (Weary, 1987). Over time, however, more and more teachers shared the materials they had created for their own students, and gradually a bank of materials became accessible when new classes were opened. The teachers also organized a very active special interest group (SIG) within the provincial ESL teachers' association SPEAQ (la Société pour la promotion de l'enseignement de l'anglais – langue seconde – au Québec). This group, which called itself IntenSIG, became both an inspiration and a resource for teachers who were faced with the challenges of teaching a program for which there were no ready-made materials or curriculum.

Having started as an experiment in two school boards in suburban Montreal in the 1970s, intensive ESL expanded to include more than 30 school boards by the late 1980s (Lightbown *et al.*, 1988). In the 1980s, my colleagues and I became involved in a project to evaluate the learning outcomes for students in the school board that had first implemented the grade 5 immersion program based on principles of communicative language teaching. This initial invitation led to a series of research projects that allowed us to become very familiar with the successes and challenges of the intensive classes not only in this school but also in other schools and school boards as well. Our research involved the collection and analysis of data on students' ability to understand and use English. We also observed many hours of classroom interaction as we sought to discover why some groups were more successful than others. Based on the extensive descriptive work, we designed some quasi-experimental studies exploring relationships between classroom activities and students' ability to use certain features of English in tasks and tests set by the researchers.

Among the findings of the many research studies that have been carried out in Quebec's intensive ESL classes are the following:

- Students in intensive ESL classes achieved levels of English ability that far surpassed that of their peers in the regular 120 minute per week programs. This is not a surprising finding, given the greater number of hours of instruction in intensive classes. More impressively, they outperformed students at the secondary level who had received a comparable number of total hours of instruction, spread over a period of several years (Spada & Lightbown, 1989).

- When they reached the end of secondary school, even though the secondary schools had offered no special program tailored to their more advanced knowledge of English, students who had experienced 5 months of intensive ESL continued to do better than their age peers on measures of English language ability and were more likely to seek opportunities to use English outside of school than students who had not had this experience (Lightbown & Spada, 1991).
- Classroom observation revealed that students in classes where instruction included both meaningful communicative interaction activities and opportunities to focus on the language itself did better than those in classes where teachers avoided all focus on language form and corrective feedback (Lightbown & Spada, 1990).

By the late 1990s, intensive ESL had become widespread throughout Quebec. Once again, what had begun in just a few schools in suburban Montreal became a feature of education across the province. As it spread, it was also adapted to local conditions and preferences (Collins & White, 2011; Collins *et al.*, 1999; Watts & Snow, 1993; White & Turner, 2005). In some schools, the intensity was achieved by offering English for half-days throughout a school year. Other schools offered shorter periods of intensive instruction for two consecutive years. One exceptional school was devoted entirely to a grade 6 intensive program and all 10 classrooms in the school were engaged either in intensive ESL instruction or in the intensive completion of their regular grade-level subject matter (Lightbown & Spada, 1997).

It is worth noting that, when intensive ESL was first offered in a few schools and was gaining support in others, some groups raised strong objections to the approach (Syndicat de l'enseignement de Champlain, 1992), arguing that it would have negative effects on students' French language skills. Another argument was that students would fall behind in their academic work since, by law, students would not be continuing their study of academic subjects other than English itself during the period (usually 5 months) of intensive ESL instruction. Indeed, the early research on intensive ESL included little in the way of verifying that students did not fall behind in their academic work, including their French language literacy skills. Eventually, some school boards did do this research and were able to show that students were willing and able (with their parents' support) to complete the academic part of their grade-level studies and to perform as well as or better than their peers in regular classes on their other subjects (e.g. Raymond & Bonneville, 1995).

Interest in expanding the availability of intensive classes reached the offices of the Ministère de l'Éducation du Québec, where the benefits of increasing and intensifying the number of hours of instruction in grade 5 or 6 was recognized by several Ministers of Education over the years (see, for example, a document published by the Ministère de l'Éducation du Québec,

2001). Nevertheless, the political pressure to lower the starting age for ESL instruction proved stronger than the research evidence that an intensive course in the late elementary years would be more effective than a drip feed approach that started earlier. Since the early 2000s, the starting age for ESL has been lowered from grade 4 to grade 3 and then to grade 1, with students receiving one hour a week of exposure to English, prompting the quip that students got several more years of instruction but not another minute. Eventually, however, the mounting popularity of this approach and the strong networking efforts of teachers, researchers and educational administrators seem to have borne fruit.

In 2011, a proposal to make intensive ESL available in all schools was approved for gradual implementation, with the expectation that it will be available to all students in grade 6 by the 2015–2016 school year (Gouvernement du Québec, 2011). This proposal will be watched closely by educators and parents in Quebec. As noted above, this is not the first time that provincial education officials have shown interest in this idea, but until now, the expansion of intensive ESL has continued to be based on local initiatives rather than a province-wide mandate. Although much has changed in Quebec with regard to the status of French, some parents and educators remain watchful and concerned about ensuring that young Québécois maintain and develop their French language and culture. While the research on intensive English has given no basis for such fears, it will be important to continue to emphasize that developing skill in the second language does not come at the expense of the first.

Intensive French

Intensive ESL in Quebec was a response to the frustration felt by many parents and some teachers and school administrators about the poor English language skills of students who had spent years trying to learn English in one or two hours a week. Because Quebec's language laws prohibited the implementation of English immersion for francophone students, intensive ESL was seen as a way to expand students' opportunities for learning English. For anglophones in other Canadian provinces, French immersion has been widely available as an alternative to 'core French' instruction. However, immersion was not an option in all locations. In spite of its high profile, especially in Canada's major cities, Netten and Germain (2004) found that only 15% of students receiving French instruction in Canada were in immersion programs. In addition, as noted above, in most of Canada outside Quebec, the use of French as a language of daily communication is relatively rare. Thus some parents and educators question the appropriateness of investing so heavily in French for students who are unlikely to encounter the language outside the classroom. In these locations, a high level of French proficiency is not seen as a pressing need, at least not for students at the elementary school level.

In the mid 1990s, some schools in Ottawa implemented a *bain linguistique* for French, drawing on the Quebec intensive ESL experience. Researchers found that students developed greater confidence in their ability to learn French as well as more positive attitudes toward that learning (Peters *et al.*, 2004). About the same time the option of intensive French was proposed for schools in an area of Newfoundland and Labrador, a province where fewer than 4% of the half-million residents said, in the 2006 census, that they speak both French and English and where fewer than 100 individuals declared themselves to speak French only. As is typical in much of Canada, most students in Newfoundland learn French in 'core French' classes, that is, in classes that meet for a few hours a week. Unlike intensive ESL in Quebec, this intensive French program was first implemented in the late 1990s as a research project, planned and followed carefully by a team of researchers from the Université du Québec à Montréal and the Newfoundland Ministry of Education (Netten & Germain, 2004). It was based on clearly stated principles drawn from research and theory in language teaching and learning, and was undertaken with a fully outlined curriculum and opportunities for teachers' professional development from the outset. The principles on which the intensive French curriculum was based emphasized both communicative interaction and the development of accurate language use. In general, more attention was paid to the development of literacy skills than had been the case in most intensive ESL classes, based on the assumption that the skills of second language literacy and first language literacy would be mutually reinforcing.

The implementation of intensive French in Newfoundland and Labrador was accompanied by an extensive evaluation study. Student outcomes surpassed expectations for both oral and written performance in French (Germain *et al.*, 2004; Netten *et al.*, 2004). As a result, educators from other Canadian provinces have begun to offer intensive French classes as an alternative to core French (Netten & Germain, 2004).

Dual Immersion in US Schools

One thing that intensive and immersion models of education have in common is that, with relatively few exceptions, students use their second language only in school, often indeed, in only one classroom, with all other school interactions conducted in the local majority language. As a result, students may have little familiarity with varieties of language that are typical of students their own age who speak their L2 as L1 (Mougeon *et al.*, 2010; Tarone & Swain, 1995). In Canada, immersion programs for English speakers in Quebec represent the exception to that rule. Students have opportunities to interact with the second language in their daily lives – on local sports teams, in mixed-language neighborhoods and, as they grow older, in the workplace and commercial establishments, where French has become the expected medium of interaction. As noted above, this has resulted in a degree of bilingualism among young anglophones in Quebec that would not have been reached if their use of French had been limited to the classroom. In addition, the demographic profile of Quebec is such that more and more school-age children come to school already speaking both French and English, either because they come from families where both languages are spoken or because their families have sought opportunities for them to interact with speakers of both languages before they reach school age – in day care or nursery schools. As a result, a number of French immersion classes in Quebec now have groups of students with more diverse language backgrounds. This does necessarily mean that there is extensive contact between the two languages, but there have been some suggestions regarding how teachers can take advantage of this opportunity (see Lyster et al., 2009).

In the USA, educators have also sought ways of expanding opportunities for communicative interaction for students learning a second language. An approach that is growing in popularity there is known as 'dual' or 'two-way' immersion, and it has been shown to work well for both minority language children learning English and for native speakers of English learning the language of their minority language peers. Dual immersion has proven to be very effective in fostering academic achievement for students from both minority and majority language groups (Howard et al., 2003; Lightbown, 2007; Lindholm-Leary, 2001). This approach has been adopted in areas where there is a substantial minority group, but where members of the majority group may have relatively little need or opportunity to use the minority language. There are scores of dual immersion programs in US schools. A substantial number of them bring Spanish- and English-speaking students together, but there are also dual immersion classes that involve other languages, including Korean and Navajo. A large number of publications provide both information about the extensive research that has been carried out in dual immersion and support for teachers and administrators who wish to implement these programs (see Center for Applied Linguistics, 2011).

Dual immersion can create motivation for language use beyond academic discourse and also provide students with age-appropriate models of the language. By bringing students from these two groups together in the classroom, dual immersion programs offer both groups the chance not only to receive their subject matter instruction in their second language, but also to interact with peers who are native speakers of that language. However, such benefits from interaction cannot be taken for granted, even where there are mixed groups of students. Ballinger and Lyster (2011) review a number of studies of interaction in dual immersion classes in the USA showing that students often see one language as the language of instruction and the other as the language of peer communication. When the two languages are seen as having very different community status, it is sometimes difficult to ensure that students from both language groups appreciate the value of developing true bilingualism.

For minority language students, whose first language is not fully supported by the education system or the larger community, dual immersion programs hold much promise. There is substantial evidence that such programs are more effective than so-called 'submersion' or mainstream approaches in helping minority language students develop skill in the majority language (Lindholm-Leary, 2001). Unfortunately, it is often the case that the educational systems within which dual immersion programs operate give little attention to students' progress in the minority language. It remains to be seen whether these programs provide the means for minority language students to acquire bilingualism that includes the long-term development of their first language.

Summary and Conclusion

Around the world, educators, families and politicians face the challenge of ensuring that their citizens receive the kind of education that is best for them and for their society. In Canada, the challenge is shaped by the presence of two official languages, each representing one of the founding communities of the country, as well as those of indigenous people, whose languages and cultures are at risk of disappearance,[4] and a large immigrant population, whose languages and cultures enrich the country's demographic diversity. The interests of these different communities will not be served best by the imposition of a single approach to language in education. For anglophone students in some areas, French immersion will continue to be an effective and popular choice. In other areas, the perceived language needs and the available resources will make an enriched core or intensive French approach both more practical and more easily accepted.

In Quebec, French is well established as the principal language of public life and English remains a high-prestige language in the larger society. In this context, French immersion in an English-medium school has allowed many young anglophones to reach high levels of proficiency while maintaining their first language ability and identity. For francophone students, the community continues to recognize the importance of ensuring that students get a strong grounding in French. For this reason, many, though by no means all, parents, educators and politicians see intensive English in the late elementary school as a better option than an early intensive or immersion program. For students who come to school speaking a language other than French or English, the priority is given to French, as educators seek to prepare newcomers to function in the French social and economic environment. The commitment to ensuring that all Québécois develop strong French language proficiency has led to a preference for approaches to teaching English that allow students to develop language and literacy skills first in French. Intensive ESL is such an approach.

It is important to acknowledge that, as successful as they have been, neither immersion nor intensive instruction on its own produces students who are native-like speakers of their second language. Nevertheless, each in its context has the potential to help students reach a level of proficiency and communicative confidence that will allow them to pursue further learning opportunities if they choose to do so, both inside and outside the classroom.

Notes

(1) When the Charter was passed in its original form in 1970s, access to English-medium schools was limited to children whose parents had attended English-medium schools in *Quebec*. Legal challenges eventually led to a modification of this provision, such that children whose parents were educated in any Canadian province were deemed eligible to attend English-medium schools. The fundamental requirement that students be educated in French still applies to the children of immigrants from English-speaking countries as well as those from other countries who, for many years, had preferred English-medium education for their children. Over the years, some immigrant families have fought the requirement that their children to attend French-medium schools, but it has now become widely accepted. One interesting result of this is that the French-medium schools, which were once linguistically and culturally homogeneous, have become far more diverse.

(2) Anecdotally, I recall being at a conference in the late 1970s or early 1980s at which videos of some students from these intensive ESL programs were shown. The students seemed to be producing language learned by rote rather than speaking spontaneously in response to genuine questions. Such an impression is consistent with information I was given at the time about the nature of the instruction, which appeared to reflect an essentially audio-lingual approach, with considerable repetition and memorization.

(3) A less strict interpretation of the charter is that subject matter from the grade level curriculum can be incorporated into the content of lessons in another language but that students cannot be evaluated on their knowledge of this subject matter for purposes of completing the grade level. Most intensive classes, especially in the early years, were careful to adhere to the strict interpretation, which meant that lesson content sometimes lacked the age-appropriate cognitive challenges that might have made the instruction more interesting, at least for some students.

(4) The language learning experience of young indigenous people is often overlooked. In some cases, their education continues to be entirely in the official language that is spoken by the majority in the province or territory where they live. In some cases, however, students receive at least some of their schooling in the language of their heritage. In cases where there are few remaining speakers of this language, this can mean that students experience a kind of immersion in a language that they do not already speak (Sarkar & Metallic, 2009). In other cases, the language is still spoken in families and communities, and the school programs allow children to begin their schooling in their first language, before moving into full or partial immersion in French or English (Spada & Lightbown, 2002). In general, educational outcomes for

these students are below Canadian averages, and there is considerable concern for finding better ways to provide the kind of schooling that will permit them to achieve success in educational institutions, including opportunities to enhance their knowledge and use of their heritage language as well as their proficiency in one of the official languages (see e.g. Ball, 2009).

References

Ball, J. (2009) Young indigenous children's language development in Canada: A review of research on needs and promising practices. *Canadian Modern Language Review* 66, 19–47.

Ballinger, S. and Lyster, R. (2011) Student and teacher oral language use in a two-way Spanish/English immersion school. *Language Teaching Research* 15, 289–306.

Billy, L. (1980) Expérimentation d'une nouvelle approche en immersion. *Canadian Modern Language Review* 36, 422–433.

Center for Applied Linguistics (2011) Two-way immersion. Online document, http://www.cal.org/twi/ (accessed 4 November 2011).

Collins, L. and White, J. (2011) An intensive look at intensity and language learning. *TESOL Quarterly* 45, 106–133.

Collins, L., Halter, R., Lightbown, P.M. and Spada, N. (1999) Time and the distribution of time in L2 instruction. *TESOL Quarterly* 33, 655–680.

Cummins, J. (1992) Empowerment through biliteracy. In J.V. Tinajero and A.F. Ada (eds) *The Power of Two Languages: Literacy and Biliteracy for Spanish-Speaking Students* (pp. 1–17). New York: McGraw-Hill.

Genesee, F. (1987) *Learning through Two Languages: Studies of Immersion and Bilingual Education*. Rowley, MA: Newbury House.

Germain, C., Netten, J. and Movassat, P. (2004) L'évaluation de la production orale en français intensif: Critères et résultats. *Canadian Modern Language Review* 60, 309–332.

Gouvernement du Québec (16 September 2011) Press release. Online document, http://communiques.gouv.qc.ca/gouvqc/communiques/GPQF/Septembre2011 (accessed 1 November 2011).

Government of Canada, Office of the Commissioner of Official Languages (2009) Annual Report 2008–2009.

Harley, B. and King, M.L. (1989) Verb lexis in the written compositions of young L2 learners. *Studies in Second Language Acquisition* 11, 415–439.

Harley, B. and Swain, M. (1984) The interlanguage of immersion students and its implications for second language teaching. In A. Davies, C. Criper and A.P.R. Howatt (eds) *Interlanguage* (pp. 291–312). Edinburgh: University of Edinburgh Press.

Howard, E.R., Sugarman, J. and Christian, D. (2003) *Trends in Two-Way Immersion Education: A Review of the Research*. Washington, DC: Center for Applied Linguistics.

Jensen, J.V. (1962) *Effects of Childhood Bilingualism*. Champaign, IL: National Council of Teachers of English.

Lambert, W.E. and Tucker, G.R. (1972) *The Bilingual Education of Children*. Rowley, MA: Newbury House.

Lightbown, P.M. (1988) Educational research and theory in language policy: ESL in Quebec schools. *TESL Canada Journal* 5, 27–32.

Lightbown, P.M. (2007) Fair trade: Two-way bilingual education. *Estudios de Lingüística Inglesa Aplicada* 7, 9–34.

Lightbown, P.M. and Spada, N. (1990) Focus-on-form and corrective feedback in communicative language teaching: Effects on second language learning. *Studies in Second Language Acquisition* 12, 429–448.

Lightbown, P.M. and Spada, N. (1991) Étude des effets à long terme de l'apprentissage intensif de l'anglais, langue seconde, au primaire. *Canadian Modern Language Review* 48, 90–117.

Lightbown, P.M. and Spada, N. (1994) An innovative program for primary ESL in Quebec. *TESOL Quarterly* 28, 563–579.
Lightbown, P.M. and Spada, N. (1997) Learning English as a second language in a special school in Quebec. *Canadian Modern Language Review* 53, 315–355.
Lightbown, P.M., Conan, H., Bolduc, I. and Guay, S. (1988) L'enseignement accru de l'anglais, langue seconde, dans les écoles primaries au Québec. Report prepared for SPEAQ (Société pour la promotion de l'enseignement de l'anglais, langue seconde, au Québec), Montreal.
Lindholm-Leary, K.J. (2001) *Dual Language Education*. Clevedon: Multilingual Matters.
Lyster, R. (1987) Speaking immersion. *Canadian Modern Language Review* 43, 701–711.
Lyster, R. (2007) *Learning and Teaching Languages through Content*. Amsterdam: John Benjamins.
Lyster, R., Collins, L. and Ballinger, S. (2009) Linking languages through a bilingual read-aloud project. *Language Awareness* 18, 366–383.
MacLennan, H. (1945) *Two Solitudes*. Toronto: Collins.
Ministère le l'Éducation du Québec (2001) Lire, écrire, communiquer... reussir: Plan d'action pour améliorer l'apprentissage de la langue seconde. Report no. 2001-01-01103.
Mougeon, R., Nadasdi, T. and Rehner, K. (2010) *The Sociolinguistic Competence of Immersion Students*. Bristol: Multilingual Matters.
Netten, J. and Germain, C. (2004) Introduction: Intensive French. *Canadian Modern Language Review* 60, 263–273.
Netten, J., Germain, C. and Séguin, S.P. (2004) L'évaluation de la production écrite en français intensif: Critères et résultats. *Canadian Modern Language Review* 60, 333–353.
Peal, E. and Lambert, W.E. (1962) The relation of bilingualism to intelligence. *Psychological Monographs* 76, 1–23.
Peters, M., MacFarlane, A. and Wesche, M. (2004) Le regime pédagogique du français intensif à Ottawa: le bain linguistique. *Canadian Modern Language Review* 60, 373–391.
Raymond, A. and Bonneville, S. (1995) *Recherche en enseignement intensif, 1987–1995*. Asbestos, QC: Commission scolaire de l'Asbesterie.
Sarkar, M. and Metallic, M.A. (2009) Indigenizing the structural syllabus: The challenge of revitalizing Mi'gmaq in Listuguj. *Canadian Modern Language Review* 66, 49–71.
Spada, N. and Lightbown, P.M. (1989) Intensive ESL programs in Quebec primary schools. *TESL Canada Journal* 7, 11–32.
Spada, N. and Lightbown, P.M. (2002) L1 and L2 in the education of Inuit children in northern Quebec: Abilities and perceptions. *Language and Education* 16, 212–240.
Stern, H.H. (1985) The time factor and compact course development. *TESL Canada Journal* 3, 13–27.
Swain, M. (1988) Manipulating and complementing content teaching to maximize second language learning. *TESL Canada Journal* 6, 68–83.
Swain, M. and Johnson, R.K. (1997) Immersion education: A category within bilingual education. In R.K. Johnson and M. Swain (eds) *Immersion Education: International Perspectives* (pp. 1–16). Cambridge: Cambridge University Press.
Syndicat de l'enseignement de Champlain (1992) L'enseignement intensif de l'anglais, langue seconde, au primaire: position de l'exécutif de la section Longueuil-élémentaire.
Tarone, E. and Swain, M. (1995) A sociolinguistic perspective on second-language use in immersion classrooms. *Modern Language Journal* 79, 166–178.
Tedick, D.J., Christian, D. and Fortune, T.W. (eds) (2011) *Immersion Education: Practices, Policies, Possibilities*. Bristol: Multilingual Matters.
Watts, W. and Snow, S. (1993) L'anglais intensif au Québec 1976–1993. Report prepared for SPEAQ (Société pour la promotion de l'enseignement de l'anglais, langue seconde, au Québec), Montreal.

Weary, K. (1987) An evaluation of the pedagogical materials of an intensive ESL program used by a francophone Quebec school board at the Grade 6 level. Unpublished master's thesis, McGill University, Montreal, QC.
White, J.L. and Turner, C.E. (2005) Comparing children's oral ability in two ESL programs. *Canadian Modern Language Review* 61, 491–517.

3 Closing the Gap: Intensity and Proficiency

Laura Collins and Joanna White

To set up the context for the issues we wish to explore in this chapter, we begin with narratives written by two young francophone learners of English in the early stages of a five-month intensive English as a foreign language (EFL) experience. They were written in response to a picture prompt showing a young child and a grandmotherly woman standing beside a basket containing a mother cat and her kittens. Please note that both names are pseudonyms.

Annie: Is the girl qui [French for who] have one cat and the cat have baby. The cat a accouché [French for gave birth] and is four baby cats. The girl is very happy and she's garde [French for keep] the baby cats. She give the name for each baby cats and is very happy.

Antoine: My name is Jacques. My grandmother have a cat, it's a female and it is big because it is enceinte [French for pregnant]. My grandmother love her cat but she can't have four kittens plus one cat. For this reason I demande [French for ask] at my grandmother si [French for if] I can take a kitten but she is not sure because kitten it's a big responsibility and I said 'Please grandmother I love kitten, I love responsibility and I love you!' and my grand mother say 'That's Ok Jacques a give a kitten' 'Thank you, I said, you are the best grandmother in the world!' This is the end of my story.

The two learners who produced these texts were at the same school, were the same age (11 years old), had similarly limited contact with English outside of class (the school was in a francophone region of the province of Quebec and both sets of parents were francophone speakers), and they had experienced the same type and amount of prior EFL instruction (two years of 90 minutes a week of communicative language instruction). However, they had clearly extracted different amounts of EFL learning during this prior limited, or drip-feed (Skehan, 1986; Stern, 1985), exposure.

We now present narratives by the same two learners, written almost four months later, during the final weeks of their intensive program. In this case, the picture prompt shows a playground altercation between a boy and a girl.

Annie: The story is about a girl. Her name is Marie-Pier. She is twelve years old. One week ago, Marie Pier was very tired because her father was die. And all the time, during the days and the nights, she was sad. She wanted to talk to anybody. But one time, her teacher started to talk with her. 'Why are you sad like this Marie-Pier? You don't eat, you don't do your homework ... What happen?' said the teacher. Marie-Pier started to be angry against her teacher because she didn't want to talk about this. So, she told her teacher 'I don't want to talk!' She went in the school yard. Some students started to told her some nouns that she don't like. They named her a dog and a stupid student so she punch one student with her hand and another with her feet. When she went at her home, her mother told her that the principal called. So, Marie-Pier tell her mother 'why' and her mother talk with her. Marie-Pier tell her that she will never start again and she will stop to be angry against her teacher and stop to punch boy or peoples.

Antoine: One time in a school there was a new girl name Amy. At school everybody was laughing of her because she was new and always alone. But one day a boy said to her that she was stupid and other things like that, then he received a foot in the stomach. Poor him, he was on the floor and everybody was laughing at him. It was the last time that he said bad things to somebody. Now Amy has a lot of friend because she gave a lesson to the boy and he know that if he continue to ecoeurer [French for annoy or 'bug'] other people they will be angry and don't have control of their feet.

By the end of the intensive experience, the differences between the two learners are much less apparent. Both use various grammatical and lexical devices appropriately and are able to construct a narrative in their second language (L2) that contains a beginning, middle, and an end.[1]

One explanation for the closing of the proficiency gap between the two students is that the increase in the amount and the intensity of instruction has minimized the role that individual differences, such as language learning aptitude (including its different subcomponents), may play in more limited exposure situations. Skehan (1986) hypothesized that high-aptitude students may be able to extract the maximum amount of learning in time-pressured situations, which, arguably, characterized the limited exposure to English that the students had had during their 90 minutes a week in the previous two grades. Since Skehan's seminal article on aptitude, there has been considerable work on the different components of aptitude that may predict performance in a variety of situations. These include the importance of memory for younger learners and analytic ability for older learners (Harley & Hart, 1997); the relationship among working memory, noticing and L2 development (Mackey et al., 2002; Ranta, 1998); and the relative contributions of first language (L1) skills and L2 aptitude in predicting L2 learning (Sparks et al., 2009). However, there has been considerably less research on the interaction between the intensity of instructional time and the individual learner. This is the issue we explore in this chapter. Our research question was: does an intensive L2 experience, which removes the time pressure factor present in the limited exposure contexts, make the L2 more accessible to a wider range of learners?

Background

Two bodies of previous research are relevant to the issues we are exploring in this paper. The first is the extensive literature on the benefits of concentrated instruction when the primary contact with the L2 is in the classroom, that is, in what is often referred to as foreign language contexts. The second is the much more limited literature on individual differences and concentrated instruction.

Research findings show that the opportunity to experience the available time for instruction in a concentrated form allows students to make considerable gains in different aspects of language learning, even after a single intensive course (e.g. Collins et al., 1999; Collins & White, 2011; Germain et al., 2004; Lapkin et al., 1998; Lightbown & Spada, 1994; White & Turner, 2005, this volume). There is even evidence that a well-designed intensive course offered in a foreign language context can be more beneficial for oral fluency than a study-abroad experience in the target language context (Freed et al., 2004). Thus, previous research demonstrates that, when learning an L2 in an environment that affords limited contact with the target language outside the classroom, experiencing the instruction in an intensive format can yield positive results.[2]

Although a considerable amount of research has looked at the role of individual differences in L2 classroom learning in general, the degree to which these factors are operative in the 'successful' intensive contexts has not received much research attention. Ranta (1998, 2002) investigated the extent to which L1 language analytic ability (as measured by an error detection and correction task in the L1) may have positive effects on learning when the intensive instruction consists of a communicative approach focused on oral interaction and listening comprehension. The French L1 students in her study were from a population similar to the one in the current study, that is 11- to 12-year-old EFL[3] learners. Using a principle components analysis, Ranta found that, for the strongest and weakest students, L1 language analytic ability predicted successful performance on a range of L2 measures (including two of the listening measures we used in the current study) at the beginning and end of their intensive program. These results suggest that an intensive experience in which little explicit attention is given to language analysis in the L2 may be enhanced for students who demonstrate an ability to take an analytical approach to language (at least in their L1). Ranta (2002: 176) also pointed out that 'different aspects of aptitude may come into play at different stages of language learning' (cf. Skehan, 1998). She speculated that problems with lexical retrieval during their prior drip-feed English program may have hampered some students' overall language development, which may explain their relatively poor performance on an aural vocabulary test at the beginning of their intensive program. It is important to note, however, that even the weaker students in Ranta's study still made substantial progress in their L2 after five months of intensive exposure.

When abilities in the L1 are defined more globally as 'academic ability', there is evidence that this may in fact be more relevant to L2 learning success in drip-feed contexts than in intensive contexts. In a large-scale study comparing different models of intensive EFL instruction in Quebec among the same population of learners as Ranta and the present study, Collins *et al.* (1999) noted that, in one of the three models, participation in the grade 6 intensive program had been restricted to students who had demonstrated above-average academic ability (across all school subjects, including EFL) in their previous year of schooling. At the pretest, these students were significantly stronger in English than the students in the other two models, in which academic ability was not a criterion for participation. Although language learning aptitude was not measured in the study, the authors argued that the academically successful students may have been able to learn more English in the limited exposure they had had to their L2 in their previous years of schooling (usually only 90 minutes a week). However, by the end of the intensive experience, there was no longer a difference between these students and another group representing a much wider range of academic ability. Both groups of students had experienced the most concentrated form of intensive instruction (massed into five months as opposed to spread out over half-days for the full 10 months of the school year), and they showed similar amounts of learning. Collins *et al.* (1999) argued that the intensive experience appeared to allow 'students of various abilities sufficient time for language learning' (p. 673). It is important to note, however, that the students in the non-selected group were also exposed to more English outside the class; there were no comparisons made in the 1999 study between students of different academic abilities and/or with different amounts of English proficiency at the outset who were following the same intensive program.

In the present study, we take a new look at data from a recent longitudinal study of different models of intensive EFL that allow us, albeit indirectly, to examine whether intensifying instruction does in fact level the playing field for L2 learning. These data also give us somewhat greater control over some of the intervening variables in previous research, highlighted above, such as amount of exposure to the L2 and type of intensive program. It is important to note that the data we will be presenting come from a *between-*program comparison of different distributions of intensive EFL (Collins & White, 2011). The data permit an additional *within* program investigation of the effects of intensity on individual learners' performance, but because the within-program comparison was not the focus of the original study, we did not collect potentially useful data, such as aptitude measures of the participating students. We believe, however, that the data we do have allow us to take some important first steps in addressing the issues we raise, and that they should generate ideas for future research more narrowly focused on some of the questions that emerged from our findings. We will return to this point in the discussion section of the chapter.

Methodology

Context

The learners we worked with for this study were similar in a number of ways. They were all grade 6 (11–12 years old) francophone students attending the same school in a region of the French-speaking province of Quebec where the dominant language of the community was French. This school housed only grade 6 students, 10 classes in total, who were all enrolled in a special intensive EFL program in which students completed the regular part of their grade 6 curriculum in French (math, science, etc.) in just five months rather than the usual 10 months, and devoted the remaining five months to EFL. Five classes did the French curriculum in the first five months, and then started intensive EFL (the students in our study); the other five classes started with EFL and finished with the French curriculum. This is an unusual situation, as normally elementary schools in Quebec contain all grades (kindergarten through to grade 6) and typically have no more than two grade 6 classes at a given time.

For research purposes, having all of the groups at the same school presented a number of design advantages. The students not only experienced the same type of instruction (a communicative-based program emphasizing oral and listening skills and the acquisition of vocabulary and fluency) for the same number of hours (approximately 400), but they also worked with the same materials and many of the same activities as there was a high degree of cooperation among the five EFL teachers at the school. In addition, they came from a similar socio-economic backgrounds and had been exposed to the same type and amount of prior EFL instruction (60–90 minutes per week in each of grades 4 and 5, for a total of approximately 70 hours).

Unlike many other intensive programs, this school did not impose any selection criteria based on previous academic performance, which resulted in a key difference of interest to the current study: the students represented a range of academic ability, and, as the pretest scores below will reveal, had learned different amounts of English in their prior, similarly limited exposure to the target language.

The larger study followed all 136 students longitudinally over the course of their 400 hours of instruction, comparing their performance with students in a different distribution of intensive EFL instruction (see Collins & White, 2011). For the current study, we focused on students drawn from all five classes who met the following criteria:

- They were not bilingual or highly proficient speakers of English (self-reported and/or reported by teachers).
- They were present at all five data collection points (explained in more detail below).
- They had very limited access to English outside the school: they reported living in homes with parents and/or guardians who spoke French (i.e. were not proficient or bilingual speakers of English) and they had not attended an English-medium school at any point in their prior schooling.

This yielded a subset of 55 students whose performance was followed for the current study.

Instruments and procedure

There were five data collection points. Pretests were administered during the first week of the intensive EFL program, one of which was used as the grouping variable for the current study. Following this, the students' developing L2 knowledge was assessed four times at regular 100 hour intervals of instruction on a range of measures. Below we give basic descriptions of the tasks; for sample items and more detail please see Collins and White (2011). Table 3.1 provides a summary of the data collection schedule.

Pretest measures

There were three pretest measures, the aural vocabulary recognition task (AVR), a cloze task and a dictation task. The measure used to group the students into different levels of knowledge of English at the outset of their intensive experience was the 80-item AVR task, which required that students match the spoken words they heard to pictures on a page. The AVR tests familiarity with basic vocabulary to describe common objects and has

Table 3.1 Overview of assessment measures

	Pretest	Time 1 (100 hours)	Time 2 (200 hours)	Time 3 (300 hours)	Time 4 (400 hours)
AVR	×	×			
Cloze	×			×	
Dictation	×			×	
Vocabulary Recognition		×	×	×	×
Written narratives: inflections		×	×	×	×
Written narratives: length		×	×	×	×
Listening: sentence			×		
Listening: general					×

AVR, Aural vocabulary recognition task

been shown to discriminate well among beginner learners of this age (Collins et al., 1999; Ranta, 1998, 2002). We grouped the learners into low, mid and high groups based on their scores on this task: low represented a score range of 37–47 (mean 43.39, $n = 14$); mid 48–58 (mean 52.94, $n = 17$); and high 59–69 (mean 64.62, $n = 21$).[4]

The cloze task asked students to complete 10 blanks in a short passage with an appropriate word. It measured the students' knowledge of basic sentence structure (word order, parts of speech). The dictation task was adapted from one used by the Barcelona Age Factor team (Muñoz, 2006) and consisted of 50 items. It measures listening skills, knowledge of basic word order, awareness of sound/symbol correspondence in English and the ability to segment words. One point was given for each correctly spelled word.

Longitudinal measures (at 100 hour intervals)

After four approximately 100 hour intervals of instruction, students' knowledge of various aspects of English was assessed. At all four times, knowledge of the 1000 most frequent words of English was measured using different versions of the yes–no vocabulary test (from Meara, 1992). Students were presented with 180 words in lists of three columns per page, of which 120 were real words and 60 were nonsense words (included to prevent guessing). Their task was to check whether or not they recognized each of the words. Students also wrote picture-prompted narratives at each testing time. The instructions were the same across the testing sessions ('Imagine what is happening now, what happened before, and what is going to happen next'), but the pictures differed. These writing samples were analyzed for use of verb inflections (a measure of grammatical knowledge) using a four-point scale ranging from no use of inflections (1) to productive use (4). The length of the narratives, a fluency measure, was assessed using a five-point scale, representing increments of 50 words.

Different tasks were used across the testing intervals to measure listening skills because this aspect of the learners' proficiency changes quite dramatically over the five-month intensive experience. Consequently, a measure that is appropriate for the low level of the students at time 1 will show ceiling effects later. Similarly, a task that is appropriate to measure their comprehension skills at the end of the intensive experience is far too difficult (and frustrating) for the students at the outset. At time 1 we re-administered the AVR from the pretest; at time 2 we used an aural sentence comprehension task in which students matched 20 sentences they heard to appropriate pictures (Muñoz, 2006); at time 3 we re-administered the cloze and dictation tasks from the pretest; and at time 4 we used a 32-item general listening comprehension task in which students listen to short statements and choose appropriate interpretations (from either text or pictures representing what they have heard). This task has been used in many studies with intensive EFL students in Quebec (e.g. Collins et al., 1999; Ranta, 1998, 2002; Spada & Lightbown, 1999).[5]

Analyses and Results

For all tests that were repeated twice or more across time, we conducted separate mixed between–within ANOVAs with the α level set at 0.01 to adjust for multiple comparisons for main effects and interactions. Following the American Psychological Association Style Manual (APA), pairwise comparisons are only discussed where a significant interaction was found. For the tests that were administered only once (the two different listening tasks at times 2 and 4), we performed one-way ANOVAs, again with the α level set at 0.01. The Bonferroni adjustment was applied to all *post-hoc* pairwise comparisons.

AVR: Pretest to time 1

There was a significant interaction between time and group (low, mid, high), $F(2,49) = 21.72$, $p < 0.01$. The pairwise comparisons (see Table 3.3 in the Appendix) show that at the pretest there was a significant difference between all groups ($ps < 0.01$), which is to be expected; as this was the grouping variable (see above), there was no overlap of scores. At time 1 (100 hours later), there was still a significant difference ($ps < 0.03$), but as Figure 3.1 shows, the gap between the groups has closed considerably, with the low group making the greatest gains.

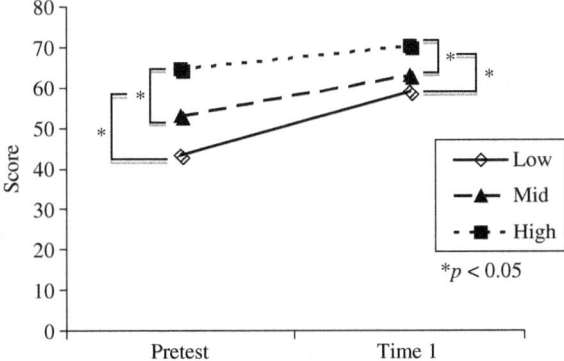

Figure 3.1 Aural vocabulary recognition over time

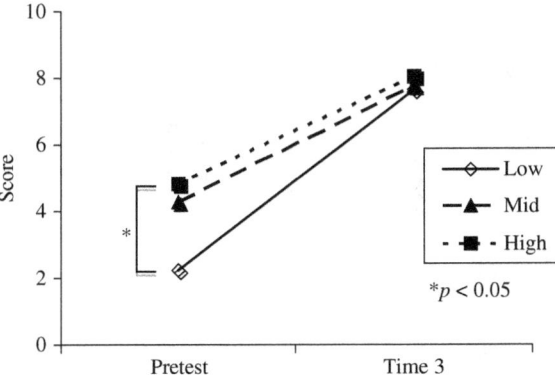

Figure 3.2 Cloze over time

Cloze task: Pretest to time 3

There was a significant interaction between time and group, $F(2,49) = 10.27$, $p < 0.01$. The pairwise comparisons (see Table 3.4 in the Appendix) show that at the pretest, the low group was significantly different from the mid and high groups ($ps < 0.01$). By time 3, there were no significant differences among the groups (see Figure 3.2).

Dictation: Pretest to time 3

The interaction between time and group was not significant; that is to say, progress over time was not mediated by the group effect. However, as Figure 3.3 shows, the modest (but insignificant) differences between the scores at the pretest did follow the trend for the other pretest tasks. In addition, the scores for all three groups were converging by time 3.

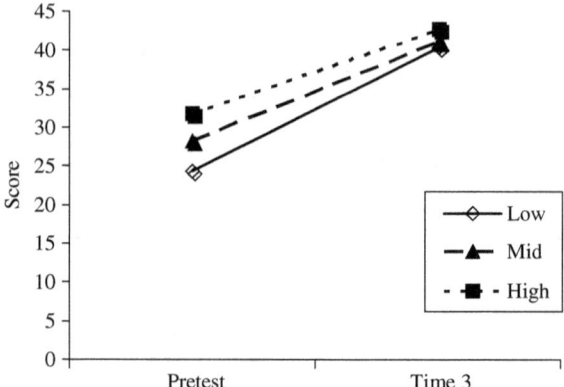

Figure 3.3 Dictation over time

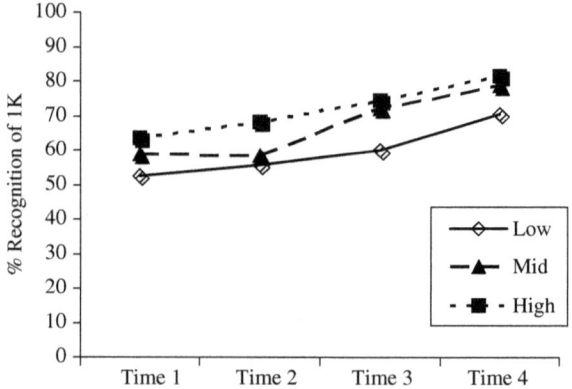

Figure 3.4 Yes–no vocabulary test

Yes–no vocabulary task: Times 1–4

The interaction between time and group was not significant. Figure 3.4 seems to suggest a difference between the low and the upper two groups at time 3, but perhaps owing to the variability within the mid and high groups on this task, the differences were not substantial enough to result in an effect of group on performance over time.

Narrative task (verb inflections): Times 1–4

The interaction between time and group was not significant. Figure 3.5 seems to suggest superior performance by the high group at time 4, but there was considerable within-group variability in the use of verb inflections. As Figure 3.5 also shows, there was very little productive use of this aspect of

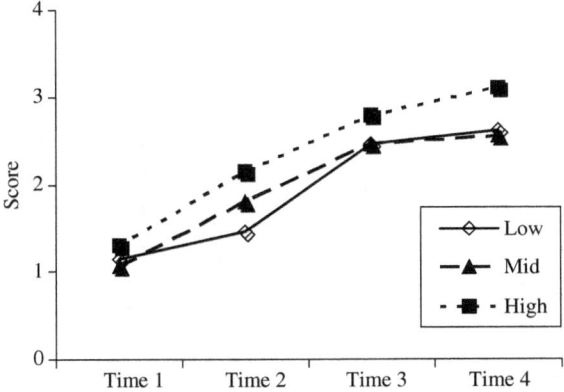

Figure 3.5 Written narratives: Inflections

English in the initial stages of intensive. It was not until the latter half of the intensive experience that some students began showing some knowledge of verb inflections, but the absence of an interaction effect suggests that this knowledge did not develop as a function of group membership (as defined in this study).

Narrative task (fluency): Times 1–4

There was a significant interaction between time and group, $F(2,47) = 4.75$, $p < 0.01$ (see Figure 3.6). The between-group comparisons (summarized in Table 3.5 in the Appendix) showed no significant differences until time 4, and they were between the low and the mid and high groups, this time in favor of the low group. The within-group comparisons demonstrated that the gains for the low group were significant across all times.

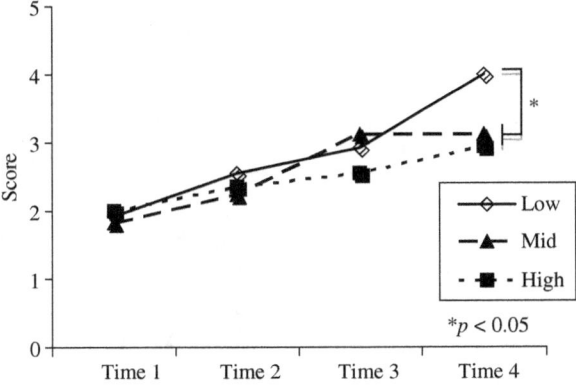

Figure 3.6 Written narratives: Length

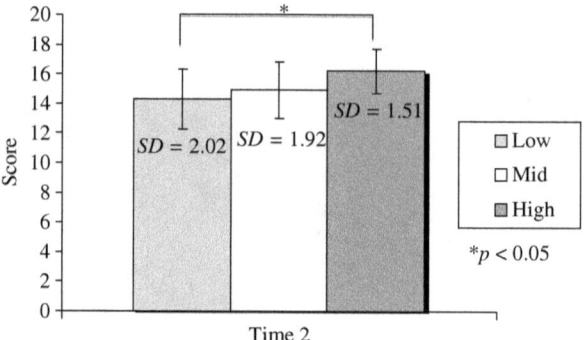

Figure 3.7 Listening comprehension (sentence comprehension)

For the mid and high groups, the significant gains did not occur until the latter half of the intensive experience.

Listening comprehension (sentence comprehension): Time 2

Figure 3.7 displays the results from this analysis. Although performance on this task did not differ dramatically between groups, there was a significant between-group difference, $F(2,51) = 5.45, p < 0.01$. The Tukey HSD (see Table 3.6 in the Appendix) shows that the difference was between low and high groups; there was no significant difference between low and mid groups (or between mid and high).

Listening comprehension (general): Time 4

As Figure 3.8 shows, the scores did not differ greatly between the groups, but there was a significant between-group difference, $F(2,51) = 4.78, p < 0.01$.

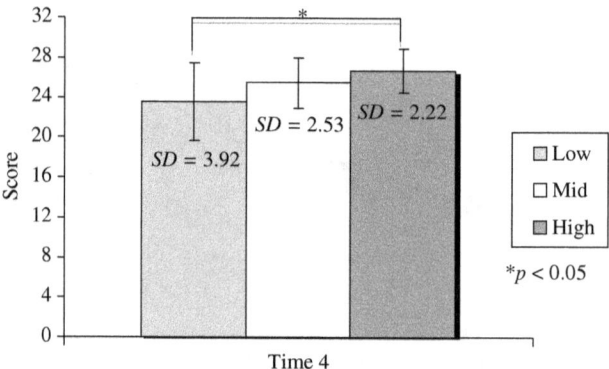

Figure 3.8 Listening comprehension (general)

The Tukey HSD (see Table 3.7 in the Appendix) shows that the difference is between low and high groups only; there is no significant difference between low and mid groups (or between mid and high).

Summary of analyses

Table 3.2 provides a summary of the significant findings from the perspective of the low group, as it is this group's progress over time that allows us to see whether the gap between their knowledge of English and that of their peers is closing. At time 1, the low group's performance on most tasks was already similar to that of the mid and high groups; only one task showed a significant difference. For the rest of the assessment measures, it was only on the listening comprehension tasks at times 2 and 4 that the low group showed somewhat lower performance; this was in comparison with the high group only. At time 4 there was also a significant difference in favor of the low group on the fluency measure (the length of narratives produced).

Discussion

The research question that we set out to explore through these data was whether the different amounts of EFL knowledge the grade 6 students had

Table 3.2 Performance of low group relative to the mid and high groups

	Pretest	Time 1 (100 hours)	Time 2 (200 hours)	Time 3 (300 hours)	Time 4 (400 hours)
AVR	L < M, H	L < M, H			
Cloze	L < M, H			NS	
Dictation	NS			NS	
Vocabulary recognition		NS	NS	NS	NS
Written narratives: inflections		NS	NS	NS	NS
Written narratives: length		NS	NS	NS	L > M, H
Listening: sentence			L < H		
Listening: general					L < H

NS, No significant difference (no interaction between group and time); blank = no data collected at that time gained from their prior, drip-feed exposure would continue to predict performance in a program that afforded students considerably more time on task, concentrated in an intensive format. The results show that pretest performance did not prove to be a consistent predictor of learning across the intensive experience.

At time 1, the low group's performance on most tasks was already similar to the mid and high groups; only one task, AVR, showed a significant difference. For the rest of the assessment measures, it was just on the listening comprehension tasks at times 2 and 4 that the low group performed differently, and this was in comparison with the high group only. At time 4 there was also a significant difference in *favor* of the low group on the fluency measure (the length of narratives produced). We now turn to a discussion of these findings.

When comparing the low-level students' performance on the pretest measures with their performance on the same measures later on in the program (time 1 for the AVR, time 3 for the cloze and the dictation), we see that the gap between the low group's performance and that of the other two groups was already beginning to close after the first 100 hours of instruction (time 1), and had indeed closed by time 3. The interactions between time and group on both the AVR and the cloze are explained at each point by the greater gains made by the low group over time, in comparison with the other two groups. Thus, the low-level learners made impressive progress in their knowledge of the meaning of common vocabulary and of basic sentence structure in English. The dictation task was challenging for all learners at the pretest; it requires a more sophisticated knowledge of vocabulary, sentence structure and sound–symbol correspondence in English than the AVR or cloze. Although there was no interaction between group and time on the dictation, the trend in the mean scores for the three groups at the pretest was in line with the other two tasks and represents a seven-point spread (from 24 to 31.5). By time 3, the range in scores had decreased considerably to a two-point spread (40.5–42.5), such that the lower-level group showed comparable development of the skills measured by this task. Similar development was also observed in the students' improvement in their recognition of the 1000 most common words of English, as measured by the yes–no vocabulary test.

The use of verb inflections on the narrative task was one of only two measures for which the within group variability actually *increased* over time. There was in fact very little use of temporal morphology of English across all groups in the initial stages of the intensive program. However, as students' knowledge began to develop, it did so at different rates within groups, and this high degree of variability made the mean scores an unreliable indicator of group behavior (this is why apparent differences between group mean scores seen in Figure 3.5 did not turn out to be significantly different). These results provide evidence that the pretest grouping did not predict development of the use of verb inflections.

Somewhat surprisingly, fluency, measured in terms of the number of words used in the narratives, yielded a significant difference in favor of the low group at the final testing time. We do not interpret this finding as strong evidence that the lower-level students became more fluent than their peers, as this was the other measure for which variability increased over time. Rather, a more appropriate interpretation is simply that group membership at the outset of intensive was not a strong predictor of the ability to produce a sustained narrative in the L2. Figure 3.6 shows, overall, that the students were not able to write very much in English at time 1 (see the sample at the beginning of this chapter for an example). One possible explanation for the considerable within-group variability is that proportionally less time is devoted to written production than to oral production in the intensive classes at this school. However, teachers did read aloud regularly to the students, and students did a considerable amount of reading on their own. This familiarity with stories and story structure may have contributed to our observation that, overall, the children were able to produce a good story at each testing time. Even the very short narratives were well structured, with a beginning, middle and end.

The one aspect of language development for which the pretest groupings did predict performance was listening comprehension, notably on the measures that required some interpretation of the message (at the sentence level at time 2 and somewhat beyond sentence level at time 4). The low group appeared to catch up to the mid group on these measures, but not to the high group. The differences were not dramatic, but they were significant.

Two points are relevant to the discussion here. First, students came into the intensive program from different schools in the district. While we can assume that they had all experienced a communicative approach in grades 4 and 5, the exact nature of their prior classroom exposure is unknown. Thus, variation in the range and type of vocabulary instruction and listening activities during their drip-feed program may have contributed to differences in students' pretest performance on the AVR measure. Once in the intensive program, where everyone was engaged in English activities all day long and oral interaction and vocabulary building was a priority, some of these students may have been able to catch up quickly, closing the gap between them and the mid or high performers.

For others, we offer another explanation. Given the overwhelming emphasis on oral skills in the previous drip-feed classes, students who were less successful at learning EFL in this time pressure situation may have been disadvantaged by auditory processing factors. This is an empirical question of course, but it is one raised by our findings and supported by Ranta (2002), who noted the important contribution that L2 vocabulary knowledge made to successful performance on the L2 post-test measures in her study. She speculated that, without automatized lexical access, students with low vocabulary scores were allocating excessive attentional resources to understanding the input in their intensive classes and that this had had a negative impact on their interlanguage development overall.

Conclusion

The findings from this study confirm the intensive EFL teachers' own perspective of the progress made by their students in these programs. At the end of the intensive program in June, all participating teachers completed a questionnaire in which they commented on various aspects of their intensive experience, including student progress. One teacher wrote: 'There are no really weak students in this class, not now in the fifth month. There appeared to be weaker kids in January and February but by March they started catching up ... they all seem to be more or less at the same level now. There are differences, but they're not major'.

We recognize that our interpretation of the findings is limited by the fact that we have no measures of aptitude or academic performance; that is, we do not know whether the low-group participants were actually poorer academically or what their aptitude scores would have been. As explained at the outset of the study, this is because these questions were not the motivation for the original study from which the data have been taken. However, it appears that the intensive experience, which offered both substantial and sustained time for learning, minimized the effects of whatever individual differences may have been operative in the students' prior drip-feed (time pressure) situations, perhaps giving 'more opportunity and less penalty for learners to learn at their own pace' (Skehan, 1986: 193).

We note that the finding of substantial gains for the lower proficiency learners in our study is consistent with findings from research in study abroad contexts, when the learning experience consists of rich exposure to the L2. Although the students in our study were not in contact with a native-speaking community, they were certainly immersed in the target language for several hours a day, five days a week, over five months. Muñoz's (2010) longitudinal study of two Spanish-Catalan children's year-long immersion in an English community, in which the children attended an English-medium school and interacted regularly in English with native-speaking peers, showed that the gap between the two children's initial knowledge of English lessened considerably over the course of the stay. Other examples of impressive gains among lower-proficiency learners who are immersed in the L2 include several of the contributors to Freed's (1995a) edited volume on study abroad (e.g. Brecht *et al.*, 1995; Freed, 1995b; Lapkin *et al.*, 1995), although there is some concern that the assessment instruments in these contexts may not have been sufficiently sensitive to capture the gains made by more advanced learners (Freed, 1998; see also Muñoz, 2010).

A related point from the study abroad 'immersion' research that is relevant to the current study is the finding that progress made in listening and speaking is not correlated with scores from the Modern Language Aptitude Test (Brecht *et al.*, 1995; Freed, 1998). This does not necessarily mean there is no relationship between aptitude and language abilities such as listening and speaking, but rather that the Modern Language Aptitude Test may not be the best instrument to capture such a relationship (see also Lightbown & Spada, 2006), It will thus be important in future research to isolate different components of aptitude and L2 learning abilities to examine the relative contribution the factors play in different aspects of L2 development under intensive conditions.

In fact, changes to the context in which the original data were collected may provide us with an ideal opportunity to address these issues. The Ministry of Education in Quebec is currently implementing a plan to offer intensive EFL to all francophone elementary students in Quebec by the 2015–2016 school year. (Previously intensive EFL was an optional program available to a minority of students across the province; most students received just 60–90 minutes of EFL a week.) With the likelihood of students with a greater range in ability and knowledge than in the current study, the new situation will allow for a more fine-grained examination of the relationship between intensity of instruction and individual factors such as memory, auditory processing and analytical ability. Equally important will be qualitative measures that track students' perspectives on their own learning of EFL in intensive programs over time. In our previous large-scale studies we have tended to administer end-of-program questionnaires to the students, and the responses consistently show high levels of enthusiasm among all students and considerable confidence in their newly acquired abilities to express themselves in their L2. However, we have not explored how these attitudes develop over time across different learners. This could be yet another potentially revealing source of information on the interaction between intensity of instruction, individual differences and L2 development.

Acknowledgments

We are grateful to a number of colleagues and students for their assistance with the study reported on here. They include our research associate and statistical advisor, Randall Halter; our graduate student project manager, Suzanne Springer, and the graduate student testers, Suzie Beaulieu, Veronica Frediani and Isabelle Morin. We also thank Philippa Bell and Victoria Dwight for their feedback on draft versions of this chapter. Funding for this project was provided through two grants: the TESOL International Research Foundation (co-awarded to us and to Carmen Muñoz and colleagues at the University of Barcelona) and a team grant from the Quebec Ministry of

Education (Fonds Québécois de la recherche sur la société et la culture), awarded to the authors and three Concordia colleagues.

Notes

(1) In fact, Annie's text is actually somewhat longer and more developed than Antoine's, perhaps because she was more inspired by the picture than Antoine.
(2) There is some evidence that these benefits may decrease in later stages of language learning, as Serrano (2011) found that intermediate level learners profited more from an intensive experience than did advanced learners.
(3) In Quebec, the teaching of English is identified as 'ESL' (English as a Second Language) in recognition of the fact that Canada is an officially bilingual country. However, in the context in which our research was carried out, there was little access to English outside the intensive program: the school was in a francophone schoolboard, in a predominately French-speaking region of the province. We opted therefore to use 'EFL' in this chapter, to make the context more transparent to an international readership.
(4) Three students' scores were several points below the 37 cut-off: to ensure that all groups represented a similar length point range on the AVR, these students were not included in the analyses, yielding a final N of 52 for the study.
(5) In the larger study we also followed oral performance over time with a subset of learners. As the two paired tasks we used did not involve all students in the sample, and because students were paired randomly each time without consideration of their AVR scores, it was not possible to consider performance on these oral tasks in the present study. For more information on the oral tasks, see Collins and White (2011).

References

Brecht, R., Davidson, D. and Ginsberg, R. (1995) Predictors of foreign language gain during study abroad. In B. Freed (ed.) *Second Language Acquisition in a Study Abroad Context* (pp. 37–66). Amsterdam: John Benjamins.
Collins, L. and White, J. (2011) An intensive look at intensity and language learning. *TESOL Quarterly* 45 (1), 106–133.
Collins, L., Halter, R.H., Lightbown, P.M. and Spada, N. (1999) Time and the distribution of time in second language instruction. *TESOL Quarterly* 33, 655–680.
Freed, B. (1995a) (ed.) *Second Language Acquisition in a Study Abroad Context*. Amsterdam: John Benjamins.
Freed, B. (1995b) What makes us think that students who study abroad become fluent? In B. Freed (ed.) *Second Language Acquisition in a Study Abroad Context* (pp. 123–148). Amsterdam: John Benjamins.
Freed, B. (1998) An overview of issues and research in language learning in a study abroad setting. *Frontiers: The Interdisciplinary Journal of Study Abroad* 4, 31–60.
Freed, B. Segalowitz, N. and Dewey, D. (2004) Context of learning and second language fluency in French. *Studies in Second Language Acquisition* 26 (2), 275–301.
Germain, C., Netten, J. and Movassat, P. (2004) L'évaluation de la production orale en français intensif: Critères et résultats. *The Canadian Modern Language Review* 60, 295–308.
Harley, B. and Hart, D. (1997) Language aptitude and second language proficiency in classroom learners of different starting ages. *Studies of Second Language Acquisition* 19 (3), 379–400.
Lapkin, S., Hart, D. and Swain, M. (1995) A Canadian interprovincial exchange: Evaluating the linguistic impact of a three-month stay in Quebec. In B. Freed (ed.)

Second Language Acquisition in a Study Abroad Context (pp. 67–94). Amsterdam: John Benjamins.

Lapkin, S., Hart, D. and Harley, B. (1998) Case study of compact core French models: Attitudes and achievement. In S. Lapkin (ed.) *French Second Language Education in Canada: Empirical Studies* (pp. 3–30). Toronto: University of Toronto Press.

Lightbown, P.M. and Spada, N. (1994) An innovative program for primary ESL in Quebec. *TESOL Quarterly* 28, 563–579.

Lightbown, P.M. and Spada, N. (2006) *How Languages are Learned*. Oxford: Oxford University Press.

Mackey, A., Philp, J., Egi, T., Fujii, A. and Tatsumi, T. (2002) Individual differences in working memory, noticing of interactional feedback, and L2 development. In P. Robinson (ed.) *Individual Differences and Instructed Language Learning* (pp. 181–209). Amsterdam: John Benjamins.

Meara, P. (1992) *EFL Vocabulary Tests*. Swansea: University College, Centre for Applied Language Studies.

Muñoz, C. (2006) The effects of age on foreign language learning: The BAF project. In C. Muñoz (ed.) *Age and the Rate of Foreign Language Learning*. Clevedon: Multilingual Matters.

Muñoz, C. (2010) Staying abroad with the family: A case study of two siblings' second language development during a year's immersion. *International Journal of Applied Linguistics* 160, 24–48.

Ranta, L. (1998) Focus on form from the inside: The significance of grammatical sensitivity for L2 learning in communicative ESL classrooms. Unpublished doctoral dissertation, Concordia University, Montreal.

Ranta, L. (2002) The role of learners' language analytic ability in the communicative classroom. In P. Robinson (ed.) *Individual Differences and Instructed Language Learning* (pp. 159–180). Amsterdam: John Benjamins.

Serrano, R. (2011) The time factor in EFL classroom practice. *Language Learning* 61, 117–145.

Skehan, P. (1986) Where does language aptitude come from? In P. Meara (ed.) *Spoken Language*. London: Centre for Information on Language Teaching.

Skehan, P. (1998) *A Cognitive Approach to Language Learning*. Oxford: Oxford University Press.

Spada, N. and Lightbown, P.M. (1999) Instruction, first language influence, and developmental readiness in second language acquisition. *Modern Language Journal* 83, 1–22.

Sparks, R., Patton, J., Ganschow, L. and Humbach, N. (2009) Long-term crosslinguistic transfer of skills from L1 to L2. *Language Learning* 59 (1), 203–243.

Stern, H.H. (1985) The time factor and compact course development. *TESL Canada Journal* 3 (1), 13–27.

White, J. and Turner, C.E. (2005) Comparing children's oral ability in two ESL programs. *Canadian Modern Language Review* 61 (4), 491–517.

Appendix

Table 3.3 Pairwise comparisons for AVR at pretest and 100 hours

Pretest	M		Low	Mid	High	Time 1	M		Low	Mid	High
	43.29	Low					58.86	Low			
	52.94	Mid	*				63.18	Mid	*		
	64.62	High	*	*			70.33	High	*	*	

*$p < 0.05$

Table 3.4 Pairwise comparisons for cloze at pretest

Time 1	M		Low	Mid	High
	2.21	Low			
	4.29	Mid	*		
	4.81	High	*		

*$p < 0.05$

Table 3.5 Pairwise comparisons for narrative length across times

Low	M		Time 1	Time 2	Time 3	Time 4	Mid	M		Time 1	Time 2	Time 3	Time 4
	1.92	Time 1						1.82	Time 1				
	2.59	Time 2	*					2.24	Time 2				
	2.92	Time 3	*					3.12	Time 3	*	*		
	4.00	Time 4	*	*	*			3.12	Time 4	*	*	*	

High	M		Time 1	Time 2	Time 3	Time 4	Time 4	M		Low	Mid	High
	2.00	Time 1						4.00	Low			
	2.35	Time 2						3.22	Mid	*		
	2.55	Time 3						2.95	High	*		
	2.95	Time 4	*	*								

*$p < 0.05$

Table 3.6 Pairwise comparisons for listening comprehension (time 2)

Time 3	M		Low	Mid	High
	14.29	Low			
	14.95	Mid			
	16.24	High	*		

*$p < 0.05$

Table 3.7 Pairwise comparisons for listening comprehension (time 4)

Time 4	M		Low	Med	High
	23.57	Low			
	25.47	Mid			
	26.62	High	*		

*$p < 0.05$

4 When Comprehensible Input is not Comprehensive Input: A Multi-dimensional Analysis of Instructional Input in Intensive English as a Foreign Language

Laura Collins, Joanna White, Pavel Trofimovich, Walcir Cardoso and Marlise Horst

A question we are sometimes asked is why so much of the classroom research on second language learning in the French-speaking Canadian province of Quebec has been conducted in intensive classes, given that this form of second language (L2) instruction is currently available to only a very small percentage (10%) of students in French-medium schools. From a language development perspective, the answer is quite simple: there is something to study! That is, in the space of a few months, the progress made is substantial, especially in oral expression and listening skills.

The reason for the impressive amount of learning is directly related to the time on task, including both its distribution and its quality. Unlike the more typical EFL[1] classes in Quebec, where students may receive as little as an hour a week of instruction throughout elementary school (grades 1–6), students in intensive ESL receive approximately 400 hours of instruction in a single school year, usually concentrated into five consecutive months of their final year of elementary school (other distributions of the time also exist, see Collins et al., 1999; Collins & J. White, 2011). Furthermore, the instructional approach used in intensive EFL in Quebec favors the provision of comprehensible input, with emphasis on authentic language experienced through a range of media, and on meaningful interaction with peers through a variety of pair and small-group activities, such as skits, surveys and theme-based projects. In the intensive classes, minimal attention is given to the formal features of language: the main objectives are to increase exposure to and use of English for communication. Thus the intensive experience provides the French-speaking[2] children with their first 'significant exposure' (Muñoz, 2008: 584) to English. Over several decades, research in these classes has documented the impressive language learning gains that result from this exposure. Students develop from false beginners with very limited English to intermediates with considerable communicative confidence (Collins & J. White, this volume; Lightbown, this volume; see also Collins & J. White, 2011; Lightbown & Spada, 1994, 1997; Spada & Lightbown, 1989).[3]

There are features of the language that remain challenging for these students, however. Examples observed in previous research include inversion in question formation (Ammar *et al.*, 2010; Spada & Lightbown, 1993), the syntax of adverbs of frequency (L. White, 1991; Trahey & L. White, 1993), the use of the *his/her* possessive determiners (J. White, 1998, 2008) and tense-aspect morphology (Collins *et al.*, 1999; Collins & J. White, 2011). This has prompted a number of form-focused instruction studies in which different types of pedagogical approaches have been used to draw learners' attention to some of the features just mentioned. The interventions have varied in their degree of explicitness, but they all resulted in an increase in the target forms in the input to the children during the experimental treatment period. There is some evidence, however, that the success of form-focused instruction in promoting the learning of a target form may not have lasting benefits if the opportunities to experience the form in subsequent classroom exposure are limited. L. White (1991), for example, found that francophone students in intensive programs did not retain the knowledge gained from focused instruction on the syntax of adverbs of frequency (*they quickly changed the subject* rather than **they changed quickly the subject*, an L1-influenced error) when the students were tested a year after the treatment. This is in contrast to the sustained improvement observed following instruction on the syntax of question forms in a companion study (L. White *et al.*, 1991; Spada & Lighbown, 1993). An analysis of classroom speech by the teachers of these students revealed that, once the instruction had ended, students did not have many opportunities to hear the forms, as adverbs of frequency were not a very common feature in the normal instructional talk in the intensive classes. Question forms, on the other hand, were quite frequent (Lightbown & Spada, 2006).[4] As the classroom input was the students' primary source of data for learning – the schools were located in French-speaking areas where students had very few (if any) opportunities to interact with speakers of the target language in the community – it seemed reasonable to conclude that adverbs of frequency were not sufficiently available in the classroom input for students to retain the gains they had made from the focused exposure provided in the experimental treatment.

This raises the interesting questions of how much and what kind of exposure the students normally get to certain grammatical forms in their regular intensive input. These are important questions for several reasons. Knowing more about how forms (of varying degrees of acquisition difficulty) are typically experienced in the input can inform our understanding of the input–acquisition relationship (see Collins *et al.*, 2009, for a summary of different views on the input–acquisition relationship). From a pedagogical perspective, knowing more about the kind of exposure students are typically getting to key language features informs choices regarding which forms merit instructional focus in a given context and, crucially, what the focus of the instruction should be (increasing the *instances* of the forms, the *variety of contexts* in which they occur or their *perceptual salience*). These are the questions we sought to answer in our investigation of the characteristics of intensive EFL input with respect to two of the challenging features of English mentioned above: the possessive determiners *his/her* and the simple past tense. Our main objectives were to determine to what degree the comprehensible input experienced in the intensive EFL context afforded quality exposure to the two features, and to identify whether there were pedagogical activities that resulted in richer exposure to language forms than others.

This chapter is organized as follows. First, we briefly describe the two target features and summarize the acquisition findings to date. Then we explain the four research questions that guided the investigation and provide an overview of the corpus we created of intensive EFL instructional talk. The analyses are sub-divided into four sections, one for each research question. The final section summarizes the findings and suggests directions for future research.

Target Features: Past Tense and Possessive Determiners *His/Her*

There are two ways in which the simple past tense is expressed in English. The vast majority of verbs, including any new verbs that enter the language (e.g. *googled, texted, spammed*), mark past with the bound morpheme *-ed*, which occurs in three allomorphs: /əd/ as in *hesitated*; /t/ as in *knocked*; and /d/ as in *tried*. There are also a comparatively small number of verbs (approximately 180, according to Prasada & Pinker, 1993), that are irregular in their past form, many of which are very common words in English (e.g. *went, took, had, was/were*).

The acquisition of the past tense in English has been the subject of a number of studies. The three main findings to date are that: (i) it can take considerable time to acquire, relative to other tense-aspect forms in the language such as progressive (the morpheme acquisition studies, reviewed in Goldschneider & DeKeyser, 2001); (ii) its early use may be semantically restricted to the lexical category of verbs known as telics (verbs with an inherent end point, such as *started, broke*) (e.g. Bardovi-Harlig, 2000; Salaberry & Shirai, 2002); and (iii) its commonly used irregular forms become reliably productive earlier than the regular forms (Lee, 2001; Rohde, 1996; see also Dietrich *et al.*, 1995). There is also some evidence that the difficulties learners have producing regular past forms (e.g. Bayley, 1994; Goad *et al.*, 2003; Wolfram, 1985) may be related to the difficulties they have perceiving these forms in aural input (Collins *et al.*, 2011b; Solt *et al.*, 2004).

The acquisition of the possessive determiners (PDs) *his* and *her* has been studied among populations of learners whose L1 marks the distinction differently. These include several Romance languages, French, Spanish and Catalan (Muñoz, 1994, 2005; Serrano, 2011; J. White *et al.*, 2007), as well as Finnish (Poussa, 1985). Because our target EFL population is francophone, we will use the English/French comparison to illustrate the main features of this form.

In English, the pedagogical rule of thumb for third-person singular PDs is straightforward: *his* is used when the possessor is masculine (*He rode his bike*) and *her* when the possessor is feminine (*She rode her bike*). In French, the masculine form is *son* and the feminine form is *sa*. The pedagogical rule is different, but equally straightforward: *son* is used with masculine nouns, sa with feminine: *son vélo; sa bicyclette* (both synonyms for bicycle in Quebec French). There is thus a masculine and a feminine PD form in both languages, but this similarity is deceptive, since the equivalent of *his* can be either *son* or *sa*, depending on the gender of the noun, as can the equivalent of *her*.

There may also be an overall difficulty in keeping track of the referent/possessor as a clause or two may separate the possessor from the PD. This is not the case when the gender of the noun determines the PD, as is the case in French. Compare the following examples:

Charles and his sister Anne got lots of candy for Halloween. *Charles* ate most of it, but he shared some pieces with *his* little brother Paul.

Charles et sa soeur Anne ont reçu beaucoup de bonbons pour l'Halloween. Charles en a mange la plupart, mais il a partagé quelques morceaux avec *son* frère *Paul*.[5]

There is a considerable body of evidence demonstrating that the productive use of *his* and *her* is acquired in a series of stages: pre-emergence, emergence and post-emergence (J. White, 1998, 2008; J. White *et al.*, 2007). In pre-emergence stages, learners avoid using PDs altogether or use one, all-purpose form, typically *your*. As third person emerges, although there may be some target-like uses of *his* and/or *her*, one form is often overgeneralized to all contexts. Finally, learners sort out the *his/her* distinction and become increasingly accurate in its use, starting in 'kin-same' contexts, where the gender of the PD matches the natural gender of possessed entity (e.g. Bill pushed *his brother* on the swing) and eventually in 'kin-different' contexts (e.g. Bill helped *his sister* build a snowman), where the genders differ. Kin-different contexts present a persistent learning challenge, and we have observed that many learners get 'stuck' at an emergence or post-emergence stage. Indeed, PD errors persist for some highly proficient speakers of English.[6]

From this overview, we see that input profiles of the two forms should document not only frequency factors (i.e. how often the forms occur), but also contextual factors, such as types of verbs (for simple past) and collocated nouns (for PDs). In addition, the relative ease with which the contexts allow for the perception of the forms may also be revealing. These factors were formalized into four research questions. The first three addressed the distribution profiles of the simple past and the *his/her* forms across the corpus (described below) as a whole; the fourth considered the distribution profiles with reference to the type of instructional activity in which the forms occurred. The questions are:

(1) How often would students typically hear the simple past and the possessive determiners *his/her* in the instructional input of the intensive classes?
(2) How rich is the aural exposure with respect to the types of verbs (simple past) and the collocated nouns (*his/her*)?
(3) How rich is the aural exposure with respect to the perceptual salience of the *-ed* and the *his/her* forms?
(4) Are some pedagogical activities better than others in terms of the frequency and richness of the exposure to the two forms?

The investigation focused on aural language to allow us to consider aspects of speech phenomena that may influence perceptual salience.

Corpus

The corpus we developed to examine these features consists of the instructional input portions of video-recordings of whole class interactions that were part of a larger study of different distributions of instructional time in intensive ESL (Collins & J. White, 2011). The three grade 6 classes were in two elementary schools located in areas outside Montreal where students had little or no contact with English outside the classroom. All classes were taught by native or highly proficient speakers of English. Four recordings of three classes were made at intervals of roughly 100 hours, such that each class was recorded at the same point in the 400 hour intensive program. These recordings were transcribed. For this study, we examined all the aural input to students from the teacher, visitors, videos and audio soundtracks. This yielded a corpus of 110,000 words representing roughly 40 hours of instructional input. Because our focus was on the aural input from proficient speakers, we did not analyze the classroom speech of the students.

Analyses and Findings: Distribution of Past and PDs Across the Corpus

The first step in our analyses was to code all finite verbs in the corpus for tense (present and past), aspect (progressive, perfect, simple) and mood, and all possessive determiners (*my, your, our, his, her, their*) for person, number and gender. Two separate teams of coders (three for verb forms, two for possessive determiners), all graduate students in applied linguistics with strong backgrounds in English grammar, coded an equivalent portion of the transcripts, and then verified the coding of the other member(s) of the coding team. As conjugated verbs and possessive determiners are low-inference categories, the only differences in coding tended to be the occasional missed instance of the target forms, rather than mis-identified forms. This process yielded 15,130 finite verb tokens and 2398 PD tokens.

Frequency of the past and PDs

To answer the first research question, we looked at the distribution of the simple past and the PDs relative to the other forms in their respective paradigms. We initially considered each of the four instructional times separately, but as Figures 4.1 and 4.2 show, the frequency of simple past and *his/her* forms were very similar at each time. Overall, the simple past accounted for less than 10% (1413 tokens) of the finite verb forms in the corpus. *His/her* tokens were similarly infrequent, representing 9% (223) of all PDs.[7]

What is remarkable about the frequency profile of PDs is the predominance of *your*. A closer look at the corpus revealed that *your* is the natural PD for activity and classroom management, as the following excerpt shows (/—/ denotes unintelligible speech):

Teacher: Okay. I will give each team a pack of cards like this. Put *your* pencils down. Close *your* agendas /—/. Close *your* activity books. Put everything on the floor. Antoine, put that /—/. Okay. So, I will give each team a pack of cards. Okay? In each pack, you have the four seasons. Who can tell me what the four seasons are? ... Raise *your* hand.

Similarly, it was also surprising to see so few instances of simple past across 40 hours of instructional talk. However, as the excerpt above demonstrates,

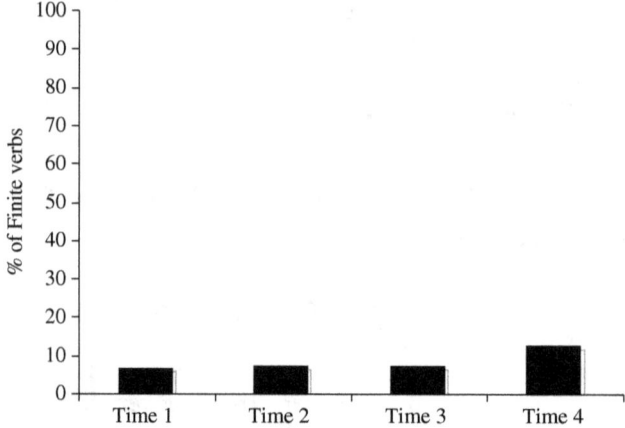

Figure 4.1 Distribution of past tense tokens by time

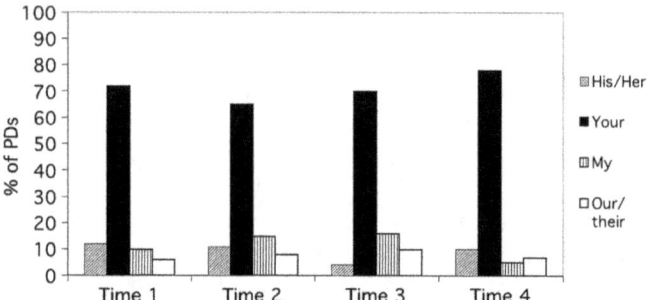

Figure 4.2 Distribution of possessive determiners tokens in instructional talk

a great deal of the talk in the classroom is focused on the here and now, and the immediate future, with limited contexts for reference to prior events. We will return to this point in more detail when we report on the analysis of pedagogical activities below.

Contexts for the past and PDs: Verb types and collocated nouns

To address the second research question, for the simple past tense we looked at the proportion of regulars vs irregulars, and the semantic category of the verbs (statives, activities and telics). For the latter, we developed a three-step operational test synthesized from previous research (Dowty, 1979; Mourelatos, 1981; Robison, 1990, 1995; Shirai & Andersen, 1995). The first step was to determine whether the verb was dynamic (*play hockey*) or stative (*feel nervous*); the second was to determine whether the dynamic verbs were activities (unbounded events with no inherent end point – *skate on the*

Table 4.1 Fifteen most common past tense verbs

was/were (258)	forgot (23)
said (121)	grew (20)
had (86)	made (19)
did (55)	came (17)
wrote (30)	saw (17)
got (29)	told (17)
went (29)	asked (15)
thought (27)	

pond) or telics (*score a goal*). The first author and a graduate student research assistant with a background in lexical semantics initially coded 25% of the verbs. There was 90% agreement on the coding, with differences resolved through discussion. The research assistant then coded the remaining tokens.

Table 4.1 shows the 15 most common past tense verbs in the corpus in order of frequency. Note that the top 14 of these are irregulars with the most frequent regular verb (*asked*) occupying only the 15th place. Indeed, irregular forms accounted for 75% of the past tense tokens in the corpus, almost all of them (98%) drawn from the 1000 most frequent words in the English language (according to lists based on the British National Corpus by Nation, 2006). Clearly, many of these verbs were repeated (in fact, of the 76 verb types that occurred more than twice in the corpus, most were irregulars). These numbers suggest that the input was relatively rich for learning irregulars: they are frequent in the corpus and frequently repeated, and they occur with familiar words. This is in contrast with the regular types, of which only slightly more than half (58%) came from the 1000 words list. Indeed, some of these verbs were quite unusual (*swayed, tangled, thumped*), and many were only encountered once in the 40 hours of recorded instruction.

As for the lexical categories of the verbs, as Figure 4.3 shows, the overwhelming majority of the past types (regular and irregular combined) occurred with telics (72%). The least frequent type was statives. These findings demonstrate that students' exposure to past was skewed towards one semantic category.

To investigate the lexical characteristics of *his* and *her*, we first examined the semantic contexts in which they occurred. That is, we were interested in whether the entity possessed was inanimate (*his* book) or animate (kin-same, as in *her* mother, or kin-different, as in *her* father), and how these contexts were distributed in the corpus. We found that inanimate contexts were the most frequent (119 tokens), followed by animate (62 tokens). Of the animate contexts, 31 were kin-same and 31 were kin-different.

We then took a closer look at the collocations for *his* and *her* in kin-different contexts. The most frequent kin-different pair in our data was *his*

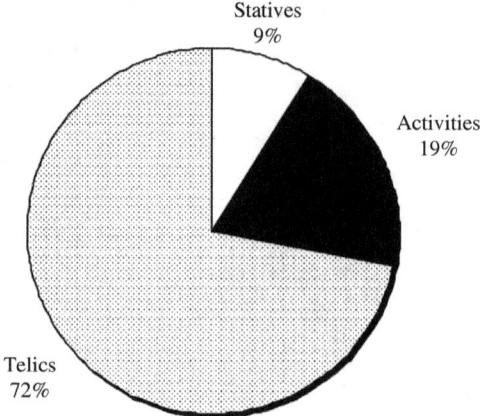

Figure 4.3 Percentage distribution of past tense by semantic category

wife, which occurred 26 times when the teacher read aloud a story. The others were *his sister, his mother, his daughter, her husband, her brother* and *her brother-in-law*. Although kin-different collocates make up a small lexical set of mostly family members, they are arguably the most informative contexts with respect to the difference between the French and English PD rules since the gender of the PD differs from that of the possessed entity. In summary, there were not only limited collocation types for PDs in our corpus, but also limited tokens of these types.

Contexts for the past and PDs: Perceptual salience

To address the third research question, we examined three aspects of the regular past allomorphs: the distribution of /d/, /t/ and /əd/; the degree of saliency (taking into account the phonetic environment following the *-ed*); and the degree of emphasis the pronunciation of the past tense verb was given, according to whether it was followed by a pause, repeated or stressed.

The most salient allomorph /əd/, as in *wanted*, was the least frequent in the data, accounting for just 22% of the regular past. Thus, the least salient allomorphs, /d/ and /t/, accounted for the majority of the regular past tense tokens: 45 and 33% respectively. Table 4.2 summarizes the findings for the immediate phonetic environment of the *-ed* forms. It shows that only 25% of the regular past occurred in the clearest contexts, that is, followed by a vowel. The remaining cases included instances in which the allomorph was followed by a consonant, co-articulated with the following consonant or deleted completely.

The majority of the forms (82%) also received no particular emphasis. They were rarely followed by a pause (12%), which occurs naturally when the verb is in sentence-final position but can also occur mid-sentence; and

Table 4.2 Perceptual saliency of regular past tense verbs

Degree of salience	Example from corpus	Percentage
clear (+ vowel)	Ah, he never complained again! Yesterday, we talked about uh, flavours, eh?	25%
somewhat clear (+ consonant, but released)	Every day Farmer Joe worked hard in the field. ... you answered well	68%
unclear (co-articulated with consonant)	Nobody noticed my mistake! No, I just wanted to say	2%
absent (deleted)	... that is the reason why I asked you to bring pictures of your family	4%

hardly ever stressed for emphasis (4%) or repeated (2%). Thus, overall, the regular past occurrences in our corpus were not very salient.

The salience of *his* and *her* was examined by means of acoustical analyses in all semantic contexts. Table 4.3 summarizes our findings for the different dimensions of saliency we considered. We considered that the salience of PDs is affected by the fact that they precede nouns and are only stressed in exceptional circumstances. For example, they may be stressed in order to contrast information (*HIS dog*, not *her* dog), or stress may serve as a pedagogical tool to increase the salience of the possessor. We found that *his* and *her* were usually unstressed, and rarely repeated. In addition, the initial sound (h) was frequently deleted (e.g. *turned _is chair*), further compromising salience.

The preceding sound affects the ease with which the /h/ in *his* or *her* is perceived. The ideal environment is a preceding pause (e.g. at the beginning of an utterance: *his dog is black*) or a preceding vowel (*see his dog*). However,

Table 4.3 Perceptual saliency of *his* and *her*

Categories	Percentage
Stressed	12%
Unstressed	88%
Repeated	3%
Unrepeated	97%
/h/ present*	16%
/h/ deleted	81%
Preceded by a vowel/pause	20%
Preceded by a consonant	80%

*Three percent of the /h/ contexts were not possible to judge

this was rare. Much more common was for *his* and *her* to be preceded by a consonant (*walked his dog*), an environment that renders the /h/ much more difficult to perceive. Thus, like the regular past, the *his* and *her* PD forms did not occur in perceptually clear contexts.

Contexts for the past and PDs: Pedagogical category

The findings reported above are based on analyses across times and types of pedagogical activity, but of course a teaching day can contain a range of activities with potentially different input profiles. Our fourth research question asked whether there were pedagogical activities that yielded potentially richer sources of aural information about the two target features. The analysis was conducted in three steps. In the first step, a team of three coders each examined a different subset of the instructional input to gain an understanding of the range of purposes it served. This data-driven approach yielded a number of precise functions such as modeling a tongue twister, preparing and monitoring an activity, explaining specific aspects of language (grammar, vocabulary, pronunciation, etc.), reading aloud, and so on. These functions were then grouped into five categories: classroom procedures, language-related episodes, text-based input, text-related discussion and personal anecdotes (defined below). The second step of the analysis, the coding of all the input by pedagogical category, was done in four phases. Two research assistants separately coded half of the instructional input transcripts from the first data collection time (time 1). They then verified each other's coding and met to resolve any differences of interpretation. This process was repeated for each of the remaining three data collection times. In the third and final step, the distribution of the past tense and the PDs within and across pedagogical categories was calculated.

Description of Pedagogical Activities

Classroom procedures, by far the most frequent category, accounted for 75% of the input in our corpus. It captured teacher talk that organized the various activities and routines, and that also managed student behavior (although discipline episodes were not very common). In the following example we see a teacher interrupting an activity in which the students are preparing menus for restaurants to provide some clarification on the procedure.

> Okay guys, can I have your attention a moment? The papers, the scrap paper that you're using is just for you to write some ideas, to invent the name of your restaurant and to write, you know. And then I will correct. You don't start making a clean copy right away with the stencil and everything. This is just after when everything is corrected and done.

Language-related episodes accounted for 17% of the aural input, and described any focus on features of the language such as morphosyntax, pronunciation and vocabulary, with the latter being the most common (see Horst, 2009, for a discussion of the vocabulary episodes and an analysis of the lexical characteristics of the corpus as a whole). This was sometimes isolated practice in which the teacher was briefly focusing on an aspect of grammar, as part of a homework activity, for example. More frequently, it was integrated into the larger lesson, in the form of feedback on error, explanation of a vocabulary item or the pronunciation of a word, provision of a grammar structure useful for completing the task at hand, and so on. In the example below, the teacher makes a comment on a student's error, providing the correction and a brief explanation.

> Okay, so here it's not he needs *a* glue. He needs *some* glue because glue is like liquid and you can't count. You see? That's why you put *some* glue. You understand?

The remaining three categories accounted for less than 10% of the input, but nevertheless represented aural language that differed in important ways from the speech that characterized the management of the class or the explanation of language features. They all focused on content beyond the 'here and now' of the classroom, often involving additional people not present in the classroom.

Text-based input accounted for 4% of the input. It described any speech involving scripted language that was read by the teacher, such as reading aloud from a storybook or the modeling of poems, songs, limericks, dialogues, and so on, as the students were learning to recite them. This was not the teacher's spontaneous speech, but it was delivered to the students by the teacher's voice. It also included audio recordings that students listened to (primarily songs). An illustration of this type of input follows, in which the teacher begins reading a story aloud.

> Once upon a time there was a boy named Bradley Flowers who lived in the Gaspé region. He liked to ski. So one day during the winter he went skiing alone and ...

Discussion of text-based input, at 3% of the data, primarily involved reflection and elaboration of the content of stories read aloud. This included elements such as plot or character and it was observed to occur prior to, during and/or after a reading. Occasionally it also focused on the content of tongue twisters or songs. In the following example, the teacher clarifies a part of the plot for the students.

> So, he quit his job. He told his boss, well I'm not continuing. So he left the ship. Lucky him! It saved his life.

Personal anecdotes were the least frequent, accounting for 1% of the input. They consisted of the teacher recounting personal experiences or elaborating upon students' own experiences during which the teacher would repeat, recast and expand the students' utterances. In the excerpt below the teacher has just explained the meaning of the expression 'break a leg' (a language-related episode) and suddenly remembers an incident that happened to her husband that she shares with her class.

> one day P, my husband, was playing in a tennis tournament and he was known to jump over the net ... instead of going on the other side, around – he would jump over the net, okay? So before the tournament I told him, I said 'break a leg'. ... So, of course, he jumped over the net and what do you think happened?

These latter three categories were sometimes the source of language-related episodes. Any attention to language during the reading/discussion of texts or the recounting of anecdotes was, of course, coded as such, to distinguish it from the language used when a story was read or elaborated upon, or when a personal experience was related. In the next example the teacher is reading aloud (text-based input), stops to explain a word (the language-focused input in italics) and then returns to the reading aloud.

> She sort of swayed ...
> *to sway is to go from side to side*
> ... like she didn't know what she was supposed to do.

Distribution of Past and PDs by Pedagogical Activity

In this section, we report on the frequency distribution of the simple past and the possessive determiners *his/her* across the five pedagogical categories. Table 4.4 shows the findings for the past tense. There are many more instances of simple past in the procedures category (871), but this is not surprising, given that it accounted for 75% of the corpus. There is, however, a substantial number of past forms in the text-based input (356, or 427 if combined with the discussion of the content of the text read aloud). There are also a considerable number of occurrences of past when anecdotes are recounted. In fact, if we tally the total number of past forms in these three categories, we see that they account for 574 instances of the simple past in the corpus, an impressive number for talk that represented less than 10% of the corpus overall. Furthermore, the number of different types of past in these three categories was much more varied than in the classroom procedures talk, as revealed by type token ratio figures in the final column of Table 4.4.

Table 4.4 Distribution of past tense tokens by pedagogical category

Category	Token	Type	Ratio
Classroom procedures	871	115	0.13
Text-based	356	90	0.25
Text-based discussion	71	23	0.32
Anecdotes	146	37	0.25
Language episodes	6	3	N/A

Table 4.5 Distribution of PDs by pedagogical category

Category	Token	Percentage
Classroom procedures	111	46.64%
Text-based	60	25.21%
Text-based discussion	19	7.98%
Anecdotes	17	7.14%
Language episodes	31	13.03%

The analysis of the PDs yielded a similar result. As Table 4.5 shows, there were again more instances of *his/her* (111) in the most common type of teacher talk, classroom procedures. However, text-based and text-based discussion also yielded a proportionately large number of tokens of *his/her* (79 combined), given the relative infrequence of these two instructional categories in the corpus. In addition, when we examine the distribution of input type by semantic category (see Table 4.6), we see that, within the crucial kin-different category, the text-based and text-based discussion input accounted for 44% of the total tokens. This figure is comparable to the 47% that are found in the classroom procedures component, but the large size of this component –which accounts for three quarters of all of the teacher speech – means that the kin-different PDs are much more concentrated in the text and text discussion categories.

Comparing Reading Aloud with Classroom Procedure Talk

The analysis above suggested that the most common source of input – classroom procedures talk – was not necessarily the richest source of exposure to the simple past and the PDs, but the variation in the proportion of talk represented by the different input categories makes it difficult to make fine-grained comparisons of the target features across the categories. We therefore decided to extract two equal segments of talk from the text-based

Table 4.6 Percentage distribution of semantic categories of *his/her* tokens by pedagogical categories

	Inanimate (n = 121)	Animate* (n = 17)	Kin-same (n = 19)	Kin-different (n = 34)
Classroom procedures (n = 111)	48.76	47.06	78.95	47.06
Text-based (n = 60)	32.23	5.88	0.00	38.24
Text-based discussion (n = 19)	11.57	11.76	0.00	5.88
Anecdotes (n = 17)	2.48	23.53	0.00	8.82
Language episodes (n = 31)	4.96	11.76	21.05	0
Totals (n = 238**)	100.00	100.00	100.00	100.00

*Animate refers to cases where the gender of the noun is not clear (e.g. student, friend) or refers to a group comprising both males and females (e.g. plural nouns like children, friends). ** This total includes 47 instances of references to body parts

and the classroom procedures categories. They were taken from the same teacher, on the same day, within the same part of the lesson. The read-aloud segment was a short story about a haunted house, and consisted of 874 words. The matched classroom procedures excerpt was a segment of 871 words.[8] We compared the frequency and the salience of the past tense and *his/her* forms in these excerpts.

For the past tense, we examined the types and tokens of both regular and irregular past forms. Table 4.7 shows that, not only were there far more instances of past overall in the story (96 vs 11 in the classroom procedures segment), but there was also a variety of different types, and a substantial number of regular past forms (roughly half of the total past tense types). For the PDs, Table 4.7 shows an even more dramatic finding: there was not a single instance of *his/her* in the classroom procedures talk. There were, however, 30 instances in the story.

As for the perceptual salience of the 34 regular past tense verbs, we found that 35% were followed by either a vowel or a pause (*decided it*), the

Table 4.7 Reading aloud: Frequency of target forms

	Haunted House story read aloud	Procedures talk
Total words	874	871
Past tokens	96 (34 regular)	11 (3 regular)
Past types	45 (20 regular)	8 (3 regular)
Possessive determiners	30 (12 his; 18 her)	0

condition that makes the -*ed* marking relatively salient. The remaining 65% contained a released consonant (*Joe worked hard*). There were thus no cases of deletion or of unreleased consonants following the -*ed*, both of which render the form difficult to perceive. In addition, all of the instances of regular past tense in the story were produced at a slower speech rate using more emphatic intonation than the regular past tense verbs in the classroom procedure talk. For *his/her* tokens in the story read aloud, we considered perceptual salience from the perspective of /h/ deletion. The analyses showed that it was deleted 37% of the time only. Recall that the overall deletion rate for the whole corpus was 81%. Thus, the reading aloud speech provided the students with substantially clearer contexts in which to perceive the *his/her* forms.

Summary and discussion of quality input

The analysis of the quantity and the quality of the occurrence of the target features in the different types of pedagogical input the students were exposed to reveals that the exposure was richer when teachers were participating in activities (e.g. commenting on stories, telling or elaborating personal experiences), and not just managing them. That is, when the role of the teacher went beyond facilitating oral interaction among students to include interacting with them herself, her own speech became a richer source of input, at least for the two features we have investigated here.

In addition, there seems to be a special status for reading aloud, both for content and salience. Stories often include events in the past, and are written in the third person; children's stories frequently also include repetition of key events and thus more opportunities for repeated exposure to PDs and the past. Furthermore, there was evidence in our corpus that teachers' speech rate was slower and clearer, potentially making aspects of language more accessible to learners.

To further explore the content point raised above, we created a corpus of 14 storybooks that were appropriate for the age and language level of the students in our study. The books included classic children's fairy tales and fables (e.g. 'Goldilocks and the three bears' and 'The tortoise and the hare'), as well as contemporary children's storybooks by authors such as Robert Munsch and Phoebe Gilman. They comprised of 8000 words. Figure 4.4 compares the PD findings for this corpus with our intensive input corpus. What is striking is the difference in the frequency of *your* vs *his/her* in the two corpora. We found that the relative proportion of instances of *his* and *her* to instances of *your* in the storybook corpus was 57 vs 17%. This is in contrast to the complete instructional talk corpus where the relative proportion of *his* and *her* to *your* was 9 vs 71%. While the absolute numbers are small – 192 instances of *his/her*, or 2% of the entire storybook corpus, compared with 223 instances of *his/her*, or 0.2% of the entire teacher corpus – it is clear that

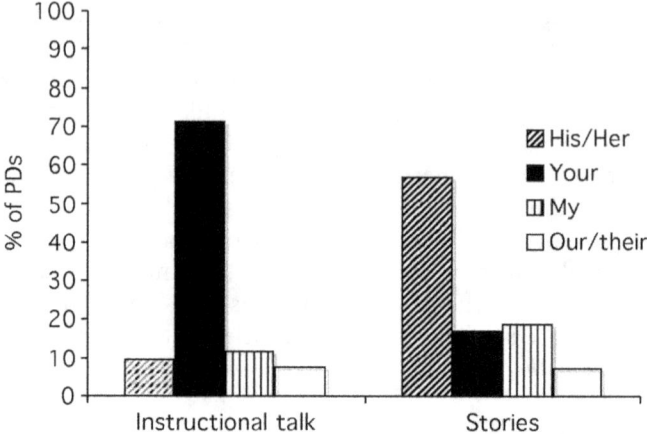

Figure 4.4 Distribution of possessive determiners in instructional talk and story-book corpus

third-person PDs occur more often and are more task-natural in stories and other narratives than in classroom input, overall.

Conclusion

To return to the questions we asked at the outset of this study, students in the intensive EFL classes had very limited aural exposure to the regular past and the possessive determiners *his/her*. The input was also lacking in terms of quality encounters with verb types (few instances of regular past or of semantic types other than telics), and with key nouns collocated with *his* and *her* (few instances of the crucial kin-different combinations). The two features also occurred frequently in contexts that would be hard to perceive.

It is important to note, however, that although the functions of the teacher talk such as 'classroom management' may distinguish it from speech in contexts outside the classroom, it nevertheless shares features observed in other contexts as well. For the simple past, there is increasing evidence that past (or perfective past, in other languages) occurs more frequently with telics than other verb types (Wulff *et al.*, 2009) and irregular past forms are much more frequent than regular past (Prasada & Pinker, 1993). Similarly, the relative frequency of *your* and the limited instances of *his* and *her* are also representative of spoken English outside the classroom. When we compared our corpus with that of the British National Corpus (2007), we found an almost identical order, with the first four the same and only those in fifth and sixth place reversed.

Intensive corpus:	your > my > his > their > our > her
BNC corpus:	your > my > his > their > her > our

In addition, the low perceptual salience of both simple past and PDs in the intensive context is consistent with speech in casual non-classroom contexts. As function words, for example, *his* and *her* are typically not stressed, and the initial /h/ is usually deleted in mid-sentence situations in connected speech, although not in sentence initial position (Mah *et al.*, 2006).

Thus the instructional input students are receiving in the intensive context is similar to 'natural' speech in a variety of ways, which is a desirable situation. However, one of the roles of the classroom is also to facilitate learning, and in our future research we will be using the insights gleaned from these analyses to explore how the comprehensible input provided by intensity may become more 'comprehensive', in terms of providing favorable conditions for acquisition.

Given our findings for the target features in the reading aloud speech – increased frequency, richer semantic contexts and superior perceptual environments – one promising avenue to explore is the design of focused listening tasks in which the targets include not only the *his/her* pronouns and *-ed* past forms, but also the surrounding phonetic environment in which they occur. A recently completed follow-up study showed significant improvement in the perception of the regular past tense among intensive students who experienced the form in different perceptual contexts (which we had manipulated) in stories read aloud (Collins *et al.*, 2011a).

Our study examined the input present in an intensive context involving francophone learners of English. The features we focused on, however, have been observed to present acquisition challenges for other populations of learners (referenced above). It is our hope that insights gained from an input study in the intensive EFL context of Quebec may guide future investigations of these (and other features) in other teaching contexts. Of particular value for understanding the input–acquisition relationship are studies that compare students' production with the input they are receiving (e.g. Rast, 2008, 2010). It will also be important in future research to explore the profiles of features that are learned more easily from the input. A follow-up study using the same corpus used in the current study examined the characteristics of the progressive *-ing*, a form that has been documented to be acquired earlier than other aspects of morphology, such as past tense (see Goldschneider & DeKeyser, 2001). The findings showed that this form was not more frequent than the simple past or PDs. However, it occurred with more varied (yet still common) verbs and was rendered more salient owing to its presence as an intact syllable (*-ing*) (Collins *et al.*, 2009).

In the current study, the attention to aural instructional input was motivated by the desire to consider speech phenomena present in connected discourse. This allowed us to create profiles for the aural exposure to the simple past and PDs in terms of both sounds and meanings. Clearly exposure to written input also merits attention, as does peer input experienced in whole class and small group situations. This is yet another worthwhile avenue to explore in future investigations of the crucial relationship between input and second language acquisition.

Acknowledgments

We are grateful to the team of student research assistants for their conscientious work transcribing the audio files and coding the various features we examined in this study. They are Concordia University students Philippa Bell, Cynthia Dery, Nancy Dytynyshyn, Jennifer Lareau, Frances MacAndrew, Christi Milsom, Josée St-Marseille and Yvette Relkoff, and McGill University student Jesús Izquierdo. We would also like to acknowledge the funding support from two research grants awarded to the team, one from the Social Sciences and Humanities Research Council of Canada, and the other from the Quebec Ministry of Education (Fonds Québecois de la recherche sur la societé et la culture).

Notes

(1) As noted in Collins and White (this volume), we have opted to use the term EFL (English as a foreign language) for our contributions to this edited volume, to reflect the absence of English in the majority of French-medium schools and communities in Quebec. This includes the research sites for the study we report on here. However, it is important to note that English L2 instruction in Quebec is normally referred to as English as a second language (ESL).
(2) For ease of reference we will refer to these students as 'francophone' with the understanding that the L1 of a small number of the students may be a language other than French or English. To date, any of these students in our intensive studies have always been highly proficient speakers of French, if not French-dominant.
(3) Recognizing the success of the intensive initiative, the Ministry of Education in Quebec has recently decided to make it available to all grade 6 EFL students (11–12 years of age) by 2015.
(4) The exact numbers are not reported in White, L (1991) or in Lightbown and Spada (2006).
(5) Sometimes an adjective may come between the PD and the noun, as in son petit frère, but even so, the distance between the PD and the noun is close, when compared to some of the contexts that arise in English.
(6) Another difference between English and French that causes problems for some learners, one that is not the focus of the analysis in this study, is use of PDs with body parts. In English, PDs are normally used (e.g. He's washing his hands). In French, it is more common to use a definite article (le, la, or les) when referring to body parts, with possession marked by a reflexive pronoun that agrees with the subject (Il se lave les mains).
(7) We also initially considered each of the three teachers separately, but the distribution patterns did not vary: there were small differences in the overall number of tokens of simple past and his/her, but the proportions relative to the other forms were the same across teacher, and across teaching time.

(8) The classroom procedures segment is 4 words shorter because to have an exact equivalent length we would have had to end the segment in the middle of a teacher's utterance. The segment we analyzed concluded at the end of the teacher's sentence.

References

Ammar, A., Lightbown, P.M. and Spada, N. (2010) Awareness of L1/L2 differences: Does it matter? *Language Awareness* 19 (2), 129–146.

Bardovi-Harlig, K. (2000) *Tense and Aspect in Second Language Acquisition: Form, Meaning, and Use*. Malden, MA: Blackwell.

Bayley, R. (1994) Interlanguage variation and the quantitative paradigm: Past tense marking in Chinese–English. In E. Tarone, S. Gass and A. Cohen (eds) *Research Methodology in Second Language Acquisition* (pp. 157–181). Hillsdale, NJ: Lawrence Erlbaum.

British National Corpus (2007) Version 3 (BNC XML Edition) Distributed by Oxford University Computing Services on behalf of the BNC Consortium. Online document, http://www.natcorp.ox.ac.uk/

Collins, L. and White, J. (2011) An intensive look at intensity and language learning. *TESOL Quarterly* 45 (1), 106–133.

Collins, L., Halter, R., Lightbown, P.M. and Spada, N. (1999) Time and the distribution of time in L2 instruction. *TESOL Quarterly* 33, 655–680.

Collins, L., Trofimovich, P., White, J., Cardoso, W. and Horst, M. (2009) Some input on the easy/difficult grammar question. *The Modern Language Journal* 93 (3), 336–353.

Collins, L., Bell, P., Dwight, V. and Trofimovich, P. (2011a) Focused listening tasks and the regular past tense in English. Paper presented at the *Task-based Language and Teaching Conference*.

Collins, L., Trofimovich, P. and Bell, P. (2011b) Kiss the boy or kissed the boy? Investigating perceptual difficulty of learning past-tense forms in English. Paper presented at the *2011 International Symposium of Bilingualism 8 Conference*, Oslo.

Dietrich, R., Klein, W. and Noyau, C. (eds) (1995) *The Acquisition of Temporality in Second Language Acquisition*. Amsterdam: Benjamins.

Dowty, D. (1979) *Word Meaning and Montague Grammar*. Dordrecht: Reidel.

Goad, H., White, L. and Steele, J. (2003) Missing inflection in L2 acquisition: Defective syntax or L1-constrained prosodic representations? *Canadian Journal of Linguistics* 48, 243–263.

Goldschneider, J.M. and DeKeyser, R.M (2001) Explaining the 'natural order of L2 morpheme acquisition' in English: A meta-analysis of multiple determinants. *Language Learning* 51 (1), 1–50.

Horst, M. (2009) Revisiting classrooms as lexical environments. In T. Fitzpatrick and A. Barfield (eds) *Lexical Processing in Second Language Learners: Papers and Perspectives in Honour of Paul Meara* (pp. 53–66). Bristol: Multilingual Matters.

Lee, E.J. (2001) Interlanguage development with two Korean speakers of English with a focus on temporality. *Language Learning* 51, 591–633.

Lightbown, P.M. and Spada, N. (1994) An innovative program for primary ESL in Quebec. *TESOL Quarterly* 28, 563–579.

Lightbown, P.M. and Spada, N. (1997) Learning English as a second language in a special school in Quebec. *Canadian Modern Language Review* 53, 315–355.

Lightbown, P.M. and Spada, N. (2006) *How Languages are Learned*. Oxford: Oxford University Press.

Mah, J., Steinhauer, K. and Goad, H. (2006) The Trouble with /h/: Evidence from ERPs. Paper presented at the *2006 8th Generative Approaches to Second Language Acquisition Conference*, Sommerville, MA.

Mourelatos, A. (1981) Events, processes, states. In P. Tedeschi and A. Zaenen (eds) *Syntax and Semantics: Vol 14. Tense and Aspect* (pp. 191–212). New York: Academic Press.

Muñoz, C. (1994) A case of frequency-based markedness. *Atlantis* 41, 165–177.

Muñoz, C. (2005) The development of the personal pronoun system in learners of English. Paper presented at *EUROSLA 2005 Conference*, Dubrovnik.

Muñoz, C. (2008) Symmetries and asymmetries of age effects in naturalistic and instructed L2 learning. *Applied Linguistics* 29, 578–596.

Nation, I.S.P. (2006) How large a vocabulary is needed for reading and listening? *Canadian Modern Language Review* 63, 59–82.

Poussa, P. (1985) The development of the 3rd person singular pronoun system in the English of a bilingual Finnish–English child. *Scandinavian Working Papers on Bilingualism* 5, 1–39.

Prasada, S. and Pinker, S. (1993) Generalization of regular and irregular morphology. *Language and Cognitive Processes* 8, 1–56.

Rast, R. (2008) *Foreign Language Input: Initial Processing*. Clevedon: Multilingual Matters.

Rast, R. (2010) First exposure: Converting target language input to intake. In M. Pütz and L. Sicola (eds) *Inside the Learner's Mind: Cognitive Processing and Second Language Acquisition*. Amsterdam: John Benjamins.

Robison, R. (1990) The primacy of aspect: Aspectual marking in English interlanguage. *Studies in Second Language Acquisition* 12, 315–330.

Robison, R. (1995) The aspect hypothesis revisited: A cross-sectional study of tense and aspect marking in interlanguage. *Applied Linguistics* 16, 344–370.

Rohde, A. (1996) The aspect hypothesis and emergence of tense distinction in naturalistic L2 acquisition. *Linguistics* 34, 1115–1137.

Salaberry, R. and Shirai, Y. (eds) (2002) *The L2 Acquisition of Tense-aspect Morphology*. Amsterdam: Benjamins.

Serrano, R. (2011) From metalinguistic instruction to metalinguistic knowledge, and from metalinguistic knowledge to performance in error correction and oral production tasks. *Language Awareness* 20 (1), 1–16.

Shirai, Y. and Andersen, R. (1995) The acquisition of tense-aspect morphology: A prototype account. *Language Learning* 71 (4), 743–762.

Solt, S., Pugach, Y., Klein, E.C., Adams, K., Stoyneshka, I. and Rose, T. (2004) L2 perception and production of the English regular past: Evidence of phonological effects. In A. Brugos, L. Micciulla and C. Smith (eds) *Proceedings of the 28th Annual Boston University Conference on Language Acquisition* (pp. 553–564). Somerville, MA: Cascadilla Press.

Spada, N. and Lightbown, P.M. (1989) Intensive ESL programs in Quebec primary schools. *TESL Canada Journal* 7, 11–32.

Spada, N. and Lightbown, P.M. (1993) Instruction and the development of questions in L2 classrooms. *Studies in Second Language Acquisition* 15, 205–224.

Trahey, M. and White, L. (1993) Positive evidence and preemption in the second language classroom. *Studies in Second Language Acquisition* 15, 225–241.

White, J. (1998) Getting the learners' attention: A typographical input enhancement study. In C. Doughty and J. Williams (eds) *Focus on Form in Classroom Second Language Acquisition* (pp. 85–113). Cambridge: Cambridge University Press.

White, J. (2008) Speeding up acquisition of his/her: Explicit L1/L2 contrasts help. In J. Philp, R. Oliver and A. Mackey (eds) *Second Language Acquisition and the Younger Learner: Child's Play?* (pp. 193–228). Amsterdam: John Benjamins.

White, J., Muñoz, C. and Collins, L. (2007) The his/her challenge: Making progress in a 'regular' second language program. *Language Awareness* 16 (4), 278–279.

White, L. (1991) Adverb placement in second language acquisition: Some effects of positive and negative evidence in the classroom. *Second Language Research* 7, 133–161.

White, L., Spada, N., Lightbown, P.M. and Ranta, L. (1991) Input enhancement and syntactic accuracy in L2 acquisition. *Applied Linguistics* 12, 416–432.
Wolfram, W. (1985) Variability in tense marking: A case for the obvious. *Language Learning* 35, 229–253.
Wulff, S., Ellis, N., Römer, U., Bardovi-Harlig, K. and Leblanc, C. (2009) The acquisition of tense-aspect: Converging evidence from corpora and telicity ratings. *The Modern Language Journal* 93, 354–385.

5 What Language is Promoted in Intensive Programs? Analyzing Language Generated from Oral Assessment Tasks

Joanna White and Carolyn E. Turner

Introduction and Background

Intensive programs for English as a second language (ESL) in elementary schools began to emerge in the mid-1970s in Quebec, Canada (see Lightbown, this volume, for history). As they grew in number, the obvious question arose as to their actual impact on language learning when compared with the *regular* ESL program (i.e. the official program that mandated, but did not always practice, 120 minutes per week).

Although a considerable amount of research had been carried out in intensive ESL classes in Quebec at the time data were collected for this study, there was no profile of the oral proficiency of students at the end of five months of intensive exposure. Since the Ministry of Education put a strong emphasis on developing students' ability to interact orally in the intensive model, the Oral Proficiency Project was designed to add information about oral skill development to the already-existing database on the development of teaching and learning in intensive ESL (e.g. Lightbown & Spada, 2000; Spada & Lightbown, 1989; J. White, 1998; L. White, 1991; L. White *et al.*, 1991). In addition, the Oral Proficiency Project was planned as a comparative study to examine the oral performance ability of students in intensive ESL as compared with that of students in regular ESL programs at the end of elementary school.

The overarching research question that motivated the study was the following:

> How does the performance on three oral tasks compare across ESL students in intensive and regular programs at the end of elementary school?

During the data collection and analysis, a secondary question of interest emerged:

> How does the nature of the discourse compare across ESL students in intensive and regular programs at the end of elementary school?

To address these questions, we used an explanatory sequential mixed methods design (Creswell & Plano Clark, 2011; Teddlie & Tashakkori, 2009). Data were collected and then analyzed in two phases: a quantitative phase followed by a qualitative phase. Initially we compared the gains in oral proficiency of students in grade 6 in intensive and regular programs in three schools during one academic year. The three oral tasks that were used corresponded to the ESL curriculum in these schools. As reported in J. White and Turner (2005), the gain scores for students in intensive classes were significantly greater than for those in regular classes. Therefore, the first phase provided us with a numeric picture of the phenomenon. What became of further interest and will be reported in more detail in this chapter were the discourse data (the qualitative data). In order to complete our understanding and enrich the quantitative results, we examined the nature of the language generated by each of the three oral tasks. We took a close look at the ways in which intensity of instruction may have affected the discourse.

This chapter will therefore provide the following: a description of the two-phase mixed methods research design of the study; the common methodology across the two phases; a summary of the first-phase quantitative procedures and results as background; a more detailed description of the second-phase qualitative procedures and results with discourse examples; and concluding remarks. The focus will be on the intensive ESL program in the second phase owing to the generous amount of language produced, but to complement and follow-up on the study's first phase, comparisons will be made with the same-age students in the regular ESL program (i.e. those who had a drip-feed experience).

Research Design

In the past two decades mixed methods research (MMR) has evolved into the third research paradigm alongside quantitatively oriented inquiry (numeric data) and qualitatively oriented inquiry (narrative data). It is interested in both quantitative and qualitative data collection and analyses and

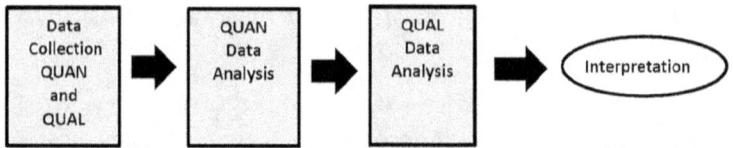

Figure 5.1 Explanatory sequential mixed method design used in this study

primarily works from a pragmatic stance to use what methods work best in order to answer research questions. The research question is central and drives the choice of design rather than a preconceived paradigm (e.g. post-positivist, positivist, constructivist). The interest and practice of MMR have emerged rapidly and have spread across many domains in the social and behavioral sciences, including applied linguistics and, in the study reported here, specifically second language acquisition and language assessment. Within this context, the movement has more recently been called 'the third research community' (Teddlie & Tashakkori, 2009).

Owing to the nature of our main and secondary research questions, we felt that an MMR design was best suited to our inquiries. The context in which we work and the audiences we wanted to be accessible to led to the decision to pursue an explanatory sequential mixed methods design (Creswell & Plano Clark, 2011; Teddlie & Tashakkori, 2009). Right after the data were collected, the quantitative question dominated in that we wanted to examine the oral language performance differences across young learners in elementary ESL intensive and regular programs (thus the notation QUAN) (see Figure 5.1). Once that performance was identified, we were interested in the nature of those significant differences, that is, the qualitative discourse (thus the notation QUAL).

It is to be noted that data for both the first and second phases (i.e. QUAN and QUAL) were the same, that is, the participants and instruments (three oral tasks) were the same. It was at the stages of data preparation and analysis where the data sets were handled differently across the two phases. We will first describe the common aspects of the methodology. Next, we will describe the aspects that are specific to each phase, including data preparation, analyses and results. The units of organization are therefore the two phases and not the instruments.

Common Methodology for Quantitative and Qualitative Phases of the Study: First and Second Phases

Context and participants

The data were collected in three French-medium schools in the Montreal region of Quebec. The three schools were similar in the following ways.

In each school, two intact grade 6 ESL classes participated in the study: one regular ESL class (September–June) and one intensive ESL class (late January–June). The students, who were aged 11–12 and in grade 6, the last year of elementary school, had little exposure to English outside of school, either at home or in their communities. They had begun studying English in grade 4, at the age of 9, and had accumulated a maximum of 144 hours (2 hours per week for 36 weeks each year) by the end of grade 5. In total, there were 73 regular-program students and 79 intensive-program students in the study. The regular and intensive teachers in the participating schools were all proficient speakers of English, used English most of the time in class, and showed evidence of planning the learning experience.

The main difference between the regular and intensive programs was the amount and intensity of instructional time in grade 6. In the regular program, students had about 60 minutes a week of English per week, for a total of 36 hours distributed over the year. In the intensive program, they had English all day, every day, for half of the academic year for a total of about 400 hours over five months.

As there was no special curriculum for intensive ESL, the teachers in the intensive model followed the Ministry-mandated program written for students in regular ESL. The regular program emphasized oral interaction over reading and writing, and teachers were encouraged to set up activities in which students worked in pairs and small groups to accomplish a variety of games and information-gap tasks. Homework, if assigned at all, usually involved finishing worksheets and activity book pages begun in class. At the time data were collected for this study, all ESL teachers – regular and intensive – were encouraged to incorporate cooperative learning into their pedagogical practices. The aim was to ensure that each pair or group member had a clear idea of what contribution he or she was expected to make to the task outcome.

Intensive teachers enriched the regular curriculum by building larger and more elaborate thematic units and projects, while maintaining the emphasis on listening and speaking through in-class activities such as information-gap games, show and tell, discussions, short individual and group presentations, role plays, skits, improvisations and reader's theater. They also assigned an average of an hour and a half of homework per day. This typically included reading, watching TV, working on projects and reviewing material covered in class. A widely used oral interaction activity done as homework was 'telephone pals', in which students called each other at home to complete a task assigned by the teacher (MEQ et al., 2003).[1] The thematic approach emphasized vocabulary building, and there was little or no explicit grammar instruction. Although strategy training was not part of the program, students were encouraged to request clarification, check comprehension and use circumlocution when they lacked precise words or expressions (see Lightbown, this volume, for more information about intensive pedagogy). An important difference between the regular and intensive program, which is directly related to the difference in instructional time, is that students in intensive ESL had much more exposure to English and many more opportunities to practice understanding and producing it than their grade 6 peers in regular ESL in the same school.

Despite the absence of a specific curriculum for intensive programs, a document prepared by the Ministry, in collaboration with SPEAQ, the provincial ESL teachers' association, specified that the goal of the intensive program is for students to be 'functional in the second language in everyday life situations by exploiting certain language learning situations' (MEQ et al., 2001: 9). It made the following distinction between the oral interaction competency outcome profiles expected for learners in regular and intensive ESL at the end of elementary school.

> Regular instruction: The student uses language limited to class situations and familiar topics.
>
> Intensive instruction: The student uses a wide range of expressions and vocabulary in various situations. He/she expresses himself/herself with ease and confidence. (MEQ et al., 2001: 10)

Our challenge was to operationalize these distinctions and then to investigate the extent to which they characterized the oral language use of learners in the two instructional models. The tasks we adapted and developed are described below.

Common tasks and data collection procedures

To obtain a variety of oral performances from each student in the regular and intensive programs, we used three different elicitation tasks: Audio-Pal, Story-Retell and Info-Gap. Data collection took place in the following manner. Pretests were administered near the beginning of the students' grade 6 ESL program (in October for the regular ESL groups and in January for the intensive groups); post-tests were administered at the end of grade 6, in late May/early June for all groups. One of the planned differences among the tasks was the type of interaction required.

Audio-Pal

In this solo, non-reciprocal task, students recorded themselves talking into a tape recorder for about one minute. They were asked to describe their families, hobbies, friends and school for an imagined English-speaking person their own age. A researcher was present to monitor the time.

Story-Retell

In this task, students watched a 2.5-minute clip from an animated film showing an episode with several characters (a woman and her three cats) and a beginning, middle and end (their peaceful life was interrupted by a sudden storm). Although the video contained some language, students did not need to understand it to tell a coherent story. Immediately after viewing the clip, students met individually with a researcher to retell the story. The students were audio-recorded and given prompts (e.g. 'What happened next?') if they had difficulty recalling the events. At the end of 2 minutes, the researcher thanked the student, whether or not he or she had already stopped talking.

Info-Gap

Working in pairs, students took turns describing items that were missing on their partner's pictures (a school at the pretest, a house at the post-test). They had 5 minutes in which to describe five items per picture (a total of 10), which their partner had to draw in the correct location of the appropriate room. Since a screen prevented them from seeing each other's pictures, they had to rely on words rather than gestures. This two-way task is similar to games the students had played in their ESL class, and many of them recognized the need to work quickly. These audio-recorded speech samples differ from those in the other two tasks in being jointly constructed (Galaczi, 2008; Gan, 2010; Swain, 2001). Students had to listen, initiate, respond and sustain the interaction. The challenges of paired scoring will be discussed below. Furthermore, since pair assignments were based on logistical matters, not on oral proficiency, the two individuals were not necessarily at the same proficiency level.

The data for the study were analyzed sequentially in two different ways (see Figure 5.1): first quantitatively and then qualitatively. In the next section we will describe the quantitative phase of the study.

Quantitative Phase: Scoring Procedures and Summary of Results

In the quantitative first phase, the researchers listened to the audio-cassette recordings to determine the scores for the three tasks. Each task was scored according to specific procedures. In this section, the procedures will be described and at the end the final gain score descriptive statistics for each group are presented to indicate the final quantitative results as reported in J. White and Turner (2005).

Scoring of the first two tasks (Audio-Pal and Story-Retell) followed procedures established by Turner and Upshur (1996, 2002) and Upshur and Turner (1999) in earlier studies, that is, empirically based rating scales. Previously developed rating scales were adapted and piloted for each task.

Audio-Pal

Using the scale to distinguish among the speech samples, two independent raters listened to the audio recordings and separately asked themselves

94 Part 2: Intensive Instruction

yes/no questions about the amount of information provided, variety of sentence patterns, linguistic accuracy, fluency and use of French. This led to ratings from 1 to 6. The scores of the two raters were combined, yielding scores that ranged from 2 to 12. Since students chose what they wanted to say about their families, hobbies, etc., the accuracy of the information provided could not be verified. Therefore, the scale that emerged from the data focused on linguistic features.

Story-Retell

Again using a scale specific to this task, two raters independently listened to the speech samples and asked themselves yes/no questions about coherence, inclusion of key story elements, fluency and use of French. This led to ratings from 1 to 6. If there were long pauses, frequent use of French and/or two or more key story elements were omitted, or if the story was just a list of words, the score ranged from 1 to 3. A coherent story with all key elements was scored from 4 to 6, depending on the lengths of pauses and the amount of French. Combining the scores of the two raters yielded total scores from 2 to 12. In this memory-based task, since the researcher knew the story, the information was predictable and could be verified. Therefore, the scale that emerged focused on the content of the story.

Info-Gap

The scoring procedure was developed by the research team, based on the speech samples that students produced during the task. To arrive at the score, two independent raters separately listened to the recorded interactions. Three points were allocated to each item: one for drawing the correct object; one if the object was in the correct room; one if the object was in the correct location. This yielded a total possible score of 30 (3×10). However, points were lost if French was used to name the item, room or location. Scores of the two raters were combined, yielding scores that ranged from 0 to 60.

From the outset, a major challenge was developing a scoring procedure for the paired oral task. We realized that we could not come up with scores for the individual students because both participants contributed to the score. Thus, the decision was made to develop a procedure to have a joint score. That is, both students received the same score.

Summary of quantitative section

To address the overarching research question, descriptive statistics for gain scores (from pretest to post-test) were calculated on all three tasks. This was followed by a two-way analysis of variance using the gain scores as the

Table 5.1 Gain score descriptive statistics for group (intensive and regular) by task*

Task	N	Minimum	Maximum	Mean	SD
Intensive group					
AP gain	75	−3.00	6.00	**2.19**	1.80
RT gain	73	−2.00	8.00	**2.37**	1.77
IG gain	70	−28.00	54.00	**20.00**	16.18
Regular group					
AP gain	69	−4.00	5.00	**0.65**	1.54
RT gain	71	−3.00	5.00	**0.09**	1.24
IG gain	62	−32.00	22.00	**−1.98**	10.27

*All scores represent the combined ratings of the two raters
AP (Audio-Pal): 6-point scale × 2 raters = 12 points. RT (Story-Retell): 6-point scale × 2 raters = 12 points. IG (Info-Gap): 30 points x 2 raters = 60 points.
The unit of analysis of IG was the pair (intensive group, $N = 35$; regular group, $N = 31$).

dependent variable. The results indicated the difference/change in performance from pretest to post-test across regular and intensive groups. As reported in J. White and Turner (2005), the gain scores for students in intensive classes were significantly greater than for those in regular classes. Table 5.1 provides the gain score descriptive statistics to give an indication of the gain score means by task.[2] It shows that the gain score mean for the task Info-Gap in the regular program is negative (i.e. students with lower posttest scores relative to their pretest had a negative gain score). This could be explained in a variety of ways, but the fact that Info-Gap was a paired task where the oral performance was co-constructed sets it apart from the other two tasks where performance was individual. The unit of analysis for scoring was the pair, which brings with it the potential that scores could have been affected by the interaction between the two students owing to several factors (e.g. proficiency levels, interpersonal characteristics, peer work ability). These interactions could have varied from the pretest to the post-test (e.g. a more proficient partner at the pretest, a less proficient partner at the post-test).

These quantitative results led us to the next phase of our study, which addressed our secondary research question. Now that we knew the numeric results of comparing task performance results across intensive and regular groups, we turned to examining and comparing the nature of the discourse generated by the two groups for each of the three tasks.

To help us compare and discuss the discourse in the next phase, we decided to carry out a further quantitative procedure to establish individual student oral proficiency levels. The students were divided into three significantly different groups according to their performance on one of the two individual tasks, Story-Retell. Using the ratings from Story-Retell, we identified three oral proficiency levels as follows. High scores were more than 1 SD above the mean (8–12); mid scores were ±1 SD (5–7); low scores were more than 1 SD below the mean (1–4). Each student could then be assigned to one of the three proficiency levels.

Following the procedure described above, we also divided the Info-Gap scores into three groups, high, mid, and low, as follows. High scores were more than 1 SD above the mean (58–60); mid scores were ±1 SD (35–57); low scores were more than 1 SD below the mean (0–34). These two classifications allowed us to examine the performance of the various pair combinations for Info-Gap.

Qualitative Phase: Procedures, Analysis and Discourse Samples

In the qualitative second phase, the audio cassettes were transferred to a computer, using Audacity 1.3 Beta software, and then were transcribed and verified by two research assistants. The discourse was analyzed in a manner similar in nature to open coding, as described in Strauss and Corbin (1998) and following guidelines from the 10 principles of interpretational analysis by Tesch (1990). The relevant and meaningful ways in which the students used language to complete the tasks were the focus of the analysis. Particular language use was identified in the tasks owing to their specific nature and demands (see Dörnyei & Kormos, 1998; Dörnyei & Scott, 1997; Long, 1983, 1996). This section describes this discourse, and segments are provided to exemplify the language use across students in both the intensive and regular programs. In order to help put into context the examples, students' scores and proficiency levels are sometimes referred to. How this information was arrived at was described in the preceding section.

Audio-Pal

In the examples below, we illustrate how students approached the task of describing themselves. Note that S refers to the student, R refers to the researcher, and three dots (...) indicate a pause.[3] Names of all students and schools are pseudonyms. The instructions to 'talk about yourself' led most students in both intensive and regular programs to begin by introducing themselves to their imagined friend: *My name is X*. For many students, this established a sentence pattern that was repeated throughout their introductions. We begin with Joel, a student in the intensive program, who provided six items of information using only the verb *is*.

Example 1: Student 87 (score = 5/12)
S: My name is Joel ... my hobby is uh car, the car. My school is uh very excellent. My friend is uh very ... gen ... [gentile] ... [long pause] ... Dominic is my best friend ... [long pause] ... my favorite car is uh Dodge/ ... / ... [long pause] ...

Tara, in the regular program, also told about her hobbies using only the verb *is*. However, in comparison to Joel, she used more French, her pauses were longer, and she provided less information about herself in the time allowed.

Example 2: Student 90 (score = 2/12)
S: Hello, my name is Tara ... uu ... I, mm ... my [passe-temp] is ... the ... computer and ... and ... [parler] to my friend ... is ... is ... my [école] my school is the ... [long pause] ... my school the ... the ...

Another characteristic of the discourse of regular-program students was simply listing friends or activities, as we see in the next example. André's score of 4 is close to the mean for students in the regular program.

Example 3: Student 46 (score = 4/12)
S: My name is André, my last name is Ouellette. Uh my [passe-temp favoris] is basketball ... uh uh friends, my friends are uh Billy uh Josep, Raoul, Sacha ... Raoul, Sacha / ... / ... [very long pause] ... uh for uh ... ba ... basketball very for school is uh ... [les] / ... / uh ... [35 seconds pause] ...

Examples 4 and 5 illustrate the mean score for the intensive groups, 6/12. We can see that Marc used four different content verbs and two forms of *to be*. He provided more information than the regular-program students in the previous examples without resorting to French content words. Audio-Pal introductions typically lacked a closure. While a few students signaled 'Finish', most simply stopped talking, as did Marc, leaving the researcher uncertain as to whether or not there was more to come.

Example 4: Student 17 (score = 6/12)
S: OK. Hi, my name is Marc. Uh my pastime [bais] I uh often play hockey in a team. I very like hockey. Uh I also play, I like the sport. I also play uh football, tennis and uh sometimes soccer. Uh I go to St Luc School. I am in uh six grade. My teacher is Lucie ... and uh that's it. Uh ... I don't uh ... I like to play uh Nintendo game and uh computer ... uh I have uh many friend uh ... [long pause] ... I ...
R: That's everything? <**S:** yes >

The next intensive student, Paul, spoke clearly and accurately and described his daily activities using a variety of content verbs. He used English pause fillers (*uh* and *uhm*) and was more fluent than Marc, who had one French pause filler (*bais*), but he also seems to have run out of things to say.

Example 5: Student 13 (score 6/12)
S: My name is Paul. Uh I am uh twelve years old. Uh I like uh to play football and hockey after school and at recess sometimes I play uh football. Uhhm, after school I watch TV and uh I uh after I do my homework. Uhmm I have many friends. My best friend is Erik uh ... I live in Montreal ... [very long pause]

We turn now to a student whose score was above the mean for the intensive groups. He spoke fluently and confidently about his interests, school and friends for the full minute he was allowed for the task.

Example 6: Student 50 (score = 9/12)
S: My uh ... my name is Luc. I, I like to play computer, go on Internet, my my school is quite big, big gymnasium, big school yard with ... big park so, uh soccer field, baseball field with big big trees, lots of trees, plants and this is it. My friend, my best friend are Maurice, Francis, and Eric. Eric is uh a pro to play drum, me I start to play guitar at ... eleven years old but I'm not good uh Patrick is good in the computer, me too. And I, I like many my friends because it's uh ss ... my best friend and I, I know they don't left me there when I am in trouble!

In summary, the Audio-Pal task discourse shows that, in comparison to regular program students, intensive students spoke more confidently. They were able to provide more information about themselves during this timed task, to do so using more varied sentence patterns, to leave fewer pauses unfilled, and to rely less on French to fill lexical gaps. We turn now to the second oral task.

Story-Retell

In both the regular and intensive programs, many students began retelling the story by identifying the characters. As we can see in the examples below, two introducer patterns predominated, both of which are typical of the way in which young French L1 learners introduce a narrative (see Lightbown, 1991). The first pattern consists of variations on the non-target-like structure, *it's a*:

It's a woman uh who have uh three cats.
Is uh a girl have a three cat.

The second introducer pattern is *there is, there are*, which Marc used to begin his story retell.

S: OK, uh there was uh a woman.
R: Yes.
S: She had uh three cats.

A typical error with this form involves the verb *avoir* (to have), probably influenced by the French equivalent, *il y a*, which is literally *it has there*.

S: Uh he have uh four uh three cat, and uh one uh woman, old woman

Many students began by establishing a time frame or a sequence of events. Joelle, an intensive student, introduced her story by situating the sequence of events in the afternoon. When she realized that she lacked a key lexical item, she hesitated and then filled the gap by pronouncing the French word as if it were English. This strategy allowed her to continue her narrative, although she needed some encouragement from the researcher.

Example 7: Student 2 (score = 6/12)
S: OK, uh at uh at uh, in the afternoon three cat um go outside to take a coffee and uh play uh on uh in the yard but uh suddenly uh ... ha um the the the wind uh ... the wind uh ha hit the ... the uh uh ... [il y a, il y a] the [orages] (anglicized pronunciation) <**R:** OK, OK> and uh and the cat uh ... the cat uh fly on the, on the sky and all the thing in the yard / ... / uh fly in the sky and uh ... and uh ...
R: And then what happens?
S: And then uh ... the the the girl, the the woman <**R:** mhm> uhm attach um, attach the, the the the cat on her and uh she walk uh uh very uh ... slow <**R:** uhum> and uh they enter in the, in the ... in the house [la]
R: Uhum, and then? What happens in the house?
S: And uh ... the ... the ... the the one cat is scared <**R:** uhum> uh he uh he hide ... itself uh under the the the carpet ... <**R:** uhum> and after on the woman and the woman uh put uh put it uh on the carpet, yeah
R: Uhum ... can you tell me about uh the objects in the sky?
S: OK, uhm ... I don't remember uh ... uh socks <**R:** yeah, there were many, yes> cloth, uh clothing

Intensive students used a number of other compensatory strategies when they lacked a key word in the story. One was to simply insert the French word and continue. For instance, after an initial long pause, Martin produced *clôture* instead of *fence* and then continued to use *clôture* each time he needed it during the retell. Another strategy is circumlocution and the use of an all-purpose word, such as *thing*, as we see in the next example from Lilianne, who did not know how to say *birdbath*. Note also that the researcher did not

100   Part 2: Intensive Instruction

need to prompt for the next events in her story, but rather confirmed that Lilianne was following what the student was saying. The performance of this student was well above the mean for the intensive group.

Example 8: Student 7 (score = 10/12)
S: There's a three cat <**R**: yes> They are always uh outside and playing, w ... the the white cat with black spot is uh always in the ... thing for the bird, <**R**: mhm mhm> for the bird ... the other cat is uh always ... doing all and the other is a ... playing in this yard. And a day there is a big win ... wind <**R**: OK> and uh all the thing uh ... fly over and, and uh their mast ... their / ... / master trying to rescue the cat ... uh she is, she is trying hard but the cat are, are flying <**R**: uhum> so, she uh take her ... her uh skirt and uh she is uh ... bringing uh the cat uh in the skirt ... so the cat won't uh fly <**R**: That's right> ... and the the cat are very scare, but they try to enter in the house ... what happen when the girl uh flying to the door and <**R**: uhum, uhum> so and everyone was in it, they were safe ...
R: That's right, good <**S**: yes> ...
S: The uh ... It's look like uh, they live in the country. <**R**: yeah, I think so> I don't think they are in the city because there's not many houses.

In contrast to the fluent performance by intensive students like Lilianne, students in the regular program had difficulty retelling the story, even with considerable prompting from the researcher. They were quick to switch into French when they ran into difficulty, as we see with Olivier in the next example.

Example 9: Student 35 (score = 2/12)
S: Uh, is the storm <**R**: yes!> in the ... in the, in the [chez eux la] <**R**: OK> is uh three beautiful cat <**R**: uhum> ... [long pause] ... [Je pas croiser]
R: Uh tell me about the grandmother, the old lady, the woman <**S**: yes> Tell me ...
S: %...% <**R**: in English> [Je pas commencer]
R: No? <**S**: no.> Nothing? Tell me about the objects in the sky, the objects
S: Oh, uh ... [long pause] ... [je pas]

Jean-Luc, in Example 10, provided more content than Olivier and had a score above the mean for the regular group on this task. However, he had to be reminded to tell the story in English.

Example 10: Student 43 (score = 4/12)
S: OK, uh the, the grandmother at uh, at the house <**R**: mhm> umm and the cat ... uh the cat and the, grandmother <**R**: mhm> go to the, to [jardin (anglicized pronunciation)] <**R**: OK> um the cat

uh/... / uh, is uh a trouble because uh, uh uh a big big big [orage (anglicized pronunciation)] <R: uhum> and uh the cat is uh, is uh [bousculade] after grandmother uhm ... scrunch to the rug <R: OK, OK> after ... [long pause] ... [indistinct speech in French] <R: Oh! in English please> OK ... and uh ... [long pause] ... <R: No¿ Can't finish¿> ... No, no, and the cat is uh is uh go at the house <R: mhm> and a big shock <R: mhm> and the cat is uh afraid.

In summary, the Story-Retell discourse shows that intensive students were able to retell the video narrative more fluently and provide more details using a narrative story structure than the students in the regular program. Furthermore, their use of compensatory strategies made them less reliant on French and contributed to their fluency when they encountered lexical gaps.

Info-Gap

In order to compare the oral interaction performance of learners in the intensive and regular ESL programs, we included Info-Gap, a paired two-way closed task. We knew that information-gap tasks were used frequently in elementary school ESL classes and would be familiar to the students in both programs. Scoring the Info-Gap task presented a challenge, however. After listening to the language generated during this task, we realized that we could not come up with scores for individual students, as the discourse was jointly constructed. Accordingly, we developed the scoring method described above, which assigns one score to each pair.[4]

Because we had not pre-arranged the proficiency levels of the pairs, we found every possible combination of proficiency among the dyads. (See the end of the quantitative section above for the procedure we used to identify high, mid and low proficiency levels.) Furthermore, when we looked at the Info-Gap scores, we became aware that knowing the proficiency combinations did not always allow us to reliably predict performance. In particular, we were struck by the fact that mid–mid pairs were represented in the high, medium and low scoring groups and that high–high pairs obtained both high and medium scores. This observation led us to go beyond the scores to examine the discourse created by various pair combinations. Our goal was to investigate what contributes to successful performance on the Info-Gap task.

The first pair, consisting of evenly matched mid-proficiency intensive students, obtained a high score on the Info-Gap task. They got right into the game mentality of doing the task quickly and finished in 3.5 minutes.

Example 12: Student A (4) and Student B (2) score = 58/60
A: OK, uh in the attic, under the bed uh, put uh in the middle under the bed put a ball...
B: Um uh ... in the living room <A: yeah¿> uh on the wall uh next to the TV <A: OK> it's a painting ...

A: OK, on the living room, uh beside the, the sofa, draw uh, on the, on the right draw a little table, coffee table ...
B: OK, umm in the, bedroom <**A**: OK> next to the uh liv ... the bathroom, at the right of the bed it's a chair ... OK ...
A: OK ... room ... OK! in the living ... dining room, on the table, put uh, put the flower ...
B: In the attic <**A**: OK> at the right of the night table, you have a, fluffy uh teddy uh teddy bear <**A**: hah!> ...
A: <**B**: OK> Umm ... number five, OK, uh in the living room, on the TV, put the pair of glasses ...
B: Uh in the bathroom, uh in front of the sink you have a little carpet <**A**: OK> ...
A: OK, umm in the bathroom uh uh on the left, of the sing, sink uh put the little basket ...
B: Wait! I'm not finish to draw. Uh in the living room <**A**: yeah?> on the sofa you have a hat ...
A: OK.

A number of characteristics of this pair's interaction contributed to their efficiency and high score: they had quick access to the specific vocabulary they needed (names of rooms, furniture, items, prepositions, left and right); because they gave each other precise instructions for drawing, no requests for repetition or clarification were needed; they confirmed with 'OK' that they were following each other; they used the same sentence frame throughout the task, contributing to the predictability of the information (room + preposition + location + verb + item); they used only English and needed no prompting by the researcher.

We turn now to extracts from the co-constructed performance between two students who were not evenly matched, Student A (mid-proficiency) and Student B (high-proficiency). As we see, Student B tried to hurry Student A along.

Example 13: Student A (118) and Student B (117) score = 54/60
A: OK uh, <**B**: fast> the ball [bais] in the attic, the ball is under the bed.
B: Go.
A: (asks for time to draw) Uh one minute
B: (gutteral noise of annoyance) Mmm –
A: OK. One minute [la] I draw ... uh 3. OK my number 4 is in the, the dining room

Indeed, they completed the task in about 4 minutes with an announcement of 'finish'. In addition to being aware of the time constraint, this pair was skilled at negotiating for meaning. In the next extract, the item to be drawn was a pair of glasses, which Student A could see on top of the television set in the living room. Realizing that Student B might think he was referring to *drinking glasses*, he specified the appropriate meaning before a misunderstanding occurred.

A: OK, my 5, in the, living room or the <**B**: yes> family room OK, on the tv, <**B**: yes> there are a little uh a glass uh no a glass of milk but a –
B: / ... /glass [la]
A: this mmhh I have it on my –
B: a glass¿
A: yeah but I have in my face.
B: OH, I think a glass of /milk/.
A: yeah, I say no a glass of /milk/ its –

The pair of glasses was problematic for a number of students and in some cases did lead to clarification requests, such as the one between another high–mid pair.

Example 14: Student A (7) and Student B (12) score = 58/60
A: OK, uh number 5, OK, there is glasses, on the tv, in the living room
B: Glasses¿
A: Yes, glasses
B: Glasses to see or to drink¿
A: To see
B: OK, number¿
A: 5
B: 5¿
A: Yes, 5

In order to avoid using French, some intensive students invented words. When Student B (mid-proficiency) could not remember *living room*, he tried out *relaxing room* on his partner. Student A (mid-proficiency) not only understood this newly minted word, but he used it himself!

Example 15: Student A(69) and Student B (64) score = 34/60
B: [oui]it's a picture, on the [cadre] <**A**: OK, OK, OK, OK>, OK, it's the the, it's uh the relax room, the relaxing room, it's uh, under, under the tv and the the next wall, the the picture <**A**: OK> ... do you understand¿
A: Yes ... OK ... number 3, is uh, on the relax room, <**B**: uhm> uh is a small desk, uh on the, on the right uh, the, on the right uh, the [divan]

Task success did not necessarily require verbs, as shown in the next example from a high- and mid-proficiency pair.

Example 16: Student A (126) and Student B (127) score = 56/60
A: OK ... OK, uh number 6, uh, a garbage c[e]n, <**B**: uhuh> next to the sink, in the wash – in the bathroom
B: Next to the sink in¿
A: In the bathroom.
B: OK, left or right¿
A: Left.
B: A garbage can¿
A: Yes.

We have focused so far on the paired performance of intensive students, and we have shown that students who obtained high scores on this task had quick access to the vocabulary they needed. That is, they could name the rooms, furniture and objects in the house and could use and understand prepositions of location. This speed allowed for task completion. In addition, they used only English and were able to draw the missing items quickly and clearly, and in some cases were able to anticipate their partner's comprehension problems. Task success did not require accurate grammar, sentence structure, artistic ability or even verbs. Students could compensate for lexical gaps with communication strategies, such as circumlocution and word coinage, but they had to be fast. Extended negotiations took time and reduced the likelihood of finishing the task within the 5 minute time limit.

In the Info-Gap example below from the regular program, we see that some of the key features of success were missing from this pair's performance. Of particular note was the frequent use of French, including *lunettes* for *glasses,*

Example 17: Student A(97) and Student B (96) score = 26/60
A: Number two is ... [ballon] under the ... [long pause] ... uh ben ... baby bedroom ... (indistinct whisper)
B: OK hmm hush! Oh! ... uh ...
R: Number two is the number
B: Number two uh uh ... uh ... [very long pause] ... uh ... [long pause ... in the TV, a card ... [very long pause]
A: Number three ... [very long pause] ... desk ... under the light, in uh ... [comment on dit salon en anglais¿]
R: Imagine I'm not here
A: [dans le salon] ... <**B**: desk> Ah! [c'est quoi¿] (laughing)
B: Uhhh number three, chair in the bedroom, on the uh ... upper / ... / the, the bed <**A**: and¿> uh it's in uh on the ca ... car ... ca ... cable ... OK! ...
R: But use your voice not the actions with your hands!> ... [long pause] ...
A: [bon] Number four ... uh ... flower ... in kitchen, flower, on the table ...

B: Number five? ... uh ... a bear ... bear, opposite the desk in the uh uh baby bedroom ...
A: Uhm ... [very long pause] ... number five ... [long pause] ... mm ... in ... [la salon / ... /] ... [lunettes] ... glasses ...
B: What?
A: Glasses
B: [ah oui] Glasses
R: OK, that's 5 minutes. So ... stop!

The long pauses in the transcript indicate that this pair did not have fast access to the vocabulary items they needed to identify or the rooms in the house. We also see evidence that Student B tried to locate an object by gesturing, rather than using a verbal compensatory strategy. When Student A came to number five, *glasses on the TV in the living room*, he first named both the object and the room in French. Possibly for this reason, Student B did not need to question which of two possible meanings of *glasses* was intended. At the end of 5 minutes, they had not completed the task.

As we have seen, an important difference between students in the regular and intensive programs was the speed with which they could retrieve the task-essential language. Another difference was the extent to which they used communication strategies to fill in the gaps, rather than switching to French. The intensive students were comfortable with English and used it confidently as a tool to complete the task, whether it involved talking about themselves, describing a video clip to a researcher or playing an Info-Gap game with a partner. Although their English was not flawless, they demonstrated their ability to use a 'wide range of expressions and vocabulary in various situations' (MEQ *et al.*, 2001) as they engaged in the three oral elicitation tasks used in this study. Table 5.2 summarizes the characteristics we observed in the discourse of intensive students in the second phase of the Oral Proficiency Project.

Discussion and Conclusion

The research questions for this study were two-fold and sequential:

- How does the performance on three oral tasks compare across ESL students in intensive and regular programs at the end of elementary school?
- During the data collection and analysis, a secondary question of interest emerged: How does the nature of the discourse compare across ESL students in intensive and regular programs at the end of elementary school?

The first question was quantitative in nature and the second one was qualitative. This chapter has demonstrated how the explanatory sequential mixed

Table 5.2 Characteristics of the language use of intensive program students

- Fluency
- Confidence
- Predominant use of English (infrequent code switching)
- Efficient negotiation for meaning
- Little or no prompting by researcher
- Varied content words and sentence patterns
- Precise descriptions
- Quick access to most of the vocabulary needed for the task
- Effective use of strategies to fill lexical gaps
  - Circumlocution
  - Use of an all-purpose word (e.g. *thing*)
  - Inventing words
  - Anglicizing pronunciation of French words
  - Use of English pause fillers (e.g. *uh, um*)
- Effective use of strategies to exchange information
  - Asking for repetition, clarification, confirmation
  - Providing repetition, clarification, confirmation
  - Checking comprehension

methods design helped us better interpret and contextualize the differences in scores between the intensive and regular elementary ESL programs in Quebec. It was anticipated that students in the intensive program would outperform the regular students. The first phase of the study confirmed that the gain scores for students in intensive classes were significantly greater than for those in regular classes.

The second phase then allowed us to better understand the nature of the discourse generated by the two groups, which led to more insight into what students can actually do with language to communicate and complete tasks when provided more intensive instruction. Owing to the task characteristics, it also allowed us to see diverse uses of language and to be able to describe those differences. In Audio-Pal, intensive students spoke more confidently and fluently than regular students and were able to provide more information about themselves in the time allowed. They were less likely to code-switch into French when they encountered lexical gaps. In Story-Retell, intensive students again were more fluent than regular students. They provided more details about the video and used strategies more often to compensate for lexical gaps than regular students. In Info-Gap, intensive students were more efficient negotiators in their information exchanges than regular students. They asked for and provided repetitions and clarifications and checked comprehension, but they kept the beat-the-clock objective of the game in mind as they did so. Regular students, on the other hand, were more focused on the language needed to perform the task and were rarely able to use English to describe and place all 10 items correctly. In the paragraphs that follow, we offer an explanation for the differences we found between the discourse of intensive and regular ESL students.

We begin this discussion by reiterating that the fundamental difference between the regular and intensive ESL programs was the amount of instructional time offered in grade 6. In one year, the students in the intensive program had 10 times more exposure to English than the students in regular ESL: 400 hours compared with fewer than 40 hours. A second difference was the intensity of the exposure: the instructional time in the intensive program was concentrated into five months, and students were in their English class all day, every day during this period. In contrast, regular instruction was distributed over a period of 10 months, at the rate of one hour a week. There is considerable evidence that distributing small amounts of exposure and practice in a second language over an extended period of time is an inefficient route to communicative competence, and our findings confirm previous research investigating this issue (for a review of the literature on the distribution of time in language learning, see Collins & J. White, 2011).

The difference in amount of instructional time has an important pedagogical implication: it is directly related to the number of opportunities learners have to practice understanding and using the new language. In-class listening and reading activities provide important input for incidental learning, and oral interaction activities such as information-gaps, role plays, group and whole class discussions, as well as homework tasks like phone pals, enable students to practice producing new language features (e.g. vocabulary and sentence structures) in real time (see Muñoz, 2007, on the importance of practice in elementary school language programs). Clearly the greater number of opportunities to practice speaking favored students in the intensive program, as we saw in the discourse examples above. Students in the regular program also did some of the same activities, but since they had much less instructional time, they did fewer of them.

Another, less-often mentioned difference between intensive and regular ESL relates to the physical environment. Intensive teachers, like homeroom teachers, have their own classrooms because they teach the same students all day long, every day. They can arrange the furniture as they wish and typically configure the desks and chairs in ways that allow for easy group and pair work. This favors cooperative learning activities and collaborative projects involving oral interaction. Because they have their own classroom, intensive teachers can make sure that students have the resources they need, such as dictionaries, books and art supplies, as well as audio-recording devices and computers, and that they are easily accessible. During the early weeks of intensive, teachers often label the objects in the classroom (desk, pencil sharpener, computer). They can write what they want on the board because no other teacher will erase it. They can also cover the walls with posters containing expressions such as 'May I go to the washroom?', 'I don't understand, please repeat' and then expect students to use this language when they communicate within the classroom. The print environment is rich, the teacher speaks English, and students are encouraged to use all the resources available to them in order to communicate with each other. They find speaking English natural right from the beginning of their five months of intensive learning, and when they get to the end of their program, they have had hundreds of hours and thousands of opportunities to practice.

In contrast, teachers in regular ESL in Quebec rarely have their own classroom and must move from one room to another every hour, pushing their teaching materials with them on a trolley. When they arrive at the classroom door at the appointed time, the homeroom teacher stops the geography or mathematics lesson and hastily leaves the room, often saying over her shoulder, 'Please don't erase the board'. The furniture may or may not be arranged in a way that facilitates group work, and decisions about groups and pairs are often based on convenience ('work with the person sitting next to/in front of you'). The classroom, while it may be pleasant and richly supportive of the French content class, does not contribute to the scaffolding of students' oral production in English in the way that is possible in intensive programs.

Two recent changes to the Quebec ESL program offer interesting possibilities for future research. The first is that the introduction to English has been lowered from grade 4 to grade 1 since the data were collected for the study reported here. The one-hour-a-week program that was developed for grades 1 and 2 focuses on listening to stories and singing songs; it is followed in grade 3 by the regular program described in this chapter. In June, 2012, the first cohort of students to have had six years of English will leave elementary school. Anecdotal reports from ESL teachers suggest that the regular-program students who have had a story- and song-based program in grades 1 and 2 speak more confidently and are less likely to switch to French when they reach grade 6 than previous cohorts. These reports have not been empirically investigated, and if found to be accurate, the impact of stories and songs on oral proficiency outcomes in intensive is unknown. Data from the Oral Proficiency Project would be useful in future comparison studies. The second change is the Ministry-mandated phasing in of intensive ESL for students in all French schools in Quebec by 2015. The potential for research in this new context is exciting, and we look forward to the day when we can report that every elementary school child in Quebec is given the opportunity to express him- or herself in English with 'ease and confidence'.

Acknowledgments

The first phase of this study was funded by the Quebec Ministry of Education. We would like to thank Randall Halter, the statistical consultant, and the four research assistants who provided invaluable assistance in the development of the instruments, data collection and data analyses: Coreen Dougherty, Heike Neumann, Ioanna Nicolae and Christianne Rivard. The second phase was funded by the Quebec Ministry of Education (Fonds Québecois de la recherche sur la societé et la culture). We thank Tayebeh Shalmani and Joy Williams, who transferred and transcribed the audio files, for their dedication and attention to detail.

Notes

(1) In telephone pals, the teacher typically provides guidance as to the topic or task, which may include info-gap activities based on worksheets the teacher has provided, talking about a television program, practicing poems, jokes, tongue twisters or skits, and playing games such as 20 Questions. The teacher allocates class time the next day for students to report on their telephone conversations.
(2) Reprinted from J. White and Turner (2005), p. 504 (Table 5).
(3) Additional coding conventions:
... long pause – longer pauses mentioned in [ ]
[...] French word
/ ... / uncertain word or phrase
% ... % simultaneous speech
<...> interrupted speech
(...) comments
(4) It is to be noted that the scoring of co-constructed tasks remains an issue in the language assessment literature. Questions remain as to the focus of the assessment. Should it be the successful completion of the task or should it focus on the inter-related discourse, and then what should the procedure be? See Fulcher *et al.* (2011), as one attempt to address scoring in co-constructed tasks.

References

Collins, L. and White, J. (2011) An intensive look at intensity and language learning. *TESOL Quarterly* 46 (1), 106–133.
Creswell, J. and Plano Clark, V.L. (2011) *Designing and Conducting Mixed Methods Research* (2nd edn). Thousand Oaks, CA: Sage.
Dörnyei, Z. and Kormos, J. (1998) Problem-solving mechanisms in L2 communication. *Studies in Second Language Acquisition* 20 (3), 349–385.
Dörnyei, Z. and Scott, M.L. (1997) Communication strategies in a second language: Definitions and taxonomies. *Language Learning* 47 (1), 173–210.
Fulcher, G., Davidson, F. and Kemp, J. (2011) Effective rating scale development for speaking tests: Performance decision trees. *Language Testing* 28 (1), 5–29.
Galaczi, E. (2008) Peer-peer interaction in a speaking test: The case of the *First Certificate in English* examination. *Language Assessment Quarterly* 5 (2), 89–119.
Gan, Z. (2010) Interaction in group oral assessment: A case study of higher- and lower-scoring students. *Language Testing* 27 (4), 585–602.
Lightbown, P. (1991) What have we here? Some observations on the influence of instruction on L2 learning. In R. Phillipson, E. Kellerman, S.L.M. Sharwood Smith and M. Swain (eds) *Foreign/second Language Pedagogy Research: A Commemorative Volume for Claus Faerch* (pp. 197–212). Clevedon: Multilingual Matters.
Lightbown, P. and Spada, N. (2000) Do they know what they're doing? L2 Learners' awareness of L1 influence. *Language Awareness* 9 (4), 198–217.

Long, M. (1983) Native speaker/non-native speaker conversation and the negotiation of comprehensible input. *Applied Linguistics* 4 (2), 126–141.

Long, M.H. (1996) The role of the linguistic environment in second language acquisition. In W.C. Richie and T.K. Bhatia (eds) *Handbook of Second Language Acquisition* (pp. 413–468). London: Academic Press.

MEQ, RCCPALS and SPEAQ (2001) *Intensive English as a Second Language, Implementation Guide: A Teacher's Guide for Implementing Programs for Intensive English as a Second Language in Québec Elementary Schools*. Québec: Ministère d'Éducation du Québec, Société pour la Promotion de l'Enseignement de l'Anglais, Langue Seconde, au Québec.

MEQ, RCCPALS, SPEAQ (2003) *Intensive English as a Second Language, New Implementation Guide*. Québec: Ministère d'Éducation du Québec, Société pour la Promotion de l'Enseignement de l'Anglais, Langue Seconde, au Québec.

Muñoz, C. (2007) Age-related differences and second language learning practice. In R. DeKeyser (ed.) *Practice in a Second Language: Perspectives from Applied Linguistics and Cognitive Psychology* (pp. 229–255). New York: Cambridge University Press.

Spada, N. and Lightbown, P. (1989) Intensive ESL programmes in Quebec primary schools. *TESL Canada Journal* 7 (1), 11–32.

Strauss, A. and Corbin, J. (1998) *Basics of Qualitative Research: Techniques and Procedures for Developing Grounded Theory* (2nd edn). Thousand Oaks, CA: Sage.

Swain, M. (2001) Examining dialogue: Another approach to content specification and to validating inferences drawn from test scores. *Language Testing* 18 (3), 275–302.

Teddlie, C. and Tashakkori, A. (2009) *Foundations of Mixed Methods Research: Integrating Quantitative and Qualitative Techniques in the Social and Behavioral Sciences*. Thousand Oaks, CA: Sage.

Tesch, R. (1990) *Qualitative Research: Analysis Types and Software Tools*. New York: Falmer.

Turner, C.E. and Upshur, J. (1996) Developing rating scales for the assessment of second language performance. *Australian Review of Applied Linguistics* 13, 55–79.

Turner, C.E. and Upshur, J. (2002) Rating scales derived from student samples: Effects of the scale maker and the student sample on scale content and student scores. *TESOL Quarterly* 36 (1), 49–70.

Upshur, J.A. and Turner, C.E. (1999) Systematic effects in the rating of second language speaking ability: Test method and learner discourse. *Language Testing* 16 (1), 82–111.

White, J. (1998) Getting the learners' attention: A typographical input enhancement study. In C. Doughty and J. Williams (eds) *Focus on Form in Classroom Second Language Acquisition* (pp. 85–113). Cambridge: Cambridge University Press.

White, J. and Turner, C.E. (2005) Comparing children's oral ability in two ESL programs. *Canadian Modern Language Review* 61 (4), 491–517.

White, L. (1991) Adverb placement in second language acquisition: Some effects of positive and negative evidence in the classroom. *Second Language Research* 7 (2), 133–161.

White, L., Spada, N., Lightbown, P. and Ranta, L. (1991) Input enhancement and L2 question formation. *Applied Linguistics* 12 (4), 416–423.

6 Time and Amount of L2 Contact Inside and Outside the School – Insights from the European Schools

Alex Housen

Introduction

Most research to date on instructed second language (L2) learning has been carried out within the contexts of (especially college-level) English as a second language (ESL) programs in North America and (Canadian-style) immersion programs. Several authors have pointed out how SLA theory, based on the knowledge generated in such a narrow range of contexts, has limited validity (Nayar, 1997; Siegel, 2003). This situation warrants an examination of the processes and outcomes of L2 learning in other educational contexts. The specific context focused on in this chapter is that of the European School system of multilingual education (Baetens Beardsmore, 1995; Baker, 2006; Housen, 2002). The European Schools (ES) have been in operation for nearly 60 years and have gained a firm reputation as successful institutes of scholastic excellence in general and of language education and learning in particular (Baker, 2006; Wesche, 2002). Recent years have also seen a growing interest in the ES as a model for developing bilingual education and second language education elsewhere (e.g. European Parliament, 2010; Skutnabb-Kangas, 1995). In this light, it is important to draw attention to the available research on the processes and outcomes of language learning in these schools and to the lessons that can be drawn from their experience. To further this end, the next section of this chapter presents the necessary background information on the ES program, with special attention to the role of the L2 and the sequencing of and time devoted to L2 subject teaching and L2 content teaching throughout the ES curriculum. Then previous research on L2 learning in the ES is reviewed, followed by the presentation of two empirical studies that investigate the development of English L2 proficiency in the ES system. The final section discusses the wider implications of this research for L2 learning and teaching.

The European Schools

This section outlines relevant features of the ES program, with particular attention to its language component. More extensive discussions of the ES system can be found in Baetens Beardsmore (1995) and Housen (2002).

Set-up, population and objectives

European Schools are official public institutions controlled by the member states of the European Union (EU). There are currently 15 European Schools located in seven member states of the EU (Belgium, Luxembourg, Germany, UK, Spain, Italy and the Netherlands), all in or near towns with high concentrations of EU officials. European Schools cater primarily for children of EU officials but other children, including host nationals and migrant children, also attend if space is available. Approximately 30,000 children are currently enrolled in the ES system, representing over 70 nationalities and 50 different languages (http://www.eursc.eu/).

Education in the ES spans 14 years and includes kindergarten (ages 4–6), primary school (years 1–5; ages 7–11) and secondary school (years 6–12; ages 12–18). Basic education in the ES is provided in 14 different first language (L1) sections, covering the major national languages of the EU member states. All L1 sections in all ES follow a common curriculum.

ES are distinctly multilingual and multicultural, not only in terms of their pupil population, but also in their organization, ethos and goals. These goals include high levels of functional proficiency and literacy in *at least* two languages. These two languages are the child's L1 (in principle one of the aforementioned 14 languages) plus a second language (L2), a 'foreign language' of wider currency to be chosen from the three 'working languages' of the ES, namely French, English or German. ES pupils must further study a third language (L3) in secondary school, with the option of studying a fourth language (L4).

L2 learning and teaching in the ES

L2 distribution in the ES curriculum

The L2 – either English, French or German – is first taught as a subject for one 30 minute period in years 1 and 2 of primary school and for one 45 minute period a day in years 3–5. The L2 remains compulsory as a subject throughout schooling for at least three periods a week. In addition, in years

3–5, the L2 becomes a medium of general instruction and classroom communication for one to three 45 minute periods a week in physical education and an activities class called 'European Hours'. Up to 30% of the timetable can thus be taken up in the L2 in the last three years of primary school through the combination of L2-subject and L2-content teaching. In secondary school, depending on their individual study program and choice of elective courses, pupils may have up to 60% of their timetable in the L2, with subjects such as history, arts, music, religion, economics and sciences classes taught in the L2.

Classes using an L2 as the medium of instruction are explicitly intended as communal lessons for non-native speaker pupils from different L1 backgrounds, for all of whom the language is a foreign language. ES teachers are native speakers of the languages in which they teach, whether they teach L1, L2, L3 or L4 language-subject or language-content classes. All ES teachers and support staff must furthermore be bilingual and know at least one of the three ES working languages (English, French and German).

The L2 teachers in the ES follow a set of broad didactic guidelines stating the general objectives and principles for L2 teaching at the various stages of education (e.g. European Schools, 1999). These guidelines are grafted onto the communicative and functional-notional principles of foreign language teaching with some features of the direct and audio-lingual method. In the first two years of primary school, focus in the L2-subject classes is mainly on developing listening and comprehension skills while gradually introducing productive oral skills. These skills are further developed in subsequent years, while reading and writing are gradually introduced in year 3. In the two final years of primary school, emphasis is still on oral expression and fluency, with attention to basic grammar and lexis, but at this point a more systematic approach to reading and writing is also undertaken. Formal study of the L2, including its metalinguistic analysis and literature, is deferred until secondary school.

The ultimate objective of the L2 program in the ES is near-native proficiency: by the end of secondary school – but not earlier – pupils are expected to master the four skills and a wide range of registers in their L2 to a degree that approximates that of native speakers, and to demonstrate high levels of fluency and lexical and grammatical precision, complexity, accuracy and appropriacy in their productive use of the language. The minimal pass level of the L2 exam for the European Baccalaureate equates approximately level B2 in the Common European Framework of Reference for Languages, but most pupils are at C1 or C2 level (Department for Children, Schools and Families, 2009: 12–13).

In sum, the ES aim at linguistic enrichment and additive bilingualism through a transition from instruction in the pupil's L1 to instruction in both the L1 *and* the L2. In contrast to other enrichment programs that involve a radical L1–L2 switch (e.g. Canadian-style early total immersion), the transition in the ES is *gradual*. The L2 is first taught as a subject before being used as a medium of general instruction, and also continues to be taught as a subject throughout schooling. Furthermore, the L2 is first used as a medium of instruction in a small number of non-academic subjects only, then gradually increases as the pupils progress through the program. The transition is also *partial*: although the L2 may become the *prime* medium of instruction for certain pupils at the end of secondary schooling, it never becomes the *sole* medium of instruction. Finally, this transition occurs (relatively) *late*. Specifically, use of the L2 as a fully fledged medium of instruction for cognitively demanding and decontextualized subjects is deferred until secondary school when pupils have had time to acquire the prerequisite skills for academic language use (including literacy) in both their L1 and their L2.

Social engineering and extracurricular support for language learning

Crucial additional reinforcement of the formal language learning process is further provided by the multilingual environment of the ES themselves and the process of *social–linguistic engineering* that has been deliberately built into the program (Baetens Beardsmore, 1995). Social–linguistic engineering here refers to the deliberate mixing of pupils from different language backgrounds for as many subjects and activities as possible with the aim of promoting cross-linguistic peer interaction through the medium of a common foreign language both inside the classroom (during communal classes) and outside the classroom. This mixing is started in the first year of primary school in the L2-subject classes and increases as the pupils get older. The aim of socio-linguistic engineering is both to reduce the risk of fragmentation of the school population on nationalistic–linguistic lines and to enhance the foreign language learning process. Cross-linguistic interaction through a common vehicular foreign language not only provides important additional linguistic input and output but also creates a fertile socio-affective climate for language learning: it makes the language learning task more pertinent to the pupils' immediate communicative needs, increasing language learning motivation, and it lowers inhibitions for using a foreign language. In addition, as will demonstrated shortly, in some ES, these elements are given even further force through the wider out-of-school environment, which may provide further foreign language exposure (e.g. French as L2/L3 in the ESs in Brussels and Luxembourg).

Previous Research on Language Learning in the European Schools

Research on the ES is slight compared with that on some other models of bilingual education. As a result, knowledge of its outcomes is neither as detailed nor as comprehensive as in the case of, for instance, immersion programs. Particularly insightful for the purposes of this chapter are a series of studies conducted in the 1980s by Baetens Beardsmore and collaborators that compared global levels of L2 and L3 achievement in the ES of Brussels and Mol (in Belgium) and Luxembourg with the linguistic outcomes obtained in other multilingual education programs. Using standardized proficiency tests developed in Canada, Baetens Beardsmore and Swain (1985) and Lebrun and Baetens Beardsmore (1995) found that levels of L2 French proficiency of 13-year-old pupils in the ES in Brussels and Luxembourg were comparable and probably even superior to those obtained by 13-year-olds in early total French immersion in Canada and in the system of trilingual education in the Grand Duchy of Luxembourg, in spite of less classroom contact with the target language.

The researchers explained these results by the self-initiated use of French by the ES pupils inside and outside of the classroom and the presence of the language in the wider environment (Housen & Baetens Beardsmore, 1989). These two factors are lacking in many immersion education contexts. Extrapolating from these empirical findings and from ES pupils' performance on final examinations in the L2, Baetens Beardsmore and collaborators further predicted that levels of L2 proficiency in the ES approximate native-like norms by the end of secondary schooling *if* the L2 is also available in the wider environment (e.g. French-L2 in the ES in Brussels). When this is not the case, slightly lower levels of L2 proficiency should be expected (e.g. L2 German in the ES in Brussels).

These previous studies on foreign language learning in the ES leave unanswered a number of important questions. They provide information on levels of L2 proficiency at the middle stages of education (ages 13 and 14) but not on the early and final stages, nor on the development of L2 proficiency over time. They also provide no information on patterns of variation between groups of pupils, or between the different ES. We may expect the range of variation in L2 achievement in the ES to be wider than in the average immersion context because the ES cater for a more heterogeneous pupil population, both in terms of L1 backgrounds and in terms of L2 proficiency (which may range from the absolute beginner to the near-native speaker). Also, the socio-linguistic status of the target languages and the extracurricular input and output conditions vary considerably from school to school. Although previous studies have suggested that these factors have an impact on L2 development and linguistic outcomes, the extent of this impact is still unknown.

Furthermore, these earlier studies do not provide direct evidence about ES pupils' ability to perform in their target language in a communicative setting, particularly about their ability to produce grammatically and lexically precise self-sustained discourse – an ability that many immersion pupils have been shown to lack (Baker, 2006; Hammerly, 1991; Johnson & Swain, 1997; Swain, 1985).

It was in order to obtain information of this kind that a new series of studies was initiated at the Vrije Universiteit Brussels (e.g. Housen, 2002, 2003; Housen et al., 2011). Two of these studies will be reported here. Both studies, referred to here as Study A and Study B, investigate the development of linguistic proficiency by ES pupils learning English as their L2.

L2 English Development in the European Schools

Rationale

Studies A and B are part of a larger research program that aims to investigate how extracurricular factors interact with curricular factors in determining processes and outcomes in instructed SLA. Curricular factors here refer to the type(s) and amount of L2 instruction and classroom contact. The extracurricular factors under investigation include the L1 background of the learners and the status and prominence of their L2 vis-à-vis their L1. The interplay between these curricular and extracurricular factors ultimately has implications for the input and output opportunities created for L2 learning and for L2 learning mechanisms such as learners' focus of attention (cf. Housen et al., 2011).

Methodological procedures

A total of 177 L2 learners of English from the European Schools participated in the two studies, involving four different L1 backgrounds (Dutch, French, Greek and Italian), five year levels and three different European Schools (Brussels, Varese and Culham). In addition, 30 age-matched native speaker children of English (from the English L1 section in the European Schools) and 24 Italian children learning English in regular English as a foreign language (EFL) classes in Italy were included to serve as benchmarks against which the L2 outcomes of the ES pupils could be compared.[1]

In both studies English speech data were collected in two standardized oral interviews, held at one to five day intervals. Each interview lasted for about 20–50 minutes (depending on the pupil) and consisted of both informal free conversation and more guided speech tasks designed to elicit a wide variety of grammatical and lexical forms. Pupils were asked to talk about past experiences and future plans, to describe pictures, retell films and books they had seen or read, and retell three picture stories involving a variety of characters and actions. The interviews were audio-taped, transcribed, segmented into clausal units and annotated in CHAT format (MacWhinney, 2000). The data were then analyzed, including in terms of basic dimensions of L2 performance and proficiency, complexity, accuracy and fluency (CAF for short), to assess the pupils' control of linguistic features of English and to determine similarities and differences in the rate of development and level of attainment between the various groups of pupils compared (see below). The CAF analyses will be reported on in this chapter.

Briefly, *complexity* refers to the ability to use a wide and varied range of structures and vocabulary in the L2 (including cognitively complex and linguistically sophisticated structures and lexis), *accuracy* to the ability to produce target-like and error-free language, and *fluency* to the ability to produce the L2 with native-like rapidity, and without undue pausing, hesitation and reformulation (cf. Ellis, 2008; Ellis & Barkhuizen, 2005; Housen & Kuiken, 2009; Wolfe-Quintero et al., 1998).

The CAF analyses were performed on speech excerpts of 400 word tokens for each pupil (excluding filled pauses but including interjections, false starts, retracings and repetitions), made up of four smaller 100-word excerpts selected from the following types of speech tasks in each transcript: picture description, a picture-story retelling, personal narration and general conversation. The excerpts from each subject were then analyzed to produce a measure for each of the following features in the sample, which previous research had suggested might prove fruitful indices of complexity, accuracy and fluency (e.g. Ellis & Barkhuizen, 2005; Iwashita et al., 2008; Ortega, 2003; Wolfe-Quintero et al., 1998)[2]:

Complexity

The measures of complexity are (a) D, (b) λ, (c) mean length (in words) of T-unit (MLU), (d) ratio of subclauses used (SCR), (e) mean length (in words) of clause (MLC) and (f) mean length (in words) of noun phrase (MLNP). Measure (a), D, measures lexical diversity (Malvern et al., 2004) in terms of the different types of words that the learners use. D was calculated on lemmatized versions of the excerpts using the *Mor* and *VocD* programs in CLAN (MacWhinney, 2000). Measure (b) was computed with the P_Lex program (Meara & Bell, 2001), which generates a value, λ, which reflects the extent of lexical sophistication (i.e. the use of less frequent words) that the excerpt exhibits.

Measures (c)–(f) gauge syntactic complexity and elaboration, at the global level (measure *c*) and the sentence level (measure *d*) as well as at the clausal level (*e*) and phrasal level (*f*). These measures were computed with the aid of MS Excel.

Accuracy

The measures of accuracy are (g) number of lexical errors (LexErr), (h) number of grammatical (morphological, syntactic) errors (GramErr) and (i) total number of errors (TotErr).[3]

Non-self-corrected lexical errors (wrong or non-idiomatic use of content words, including prepositions), morphological errors (omissions and overextensions of inflections and grammatical function words; omissions of syntactic arguments or wrong word order patterns) were coded manually and computed with the aid of the Freq program in CLAN.

Fluency

The measures of fluency are (j) mean length of run (MLR), (k) number of dysfluent pauses (DysP) and (l) number of hesitations (Hes).

Measures (j)–(k) each assess one of the three main sub-dimensions of L2 fluency proposed by Skehan (2003), respectively *speed* fluency, *pause* (or breakdown) fluency and *repair* fluency. Mean length of run is operationalized as the mean number of word tokens (excluding filled pauses, repeated and rephrased language) between dysfluent pauses, that is, the sum of all medium length pauses (between 1 and 2 seconds) occurring outside clause boundaries and all long pauses (longer than 2 seconds) in any position. Number of dysfluent pauses (DysP) includes medium pauses occurring in positions other than clause boundaries and all long pauses. Repair fluency is measured by the number of hesitation phenomena: false starts, repetitions, reformulations and replacements.

Simple ANOVA or, in the case of non-normality of the data, the Kruskall–Wallis rank sum test, was used to assess the effect of the main factors ('context' in Study A; 'year level' and 'L1' in Study B). Scheffé tests were applied for ANOVA *post hoc* comparisons. All α levels were set at 0.05. Where non-parametric testing was required, Mann–Whitney rank sum tests were used for *post hoc* testing. Here, α levels were corrected for multiple paired testing by applying the Bonferroni correction.

A detailed presentation and discussion of the results of these two studies is beyond the scope and space limitations of this chapter (yet see Housen, 2002, 2003, 2008). For the purposes of this chapter, which is to illustrate patterns of variation in instructed L2 learning in spite of identical types and amounts of classroom exposure to the L2, overall complexity, accuracy and fluency scores were calculated by standardizing and averaging over the scores of the various measures. The mean scores of the native speakers are taken as a benchmark (representing 100%) and the mean scores of the L2 learners are expressed as a percentage score relative to the native speaker benchmark scores (Sirkin, 1995). Finally, to further facilitate comparison and interpretation, composite L2 proficiency scores were obtained by averaging the global complexity, accuracy and fluency scores. This procedure allowed us to condense a multitude of detailed results in an interpretable format. This was particularly necessary for the results of Study B which, with 12 dependent variables and two independent variables, would have required the presentation and discussion of minimally 12 tables. Although some information is probably obscured by the procedure of standardizing and averaging over the original individual scores, we feel that the trends that emerge do not substantially detract from the integrity of the original individual scores and results. All the results are presented below by means of graphs to visualize the relevant trends. The corresponding tables can be found in the Appendix. In order to give the reader some indication of the outcomes of the statistical analyses of the original scores on the CAF measures, the results of Study A are reported with the necessary statistics in Tables 6.3–6.5 in the Appendix.

The following sections present the specific objectives, research questions and designs of each of Studies A and B separately, as well as the findings that emerged from them, focusing on both general trends and patterns of variation in the domains of lexical and grammatical complexity, accuracy and fluency development.

Study A – Extracurricular L2 Exposure in Instructed L2 Learning

Objectives, design and methodology

Study A cross-sectionally examined levels of English-L2 proficiency among 72 Italian-L1 pupils in years 3 and 4 of the primary cycle of three ES: Varese (Italy, Context 2), Brussels (Belgium, Context 3) and Culham (UK, Context 4). For purposes of comparison, similar data were obtained from Italian pupils in traditional EFL classes in two regular Italian schools near Bologna (Context 1) and from native English pupils from the English L1 section in the ES in Brussels (see Table 6.1).

The principal aim of Study A was to identify similarities and differences in instructed L2 learning as a function of varying extracurricular exposure to the L2. To this end the L1 and L2 of the pupils were held constant, as were curricular variables such as type, amount and intensity of formal classroom contact with the L2. All the L2 learners in the study exclusively or predominantly used their L1 Italian at home and had had similar amounts (approximately 250–270 hours) of formal classroom contact with their L2 English at the time of data collection.[4] The main differences between the learning contexts in the three ES and the EFL classes in the Italian schools lie in the prominence, role and status of the L2 and the L1 outside the classroom, with implications for the amount and types of extracurricular input and output offered for L2 learning in each context as well as for pupils' motivations for using and learning the L2 (see Housen, 2002 and Housen *et al.*, 2011 for a fuller discussion of these issues). The four learning contexts may thus be

Table 6.1 Sample of Study A (L1 Italian, L2 English)

	Year			
Context	3	4	5	Total
Context 1 (ES Bologna, Italy)			24	24
Context 2 (ES Varese, Italy)	20	4		24
Context 3 (ES Brussels, Belgium)	20	4		24
Context 4 (Culham, UK)	20	4		24
Benchmark (native speakers, Brussels, Belgium)	10	5		15

conceived as representing four discrete points on the foreign–second language learning context continuum (Gajo & Mondada, 2000): Context 1 (C1) approximates most closely the prototypical *foreign* language (FL) context and Context 4 (C4) the *second* language (SL) context. Contexts 2 and 3 represent two different midway positions between these two extremes. The Italian pupils in the ES in Varese (C2) receive English instruction very much like in regular Italian schools (C1), the differences being that the English teachers in the ES in Varese are native speakers and the pupils hear English being used by their English-speaking peers and teachers from the English-L1 section on the playground or when attending other classes. In addition, in the ES of Varese, English is used from year 3 onwards as a medium of instruction for up to 2 hours per week during Physical Education and the 'European Hours', albeit not consistently (Italian also often used in these lessons). The Varese pupils further know that English will be increasingly used as a medium of instruction in general content classes as they progress through the curriculum. This awareness could render the learning of English more pertinent for them than for their peers in mainstream Italian schools. For the rest, the presence of Italian is strongly felt in the ES in Varese. It very much functions as a *lingua franca* among pupils and staff members from different language backgrounds.

The main difference between the European Schools in Varese (C2) and Brussels (C3) is that the Italian pupils in Brussels cannot normally use their L1 for communication in the out-of-school context, or in interactions in the school with peers from other L1 backgrounds, as French is the principal *lingua franca* in the ES in Brussels, although English is sometimes also used as a vehicular language, providing the Brussels pupils with some additional opportunities for L2 exposure.

Finally, in the context of the ES in Culham (C4), Italian plays no significant role outside the lessons in the Italian-L1 section itself, English being the dominant language inside and outside the school.

Thus, the central research question investigated in Study A was whether the differences in the role and functions of the L2 and L1 in these different contexts were reflected in the rate and outcome of L2 learning. We hypothesized that the more closely a learning context approximates the prototypical SL context, the more favorable the L2 learning conditions in terms of input, output and interaction opportunities will be and, hence, the higher the levels of L2 proficiency that will be attained. Concretely, the highest L2 proficiency levels were predicted for the learners in Context 4, followed by those in Contexts 3, 2 and 1, in that order. Specific hypotheses for the three different dimensions of L2 proficiency (CAF) are less straightforward. There is some evidence to suggest that SL contexts would be more likely to enhance the development of oral fluency and lexical complexity, whereas FL contexts would lead to higher levels of grammatical accuracy and complexity (see Collentine & Freed, 2004; Ellis, 2008; Housen *et al.*, 2011). However, at the current exploratory stage of research we refrain from formulating detailed or explicit directional hypotheses. Instead we predict similar trends for the development of complexity, accuracy and fluency, with the highest levels for Context 4, followed by Contexts 3, 2 and 1, again in that order.

Results

Tables 6.3–5 in the Appendix show the mean percentage scores for the complexity, accuracy and fluency measures for contexts 1–4 in Study A (relative to the scores of the native speaker benchmark, BM, group), with the F-values for the main effect of *context*, their corresponding significance levels (p) and *post hoc* significant contrasts ($\alpha = 0.05$) between the contexts under investigation (C1, C2, C3, C4 and the BM group). The scores are percentages, with higher scores reflecting higher (closer to native norms) levels of L2 complexity, accuracy and fluency. Statistical analysis revealed that the native speaker BM group significantly outperformed the L2 learners in all four learning contexts on all 12 linguistic proficiency measures computed. Therefore, in what follows, the discussion will focus on the differences or similarities between the learners in the four L2 learning contexts. For the sake of survey, the relevant trends are presented by means of graphs (Figures 6.1–6.3).

Complexity

Table 6.3 and Figure 6.1 show that the highest L2 complexity scores were obtained by the English learners in C4 (ES Culham), C3 (ES Brussels), C2 (ES Varese) and, finally, C1 (regular EFL in Bologna). This general trend corresponds to the predicted trend. However, statistical analyses revealed that not all differences on all measures were significant.

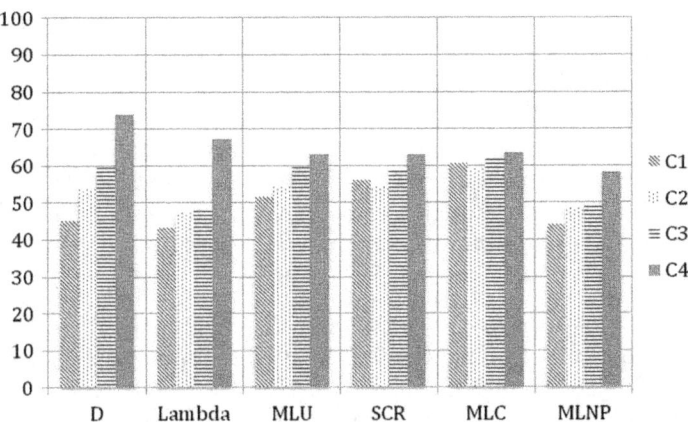

Figure 6.1 Complexity scores of Italian pupils in three ES and a regular EFL program (in percentages relative to native speaker benchmark scores of 100%)

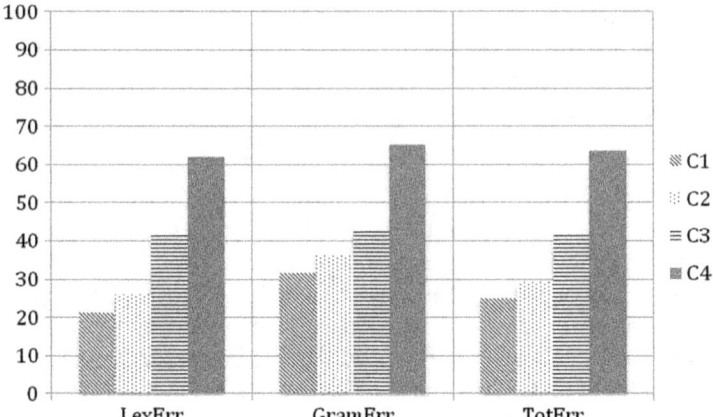

Figure 6.2 Accuracy scores of Italian pupils in three European Schools and a regular EFL program (in percentages relative to native speaker benchmark scores of 100%)

The learners in Culham and Brussels produced significantly longer T-units than the learners in Varese and Bologna, pointing to higher overall syntactic complexity. No significant contrasts between the four L2 learning contexts were found for the measures of clausal and sentential syntactic complexity (MLC, SCR). The largest, and the most significant, contrasts were found for the measure of phrasal syntactic complexity (mean length of NP) and, particularly, the measures of lexical complexity (D, λ), where the Culham learners significantly outperformed the learners in the other contexts. Furthermore, all the ES learners (C2, C3, C4) significantly outperformed the Bologna EFL learners in (C1) on these three complexity measures.

Accuracy

A consistent pattern emerges from the scores on the three accuracy measures shown in Table 6.4 in the Appendix and in Figure 6.2. Again, the native speaker benchmarks significantly outperformed the L2 learners in all contexts. The highest L2 accuracy scores were obtained by the English learners in C4 (ES Culham), who in turn were significantly more accurate than the learners in C3 (ES Brussels), who in their turn outperformed the learners in contexts C2 (ES Varese) and C1 (EFL Bologna). Finally, the pupils in C2 made fewer lexical and grammatical errors than their peers in the EFL context, but here the differences were not significant.

Fluency

The same general pattern familiar from linguistic complexity and accuracy analyses also emerges from the scores on the fluency measures shown in Table 6.5 (Appendix) and Figure 6.3. The native BM group produced significantly longer runs, significantly fewer dysfluent pauses and significantly fewer hesitation phenomena than the L2 learner groups. The highest L2

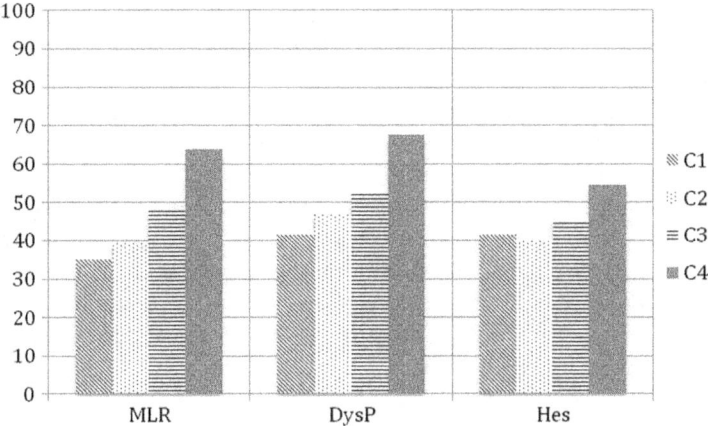

Figure 6.3 Fluency scores of Italian pupils in three European Schools and a regular EFL program (in percentages relative to native speaker benchmark scores of 100%)

fluency scores were obtained by the English learners in C4, C3, C2 and, finally, C1, in that order. The only exception to the general and predicted trend was for the number of hesitations, where the C1 learners outperformed the C2 learners in producing fewer hesitations, although the difference was slight and not statistically significant. Nor were the differences between the C1 and C2 groups on the two other fluency measures (MLR, DysP). In fact, none of the four L2 learning contexts differed significantly in terms of number of hesitation phenomena produced. The differences in speech rate (MLR) between the learners in the ESs of Culham and Brussels were not significant either, but the difference in terms of pause fluency (DysP) was.

Summary and discussion

The results of the CAF analyses presented here reflect the similarity between the traditional EFL context in Bologna and the ES context in Varese in terms of rate and outcome of L2 learning. Whatever advantages the European School pupils in Varese may have in terms of curricular or extra-curricular input and output opportunities for learning English, they do not appear to lead to faster grammatical growth or fluency development during the first three years of primary school. Only in terms of lexical development does the ES context in Varese appear to yield advantages. However, differences in the socio-linguistic status of the L1 between the Varese context and the Brussels context do affect English-L2 development in the first three years of primary school, particularly in terms of fluency and lexical development. However, differences in the prominence of the L2 are the ones most clearly felt: the Italian pupils in Context 4 have clearly developed a more fluent, a more elaborate and, particularly, a more accurate vocabulary and grammar than the learners in the other L2 learning contexts. This finding echoes those of Baetens Beardsmore and Swain (1985) on the learning of French-L2 in the ES in Brussels as well as the findings of Housen *et al.* (2011) on the learning of L2 English by German-speaking students in the ES system. The role of English as a *lingua franca* inside and outside the ES in Culham provides the English-L2 pupils in this context with additional input and output opportunities and also creates a more fertile climate for language learning. What is striking is the magnitude of these effects; after only three years of primary schooling and approximately 250 hours of classroom contact, the Culham pupils outperformed the pupils in the other learning contexts with some 16% points in fluency, nearly 13% points in the grammatical domain, and nearly 25% points in the lexical domain.

Study B – L1 Background in Instructed L2 Learning

Using the same type of data and measures as Study A, Study B cross-sectionally compared patterns of English-L2 development by 105 Dutch, French and Greek-speaking pupils across five different year levels spanning primary and secondary school (years 3, 5, 7, 9 and 11, roughly corresponding to the ages of 9, 11, 13, 15 and 17, respectively) in the ES of Brussels. Native English-speaking pupils again served as comparisons. Table 6.2 shows the distribution of the learners in this study, together with an estimation of the accumulated amount of classroom contact with English at the end of each of the five year levels involved.

The objective of Study B was to explore the limitations of the impact of curricular factors in instructed SLA, such as amount and type of L2 classroom exposure, by identifying similarities and differences in the route, rate and outcome of L2 of learners from different L1 backgrounds in the same educational context. The Dutch, French and Greek-speaking children in

Table 6.2 Sample of Study B (L1 Dutch, L1 French, L1 Greek; L2 English)

	Year level					
	3	5	7	9	11	Total
	L2 classroom contact*					
	250	370	1045	2095	2670	
L1-Dutch	7	7	7	7	7	35
L1-French	7	7	7	7	7	35
L1-Greek	7	7	7	7	7	35
L1-English		5	5	5		15

* Approximate accumulated hours of classroom contact with L2 English

Study B all learn English under the same curricular conditions. They sit together in the same English-L2 classrooms and attend the same English-L2 medium classes. They receive the same amount and kind of classroom input and the expectations about their linguistic progress are also the same. However, the three L1 groups differ in terms of the extracurricular conditions of their language-learning experience. French being the *lingua franca* in the ESs of Brussels and in the wider, out-of-school context, it was hypothesized that the French-speaking pupils perceive the learning of English as less pertinent to their communicative needs and seek out fewer opportunities to hear and use English than the Greek and Dutch pupils (Housen & Baetens Beardsmore, 1989). The Dutch pupils in turn were predicted to perceive the learning of English as slightly less pertinent than the Greek pupils because Dutch, unlike Greek, is one of the official languages in the bilingual city of Brussels, although its presence in daily life inside and outside the ESs is not strongly felt (Housen, 2002). In addition, the three L1 groups also differ in the degree of typological proximity between their respective L1 and the target language, with Dutch being the closest to English, followed by French and then Greek. Previous research suggests that this factor, too, can have a considerable impact on levels of L2 achievement in education contexts via lexical and morphological cognates, syntactic resemblances and prosodic similarities (Odlin, 2003; Swan, 1997).

Thus Study B aimed to investigate the variable effect of these two factors, 'immediate pertinence/opportunity for extracurricular L2 exposure' and 'typological proximity', on the route, rate and outcome of the L2 learning process. 'Immediate pertinence/extracurricular exposure' predicts that the Greek pupils will learn more and faster than the Dutch pupils, who in turn will outperform the French pupils; 'Typological proximity' predicts a learning advantage for the Dutch learners, followed by the French pupils and then the Greek pupils.

Results

For reasons outlined above, a detailed presentation of the analysis of the 12 CAF measures for the four groups of pupils over the five year levels is not possible here. Instead, for the sake of presentation, the general trends are illustrated by means of graphs based on the overall percentage scores (relative to native speaker benchmark scores of 100%) for the following linguistic subdomains: lexical complexity (average of the scores on the measures D and λ), grammatical complexity (average of the scores on the measures MLU, SCR, MLC and MLNP), lexical accuracy (number of lexical errors; LexErr), grammatical accuracy (number of morphological and syntactic errors; GramErr) and fluency (average of the scores on the MLR, DysP and Hes measures). A more detailed presentation of the results can be found in Housen (2003).

All three groups make at least some progress in absolute terms in all the linguistic subdomains investigated, but the gains are not always significant. The French and the Greek pupils make minimal progress in the course of primary schooling (years 3–5), in contrast to the Dutch pupils, who progress significantly during these early years, except for the measures of lexical accuracy and fluency (see Figures 6.6 and 6.8). A developmental 'spurt' can be observed for all three L1 groups after year 5, particularly in the lexical domain (see Figures 6.4 and 6.6) and for fluency (Figure 6.8). This spurt is more pronounced for the French and the Greek learners than for the Dutch learners, whose developmental pattern demonstrates a more gradual and steady climb. The grammatical development of the Dutch pupils (especially their syntactic complexity and morphological accuracy development) trails off after year 7 when they reach the 80–90% criterion level (see Figures 6.5 and 6.7).

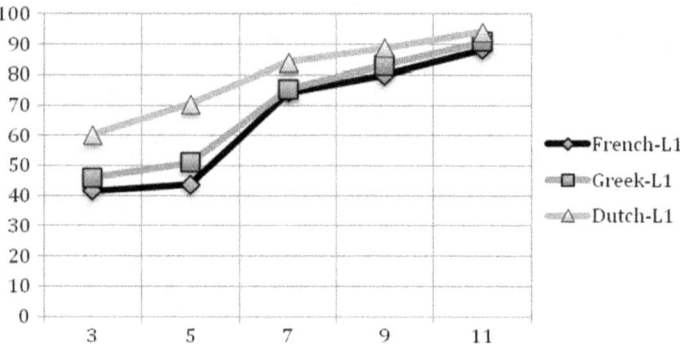

Figure 6.4 Lexical complexity development of Dutch, French and Greek learners of L2 English in the ES of Brussels (in percentages)

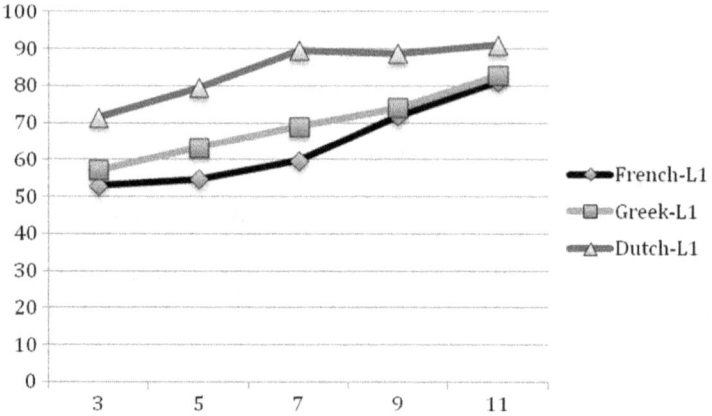

Figure 6.5 Grammatical complexity development of Dutch, French and Greek learners of L2 English in the ES of Brussels (in percentages)

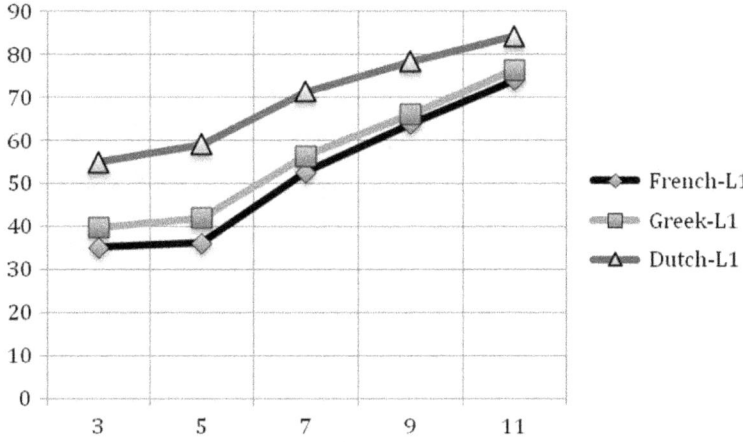

Figure 6.6 Lexical accuracy development of Dutch, French and Greek learners of L2 English in the ES of Brussels (in percentages)

The Dutch learners furthermore consistently obtain the highest scores, followed by the Greek and then the French learners. Thus, the Dutch pupils, from the start of observation, have a considerably (and significantly) more complex and more accurate vocabulary and grammar and higher fluency in English than the Greek and especially the French pupils. The scores of the Greek and the French learners are nearly always statistically comparable (except for the scores on the grammatical complexity measures MLU and MLNP in year 7 and the speech rate measure MLR in year 3, where the Greek pupils statistically outperform the French pupils at $p \leq 0.01$). With time,

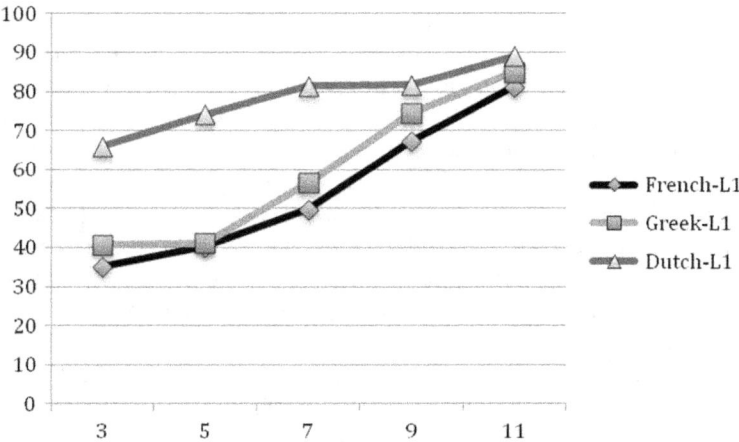

Figure 6.7 Grammatical accuracy development of Dutch, French and Greek learners of L2 English in the ES of Brussels (in percentages)

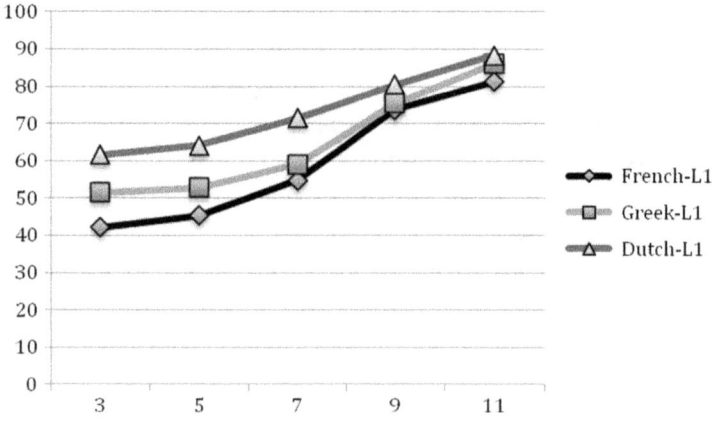

Figure 6.8 Fluency development of Dutch, French and Greek learners of L2 English in the ES of Brussels (in percentages)

however, the initial gap between the Dutch pupils and the French and Greek pupils gradually narrows. Although the Dutch pupils continue to outperform their peers on all 12 CAF measures, the differences between the three groups are no longer significant for most measures by year 9 (for lexical complexity and fluency) or by year 11 (for grammatical complexity and lexical and grammatical accuracy; at year 11 differences between the French and the Dutch pupils for the grammatical complexity measures MLU and MLNP and the lexical accuracy measure are still significant at $p \leq 0.05$).

Summary and discussion

The trends outlined above indicate the considerable range of variation in the rate and level of L2 CAF development that exists among pupils in the same L2 classroom in the European Schools, particularly in the early stages of instructed L2 learning in the ES system. The Dutch pupils have at their disposal a richer and more native-like L2 system and demonstrate greater control over their system (as reflected in their greater fluency) than the French and Greek pupils. In the course of secondary schooling these differences are leveled out to a considerable extent so that, by the end of secondary education, all ES pupils attain comparable levels of lexical proficiency which, moreover, approximate (but do not equal) those of the native speaker benchmark pupils.

Typological proximity between the L1 and the L2 emerges as the most likely factor to account for the observed differences between the Dutch vs the French and Greek pupils in the ES of Brussels. The existence of many cognate and near-cognate forms in English and Dutch probably gave the Dutch learners a considerable headstart. Although the Greek pupils in the ES in Brussels were predicted to perceive the learning of English as the most pertinent to their immediate communicative needs, this apparently did not lead to significantly faster or more extensive learning of English than the French pupils, who were predicted to perceive the learning of English as the least pertinent to their needs.

The results from Study B further suggest that, although L2 development in the ES system is on the whole a gradual and incremental process, there are periods of more extensive change. A developmental 'spurt' can be observed between year 5 and year 7. This coincides with two important developments in the L2 curriculum. The first development is the increase from year 6 onward in the use of the L2 as a medium of instruction in content lessons such as arts, music, history, geography, economy and social studies. This increases not only the amount of input available for L2 learning, but also the opportunities for pupils to produce the kind of comprehensible output that Swain (1985) and others have proposed as necessary for grammatical and lexical growth and precision in an L2. Classroom observations in the ES have revealed that there is little opportunity for pupils to produce such comprehensible output in the lessons at primary school, given the early emphasis on the development of receptive skills in the L2. This is in contrast to the L2-subject and L2-content classes in secondary school, where pupils must regularly produce self-sustained oral and written discourse in their L2, thus promoting lexical and particularly grammatical processing of the language.

The second development that may explain the developmental spurt observed in Study B is the increase in analytic, form-focused instruction in the English L2-subject lessons in secondary school in the ESs. This type of instruction is rare or absent in L2-subject lessons in primary school, where the focus is on the L2 as a means for language play and for exchanging meaning and content. Previous research has identified this type of form-focused instruction as necessary for the acquisition of lexical precision and grammatical accuracy in an L2 (Hammerly, 1991; Spada, 1997; Williams, 2005).

Implications

Although there remains much to be learned about processes and outcomes of L2 learning in the ES program, the combined information from internal assessments (e.g. exam results) and from external research such as that reviewed and presented in this chapter warrants a positive evaluation of the L2 component of the ES. The studies presented here suggest that global levels of L2 proficiency in the ESs are *at least* comparable to those attained in other tried models of bilingual education and probably close to native speaker norms by the end of secondary schooling (with some variation depending on the availability of the language in the wider context). These levels of proficiency include the ability to produce not only fluent but also grammatically and lexically accurate and precise discourse in an L2, even in contexts where additional, out-of-school support for L2 learning is sparce. This is an ability that many immersion pupils have been shown to lack (e.g. Baker, 2006). According to Johnstone (2002), ideal conditions for developing functional proficiency in a a foreign language in an instructed environment include starting at an early age (preferably between the ages of 6 and 9), minimally 45 minutes a day for 5 days a week and classes of a maximum of 15 pupils. The ES approximate these ideal conditions, which may help to account for the high ultimate levels of proficiency.

Yet the available research also demonstrates the often extensive range of variation in the rate and outcomes of foreign language learning in the ESs, particularly in early and intermediate stages of schooling. It further shows the limitations of what can be achieved in terms of L2 learning by means of curricular L2 exposure and instruction alone, no matter how 'ideal' these may be. Depending on factors such as L1 background and the status and availability of the target language both within the schools and in their wider context, different pupils experience the learning of a foreign language in quite different ways.

More generally, the findings presented here show that learning a foreign language is not always a given, not even in contexts conducive to language learning, such as the ESs, and not even for a language such as English. The high levels of L2 achievement reported in this chapter are attained only at the *end* of secondary schooling. They are the outcome of a gradual and long-term process that spans the entire curriculum and only really takes off in secondary school, after a somewhat less spectacular but probably necessary formative start in primary school.

From the insights gained so far, supported by insights from L2 development in other bilingual and L2 programs (e.g. Baker, 2006; Cenoz & Genesee, 1998; Dixon *et al.*, 2012; White & Turner, 2005), several general observations can be made about factors contributing to successful L2 learning in bi-/multilingual education and second language education in general, where successful L2 learning is defined as the ultimate attainment of high, close to native-like levels of functional proficiency in the L2.

Amount and time of L2 education

Amount of L2 education

Given that language development is primarily driven by the amount of exposure to a language (e.g Muñoz, 2011), the issue of the amount of L2 education is a matter of primary concern. In educational contexts, the time devoted to the L1, L2 and any further languages in the curriculum will depend on a variety of considerations. These include the socio-linguistic status and role of the languages involved, the availability of extracurricular input and output opportunities inside and/or outside the school, and the ultimate goals of the program (i.e. whether to develop high levels of bi- or multilingualism and biliteracy or rather more limited or partial bilingualism/biliteracy). As a general principle, there should be as much curricular support for the L1 as is necessary to avoid L1 impairment, and as much support for the L2 as possible (Skutnabb-Kangas, 1995). Concretely, this means that, unless the L1 is dominant in the wider environment of the school, it is probably advisable to devote no more than 50% of the timetable to the L2 in the first five to eight years of schooling. If the L1 is dominant both inside and outside the school (as in the case of Italian in the ES of Varese in Study A), a higher proportion of L2 teaching and teaching through the L2 could be envisaged to allow for the development of high levels of L2 proficiency (on the provision that the L1 is indeed the L1 of all or most of the pupils, which is not the case in the linguistically diverse L2 classes in the ES of Varese).

Length of L2 education and L2 contact duration

It makes sense to assume that the more and the longer the contact with the L2, the more L2 learning will be fostered and the higher the levels of L2 proficiency that will be attained. This has been shown in Study B for the ES program, but it has also been shown for many other L2 education contexts and for a wide range of aspects of language, including L2 pronunciation, vocabulary and grammar. At the same time, however, many studies on immersion education have also suggested that L2 proficiency does not necessarily increase *ad infinitum* with longer classroom contact with the L2. In fact, several aspects of L2 proficiency develop asymptotically, with development gradually trailing off as it approaches a plateau or ceiling level, in spite of continued contact with the L2. In particular grammatical abilities have been shown to prematurely 'fossilize' in immersion contexts at a below-native speaker level (Hammerly, 1991; Johnson & Swain, 1997; Johnstone, 2002; Swain, 1985). There are also more practical reasons to investigate if and how much L2 proficiency develops with increased L2 contact duration in the bilingual schools. As mentioned earlier, L2 learning is typically a gradual, lengthy and relatively slow process but parents, policy-makers and teachers sometimes have unrealistic expectations as to the amount of L2 progress that pupils can make in the course of a school year.

However, there is still a dearth of empirical information as to exactly how much progress is made within a given time period and what level of linguistic abilities may be expected at certain points in time in the course of L2 education. Until such information becomes available, it seems wise to recommend that L2 education be allowed to span both primary and secondary schooling (and preferably beyond). This has the additional advantage of providing an important element of continuity in the curriculum.

Intensity of L2 education

The level and rate of L2 development depends not only on the amount and duration of L2 contact (i.e. in number of school years, months or weeks), but also on the intensity of L2 input, that is, how the total amount of L2 input and contact is distributed over the course of the L2 program or curriculum. Most studies to date have reported L2 learning benefits for more intense or compactly distributed forms of L2 teaching in EFL and ESL programs (Collins *et al.*, 1999; Serrano, 2011; Serrano & Muñoz, 2007). For example, Curtain (2000) examined three elementary school foreign language programs in the USA that differed with respect to time overall within the program, the intensity (i.e. the number of classes per week, with 5 hour and 3 hour classes being compared) and the time actually used in teaching and learning in class. For the factor 'intensity', Curtain found that students in more intense programs fared better than students in less intense programs. Likewise, from her overview on early immersion models in Canada, Wesche (2002) concluded that an intensive dose of 'immersion' in a language is generally more effective for learning it than the same dose spread over a longer time. Compared with some other bilingual and second language programs, the ES program can be characterized as moderately intensive program, where the intensity of curricular contact with the L2 increases as the pupils progress through the curriculum. Also the intensity of *extracurricular* contact with the L2 gradually increases: whereas most primary ES pupils still select friends from their own L1 section, the majority of social relationships in the ES become distinctly cross-linguistic in the course of secondary education and are maintained via the common L2 (Housen, 2002; Housen & Baetens Beardsmore, 1989).

As mentioned above, 'intensity' is usually indexed as the number of L2 lessons or hours per week, month or year (e.g. Curtain, 2000; Wesche, 2002). However, in bilingual school contexts, other variables may also need to be taken into consideration because the curricular and extracurricular conditions generally differ from program to program and from school to school. For instance, the number and type (e.g. whether native or non-native) of L2 teachers or of other L2 input models present in a classroom, school or wider context may also have an effect on learners' L2 development (Steinle *et al.*, 2010). For instance, Wippermann *et al.* (2010) showed that the pupils in an early English immersion school where there was one L2 teacher for 60 pupils developed more slowly than those in a similar school where there were three L2 teachers for 55 children in one class. In the ES, the teacher:pupil ratio in L2 classes is fairly favorable as it ranges from 1:10 to 1:25, depending on the year and whether the L2 is taught as a subject or used as a medium of instruction in general content classes. Thus, the number of L2 teachers, and the pupil:teacher ratio, as well as the range and amount of extracurricular contacts through the L2 may also affect the overall intensity of the L2 input available for L2 learning and the intensity of specific types of L2 input in particular (e.g. pupil-directed vs classroom-directed input), as well as the diversity of the input (e.g. as a result of inter-teacher variability in terms of intonation and speech rate, pronunciation, vocabulary use and grammatical structures).

Integrating language and content in L2 education

The European School experience also underscores the importance of using the L2 as a medium for teaching general content matter. Also experiments with immersion education have shown that L2 or L3 learning is more effective when it is integrated with meaningful and significant content (Baker, 2006). In school, this means integrating language instruction with academic instruction so that students are taught academic subjects through the medium of the target language, taking into account their language needs. This provides essential input and output reinforcement for the L2 learning process and also generates the pertinence and motivation that Baetens Beardsmore and Kohls (1988) and others identified as an important factor in the success of L2 programs. In addition, content-based use of the L2 is also different from its subject-based use, extending the range of input types to which pupils are exposed. For these reasons, it is recommended that at least one general subject be taught through the medium of the L2. Activity-based lessons, like physical education, music, arts and even basic science subjects create opportunities for contextualized and cognitively undemanding input and output. They provide opportunities for introducing basic vocabulary (e.g. for elementary concepts like shape, size, color) and basic speech acts (e.g. requests for information and materials, giving instructions). At later stages teaching subjects like human sciences and social studies in the L2 provides a suitable context for introducing pupils to increasingly more decontextualized and cognitively demanding L2 (Cummins, 1991).

The need for (formal) L2-subject teaching

Research on second language acquisition suggests that the comprehensible input and output provided by content-based L2 instruction, or by informal interaction in the L2, may still not be sufficient to provide high proficiency in the L2 (e.g. Dixon *et al.*, 2012; Hammerly, 1991). The ES experience in L2 teaching provides evidence supporting the hypothesis that in many bilingual education contexts there is a clear need at all stages for 'structured exposure' to the L2. This should be in the form of L2-subject teaching to supplement the 'language in use' component of L2-medium instruction. In addition, it shows the need for this L2-subject teaching to be analytic and form-focused at some stage of schooling. This helps pupils acquire the less accessible aspects of the target language and ensures high levels of linguistic accuracy, precision and appropriateness (cf. Spada, 1997; Williams, 2005).

Withholding such analytic instruction heightens the risk of arrested L2 development (*fossilization*), particularly in instructed learning contexts where critical levels of comprehensible input, output and motivation cannot be guaranteed.

Conclusion

The ES experience shows that even in the most complex of situations the potentially conflicting demands of academic and linguistic development in L2 education can be reconciled. At the same time, the ES experience shows that such reconciliation is by no means self-evident, requiring careful planning and considerable investment. Additionally, success in L2 education is ultimately determined by myriad factors, curricular and extracurricular, some of which may well be beyond the control of program designers. More research is needed to establish the exact weight of these factors, and their interactions, in determining outcomes in the ES and in L2 education in general.

Notes

(1) For a fuller description of the sampling and data collection procedures in these studies, see Housen (2002) and Housen *et al.* (2011).
(2) Coding was done by 12 trained coders (students in a master's course on learner language analysis at the University of Brussels) in a carefully controlled procedure to ensure high inter-rater reliability. A random sample of approximately 10% of the data was also independently coded by the author. Inter-rater reliability was 93–96% agreement for complexity, 91–94% for fluency and 86–92% for accuracy-related aspects of the coding and analysis.
(3) Accuracy measures were computed for the L2 learners only, not for the native speaker benchmark pupils. In the comparative analyses (cf. below), the accuracy of the native speakers was set at 100% accurate.
(4) As a result of this requirement, the learners in the regular EFL classes were on average 26 months older than the ES pupils because English instruction in the regular Italian school system starts in year 3 rather than in year 1 as in the ES. The subsamples from the ES also include four pupils from year 4. These pupils had entered the ES system in the course of year 2 rather than year 1 of primary.

References

Baetens Beardsmore, H. (1995) The European School experience in multilingual education. In T. Skutnabb-Kangas (ed.) *Multilingualism for All* (pp. 21–68). Lisse: Swets & Zeitlinger.
Baetens Beardsmore, H. and Kohls, J. (1988) Immediate pertinence in the acquisition of multilingual proficiency: the European Schools. *The Canadian Modern Language Review* 44 (2), 240–260.
Baetens Beardsmore, H. and Swain, M. (1985) Designing bilingual education: aspects of immersion and 'European School Models'. *Journal of Multilingual and Multicultural Development* 6 (1), 1–15.

Baker, C. (2006) *Foundations of Bilingual Education and Bilingualism* (4th edn). Clevedon: Multilingual Matters.

Cenoz, J. and Genesee, F. (eds) (1998) *Beyond Bilingualism: Multilingualism and Multilingual Education*. Clevedon: Multilingual Matters.

Collentine, J. and Freed, B. (2004) Learning context and its effects on second language acquisition. *Studies in Second Language Acquisition* 26 (2), 153–171.

Collins, L., Halter, R., Lightbown, P. and Spada, N. (1999) Time and the distribution of time in L2 instruction. *TESOL Quarterly* 33 (4), 655–680.

Cummins, J. (1991) Language development and academic learning. In L. Malave and G. Duquette (eds) *Language, Culture and Cognition* (pp. 161–175). Clevedon: Multilingual Matters.

Curtain H. (2000) Time as a factor in early start programmes. In J. Moon and M. Nikolov (eds) *Research into Teaching English to Young Learners* (pp. 87–120). Pécs: University of Pécs Press.

Department for Children, Schools and Families (2009) The European Schools and the European Baccalaureate – Guidance for Universities and Schools. Online document, http://www.euroschool.lu/luxschool/ukuni/DCSF-Euro_Baccalaureate.pdf

Dixon, Q., Zhao, J., Shin, J.-Y., Wu, S., Su, J.-H., Burgess-Brigham, R., Gezer, M. and Snow, C. (2012) What we know about second language acquisition – A synthesis from four perspectives. *Review of Educational Research* 82, 15–60.

Ellis, R. (2008) *The Study of Second Language Acquisition* (2nd edn). Oxford: Oxford University Press.

Ellis, R. and Barkhuizen, G. (2005) *Analysing Learner Language*. Oxford: Oxford University Press.

European Parliament (2010) Resolution on 'Better Schools: an agenda for European cooperation'. Online document, http://www.europarl.europa.eu/oeil/home/home.do

European Schools (1999) *Report 92-D-296: Guidelines for Second Language Teaching in the Primary Section*. Brussels: Scholae Europea.

Gajo, L. and Mondada, L. (2000) *Interactions et acquisitions en contexte*. Fribourg: Éditions Universitaires.

Hammerly, H. (1991) *Fluency and Accuracy: Toward Balance in Language Teaching and Learning*. Clevedon: Multilingual Matters.

Housen, A. (2002) Second language achievement in the European School system of multilingual education. In D. So and G. Jones (eds) *Education and Society in Plurilingual Contexts* (pp. 96–128). Brussels: Academic Press.

Housen, A. (2003) Processes and outcomes in the european schools model of multilingual education. *Bilingual Research Journal* 26 (1), 43–62.

Housen, A. (2008). Multilingual development in the European Schools. In R. De Groof (ed.) *Brussels and Europe – Bruxelles et l'Europe* (pp. 455–470). Brussels: Academic and Scientific Publishers.

Housen, A. and Baetens Beardsmore, H. (1989) Curricular and extracurricular factors in multilingual education. *Studies in Second Language Acquisition* 9 (1), 83–102.

Housen, A. and Kuiken, F. (2009) Complexity, accuracy, and fluency in second language acquisition. *Applied Linguistics* 30 (4), 461–473.

Housen, A., Schoonjans, E., Janssens, S., Welcomme, A. and Pierrard, M. (2011) Conceptualizing and measuring the impact of contextual factors in instructed SLA – the role of language prominence. *International Journal of Applied Linguistics* 49 (2), 83–112.

Iwashita, N., Brown, A., McNamara, T. and O'Hagan, S. (2008) Assessed levels of second language speaking proficiency: How distinct? *Applied Linguistics* 29 (1), 24–49.

Johnson, R. and Swain, M. (eds) (1997) *Immersion Education: International Perspectives*. Cambridge: Cambridge University Press.

Johnstone, R. (2002) *Addressing 'The Age Factor': Some Implications for Language Policy*. Strasbourg: Council of Europe.

Lebrun, N. and Baetens Beardsmore, H. (1993) Trilingual education in the Grand Duchy of Luxembourg. In H. Baetens Beardsmore (ed.) *European Models of Bilingual Education* (pp. 107–122). Clevedon: Multilingual Matters.

MacWhinney, B. (2000) *The CHILDES project: Tools for analyzing talk*. Mahwah, NJ: Lawrence Erlbaum.

Malvern, D., Richards B., Chipere, N. and Durán, P. (2004) *Lexical Diversity and Language Development. Quantification and Assessment*. Basingstoke: Palgrave Macmillan.

Meara, P. and Bell, H. (2001) P_Lex: A simple and effective way of describing the lexical characteristics of short L2 texts. *Prospect* 16 (3), 5–19.

Muñoz, C. (2011) Input in foreign language learning: more significant than starting age. *International Review of Applied Linguistics in Language Teaching* 49 (2), 113–133.

Nayar, P.B. (1997) ESL/EFL dichotomy today: language politics or pragmatics? *TESOL Quarterly* 31 (1), 9–27.

Odlin, T. (2003) Crosslinguistic influence. In C. Doughty and M. Long (eds) *The Handbook of Second Language Acquisition* (pp. 436–486). Oxford: Blackwell.

Ortega, L. (2003) Syntactic complexity measures and their relationship to L2 proficiency: A research synthesis of college-level L2 writing. *Applied Linguistics* 24 (4), 492–518.

Serrano, R. (2011) The time factor in EFL classroom practice. *Language Learning* 61 (1), 117–145.

Serrano, R. and Muñoz, C. (2007) Same hours, different time distribution: Any difference in EFL? *System* 35 (3), 305–321.

Siegel, J. (2003) Social context. In C. Doughty and M. Long (eds) *The Handbook of Second Language Acquisition* (pp. 178–223). Oxford: Blackwell.

Sirkin, M. (1995) *Statistics for the Social Sciences* (2nd edn). Thousand Oaks, CA: Sage Publications.

Skehan, P. (2003) Task-based instruction. *Language Teaching* 36 (1), 1–14.

Skutnabb-Kangas, T. (ed.) (1995) *Multilingualism for All*. Lisse: Swets and Zeitlinger.

Spada, N. (1997) Form-focused instruction and second language acquisition: A review of classroom and laboratory research. *Language Teaching* 30 (1), 73–87.

Steinle, A., Häkansson, G., Housen, A. and Schelletter, C. (2010) Receptive L2 grammar knowledge development in bilingual preschools. In K. Kersten, A. Rohde, C. Schelletter and A. Steinle (eds) *Bilingual Preschools – Learning and Development* (pp. 69–101). Trier: WVT.

Swain, M. (1985) Communicative competence: some roles of comprehensible input and comprehensible output in its development. In S. Gass and C.G. Madden (eds) *Input in Second Language Acquisition* (pp. 235–253). Rowley, MA: Newbury House.

Swan, M. (1997) The influence of the mother tongue on second language vocabulary acquisition and use. In N. Schmitt and McCarthy M. (eds) *Vocabulary: Description, Acquisition and Pedagogy* (pp. 156–180). Cambridge: Cambridge University Press.

Wesche, M. (2002) Early French immersion: How has the original Canadian model stood the test of time? In P. Burmeister, T. Piske and A. Rohde (eds) *An Integrated View of Language Development* (pp. 357–379). Trier: WVT.

White, J. and Turner, C. (2005) Comparing children's oral ability in two ESL programs. *The Canadian Modern Language Review* 61 (4), 491–517.

Williams, J. (2005) Form-focused instruction. In E. Hinkel (ed.) *Handbook of Research in Second Language Teaching and Learning* (pp. 671–692). Mahwah, NJ: Lawrence Erlbaum.

Wippermann, I., Tiefenthal, C., Schober, A. and Gotthardt, L. (2010) Profiles of the ELIAS preschools. In K. Kersten, A. Rohde, C. Schelletter and A. Steinlen (eds) *Bilingual Preschools – Learning and Development* (pp. 239–262). Trier: WVT.

Wolfe-Quintero, K., Shunji, I. and Hae-Young, K. (1998) *Second Language Development in Writing: Measures of Fluency, Accuracy and Complexity.* Honolulu, HI: University of Hawai'i Press.

Appendix

Table 6.3 Study A – lexical and grammatical English-L2 complexity scores of Italian pupils in three European Schools and a regular EFL program (in percentages relative to native speaker benchmark scores of 100%)

	C1	C2	C3	C4
D	45.07	53.74	59.54	73.86
	$F = 25.67$; $p = 0.000$; C1 < C2 < C3 < C4 < BM			
λ	43.37	47.65	48.24	67.16
	$F = 5.23$; $p = 0.012$; C1 < C2 = C3 < C4 < BM			
MLU	51.51	54.29	59.96	63.09
	$F = 3.23$; $p = 0.023$; C1 = C2 < C3 = C4 < BM			
SCR	56.04	54.62	59.39	63.03
	$F = 8.31$; $p < 0.001$; C1 = C2 = C3 = C4 < BM			
MLC	60.58	59.33	62.12	63.43
	$F = 3.59$; $p < 0.008$; C1 = C2 = C3 = C4 < BM			
MLNP	44.13	48.77	49.45	58.14
	$F = 4.67$; $p < 0.013$; C1 < C2 = C3 < C4 < BM			
Overall complexity	50.12	53.07	56.45	64.79

F and *p* values for main effect (context); *post hoc* significant contrasts $\alpha = 0.05$

Table 6.4 Study A – lexical and grammatical English-L2 accuracy scores of Italian pupils in three European Schools and a regular EFL program (in percentages relative to native speaker benchmark scoresof 100%)

	C1	C2	C3	C4
LexErr	21.23	26.14	41.76	61.89
	$F = 59.43$; $p = 0.000$; C1 = C2 < C3 < C4 < BM			
GramErr	31.76	36.09	42.52	65.12
	$F = 41.03$; $p = 0.000$; C1 = C2 < C3 < C4 < BM			
TotErr	24.94	29.15	41.37	63.45
	$F = 72.43$; $p = 0.000$; C1 = C2 < C3 < C4 < BM			
Overall accuracy	25.98	30.46	41.88	63.49

F and *p* values for main effect (context); *post hoc* significant contrasts $\alpha = 0.05$

Table 6.5 Study A – English-L2 fluency scores of Italian pupils in three European Schools and a regular EFL program (in percentages relative to native speaker benchmark scores of 100%)

	C1	C2	C3	C4
MLR	35.22	39.41	48.78	63.76
	\multicolumn{4}{c}{$F = 23.16; p = 0.000; C1 = C2 < C3 = C4 < BM$}			
DysP	41.47	46.87	52.06	67.49
	\multicolumn{4}{c}{$\chi^2 = 49.23; p = 0.000; C1 = C2 < C3 < C4 < BM^*$}			
Hes	41.61	40.11	45.43	54.52
	\multicolumn{4}{c}{$F = 16.87; p = 0.000; C1 = C2 = C3 = C4 < BM$}			
Overall fluency	*39.43*	*42.13*	*48.76*	*61.92*

F and p values for main effect (context); *post hoc* significant contrasts $\alpha = 0.05$
*The data are not normally distributed and require no parametric testing

Part 3

Learners' Perceptions and Intensive Exposure

7 The Significance of Intensive Exposure as a Turning Point in Learners' Histories

Carmen Muñoz

The Role of Input in Second Language Acquisition

The importance of input in second language acquisition (SLA) has become a matter of contention as an issue that merits more innovative investigation. To begin, research has not consistently found a significant association between amount of input and second language (L2) outcomes. This lack of significant relationship has often been reported in studies concerned with the effects of starting age of learning, in which length of residence (LOR) does not seem to impact learners' ultimate attainment (e.g. DeKeyser & Larson-Hall, 2005). Recently, however, it has been argued that LOR may be too imprecise a measure of exposure and contact, and that in order to examine its influence, it is first necessary to obtain better estimates of L2 input (Flege, 2009) and to take account of its quality (e.g. Flege & Liu, 2001; Piske, 2007), the frequency and quality of interaction with L2 speakers (Derwing & Munro, 2012) and the domains in which the learner participates (Moyer, 2004, 2009).

Additionally, age mediates frequency and type of contact with native speakers. Findings from both immigration and stay-abroad settings show how children enjoy more contexts of L2 use and a higher number of L2-speaking friends than adolescents (Jia & Aaronson, 2003) and than young adults (Llanes & Muñoz, forthcoming). Similar results have been found by Kopečková (this volume) and Llanes (this volume).

In the area of study abroad, researchers have striven to improve the instruments used to examine the amount and characteristics of learners' input and interaction (questionnaires and calendar diaries, traditionally). An example is the Language Activity Log developed by Ranta and Meckelborg (2002) in an attempt to measure exposure in great detail and to overcome the difficulties of categorizing open-ended entries in questionnaires. By means of this instrument, Ranta and Meckelborg (2009) have revealed that the use of the second language while abroad may be extremely limited. Kinginger (2008) integrated test data with ethnographic data, exploring by means of several qualitative instruments (interviews, journals, language use logbooks and on-site observation) the degree to which individuals succeed in developing social relationships with target language speakers. The detailed case histories in Kinginger highlight the importance of the learner's motivational orientation towards the target language in understanding individual differences in achievement outcomes abroad.

The scarcity and limitations of input in typical foreign language (FL) settings have been a common concern in the area of instructed L2 learning. Rikfin (2005) suggests that there may be ceiling effects in instructed FL given the low exposure to the language (in his study, college students of FLs in the USA). In that respect, Rifkin argues that students must immerse themselves to reach advanced proficiency, either in a domestic immersion programme or abroad. Evidence for the superiority of immersion settings (at home or abroad) was gathered by Freed *et al.* (2004), who compared proficiency gains in traditional 'drip-feed' instruction, immersion programmes and study abroad, and showed that students in an input-limited FL context do not make significant gains whereas students in the latter two contexts do (see also Pérez Vidal *et al.*, this volume). Similarly, Serrano *et al.* (2011) found that learners obtained similar gains from study-abroad experiences and intensive programmes at home, whereas gains for students in a semi-intensive programme at home were lower.

Certainly, the intensive distribution of input has shown remarkable benefits for learners (e.g. Serrano & Muñoz, 2007). The research evidence accumulated from the intensive English learning programmes in Quebec confirms the significant benefits of intensive exposure (e.g. Spada & Lightbown, 1989; White & Turner, this volume). Benefits accrue both when exposure is concentrated and when it is distributed across time in short intensive experiences (Collins & White, 2011). This may partly result from the fact that intensive exposure environments probably involve implicit L2 learning processes to a greater degree than regular limited classroom exposure. In that respect, Serrano (2011) suggests that L2 classroom practice that is not concentrated does not generally facilitate remembering, let alone 'proceduralising' previously acquired declarative knowledge (DeKeyser, 2007).

The importance of intensive exposure has also been affirmed in studies focusing on age differences. Specifically, it has been seen as instrumental in explaining young learners' differential outcomes in naturalistic language learning settings and in tutored FL settings. The former foster implicit language acquisition and favour young learners, who are observed to have a long-term advantage (DeKeyser, 2000; DeKeyser & Larson-Hall, 2005). However, this advantage is not found in the latter settings, where implicit acquisition is not facilitated (Muñoz, 2006b, 2008). Along that line, Muñoz

(2009: 154) has argued that what learners – and particularly the younger ones – need is not an extremely long period of 'extended input', but a substantial period of 'intensive input' for implicit learning to take place.

However, as the studies reviewed above point out, intensive exposure or immersion does not guarantee that learners will participate in the relevant contexts of use with enough frequency and the appropriate predisposition. Factors such as cultural distance, willingness to communicate, chronological age or even individual characteristics such as openness may all affect learners' L2 outcomes. The study of learners' orientations to input may help us interpret the different benefits learners draw from language use possibilities and ultimately understand 'how and why input matters' (see Moyer, 2009: 159). One way of gaining insight into FL learners' orientations to input may be the use of language learning histories, which are increasingly utilized in SLA (e.g. Norton & Toohey, 2001). Along this line, the present study incorporates the voices of learners themselves to yield a more complete understanding of the importance of input for L2 learning.

Antecedents of the Study

The present study was inspired by previous research findings (Muñoz, 2011) that explored the long-term effects of starting age and input in an instructed language learning setting. That study was motivated in turn by recent age-related research (e.g. García Mayo & García Lecumberri, 2003; Muñoz, 2006a) that found that late learners in instructed FL settings reach higher levels of language proficiency than early learners after the same amount of instructional time. This finding was in line with results in naturalistic language learning settings, where older learners are seen to be more efficient in the short term (e.g. Snow & Hoefnagel-Höhle, 1978). In the same settings, as mentioned above, a recurrent finding has also been that early-start learners surpass late-start learners in the long run (Krashen *et al.*, 1979). However, this latter finding has not been confirmed in instructed L2 settings, allegedly because learners had not yet had sufficient input and exposure to the target language when tested (Singleton, 1995). In contrast, Muñoz (2006b) predicted that if young learners were not provided with massive exposure to the target language to allow their superior implicit learning mechanisms to operate, they would not have higher levels of proficiency than late starters in the long term and after the same amount of instruction hours. Muñoz (2011) set out to examine these opposite predictions, namely whether early learners would surpass late learners in the long term, specifically after a minimum of 10 years of instruction.

Muñoz (2011) examined the written and oral proficiency of 190 upper-intermediate learners of English as a foreign language (EFL) by means of a battery of language tests. Participants' mean length of exposure to English since the beginning of instruction was 13.9 years, and instruction began on average at age 7.8. The average age at testing was 21.3. The majority (89%) were bilingual Catalan–Spanish. Information about the learners' past and present target language use was elicited by means of an extensive written questionnaire. A number of input-related measures were derived from this information, such as instruction hours at different educational stages, length of stays abroad and current target language use. Finally, a one-on-one semi-structured oral interview was conducted with a sub-sample of learners.

The analyses showed that starting age was not a predictor of learners' language outcomes, confirming the author's prediction. Instead, several input measures derived from the questionnaire information correlated, modestly but significantly, with the scores from a general proficiency test, a receptive vocabulary test and a phonetic perception test. While these results highlight the important role played by input for these experienced learners, a more qualitative type of study was needed in order to shed light on *how* the amount and type of input impact learners' achievements in the target language over and above their starting age of learning (see Singleton & Muñoz, 2011).

A preliminary study was therefore conducted of the semi-structured interviews of 37 of these participants, specifically of the responses to a question concerned with the existence of a turning point in their learning histories. Participants' answers revealed the importance of *intensive* input experiences in their trajectories. In consequence, given the significant relationship between amount and type of input and long-term learning outcomes, and the preliminary evidence that intensive exposure experiences may play a significant role in such a relationship, more research needs to be carried out to shed light on the significance of intensive exposure for language learners.

The Present Study

The present study sets out to investigate the existence and nature of turning points in L2 learners' trajectories to investigate the role played by intensive exposure in them. For some of these learners, English is a foreign language that has been learnt only in instructed contexts, whereas some learners have also experienced shorter or longer stays in English-speaking countries. On the basis of the quantitative results obtained in the previous study commented on above, the preliminary examination of those participants' answers to the interviews about their learning histories and finally the research in the literature review that highlights the importance of language exposure and language contact, the first research question of the present study is the following:

(1) How frequently are *intensive* exposure experiences identified by learners as representing turning points in their trajectories?

In addition, with the aim of exploring learners' orientations to intensive input and to English language learning in general, this study addresses a second research question:

(2) What is the nature of the turning points related by these foreign language learners?

Participants

The participants in this study were 142 undergraduate students in an English Studies degree at a university in Spain, 111 of them female and 31 male. The sample includes participants in the previous study (see section above) and a new sample collected from the same population of students one or two years later. Most of them were bilingual Catalan–Spanish, while 8% of them had a different L1. Their range of languages varied from three to eight, and half of the sample had four. They began to learn English at an average age of 8.8 and the mean number of years of EFL study was 14.8. At the time they were interviewed their mean age was 23.5 (range 18–61), and they had studied language and literature courses in English for 2–4 years. The mean number of lesson hours per week was 15, and contact time with English could be variably increased by interaction with professors or other students. Therefore, the participants' learning milieu can be considered partial immersion in English.

Method

Data were collected by means of a semi-structured interview. The interviews were conducted in English but interviewees were told to codeswitch to their L1 if they felt the need to, although only a handful of participants did so. The interviews lasted from 15 to 30 minutes.

The interview guide consisted of 17 questions, distributed into three groups with different time references: present, past and future. The first group was mainly concerned with participants' language learning aptitude and included questions about the degree of difficulty of English learning, participants' self-perception of aptitude for learning languages and a self-evaluation of their competence in the four skills (speaking, listening, writing and reading) in each of their languages. The second group of questions enquired about their perception of their own language learning history, the factors that had been most important in their learning trajectory, and a possible turning point in their English learning history, as mentioned above. Specifically, this last question was worded in the following way:

> Was there any moment in the past when you thought you had really improved your level of English? A turning point? Why did you think so? What happened? Any particular experience?

The third group of questions asked for any plans (immediate and future) that participants had to improve their level of English, as well as for advice for a fictitious friend who had just begun learning English.

The interviews were audio-recorded and later transcribed by a trained research assistant and checked by a second one. The author and another researcher read the answers to the question concerning the existence of a turning point several times to create categories for the analysis. The responses given by the participants were grouped first in terms of whether or not they identified a turning point in their EFL learning history. Next, those answers that identified a turning point were grouped on the basis of whether or not the turning point involved an intensive language learning experience. Finally, the emerging themes in those answers were explored by the two researchers. After discussing and refining the categories, an inter-rater reliability of 0.96 was achieved; unclear cases or cases with not enough information were left out of the final count.

Analysis of participants' answers

Learners' identification of turning points

Participants' answers were first of all classified in terms of whether or not they identified a specific turning point (see Table 7.1). The first category corresponds to those participants who did not identify any turning point or critical event in their learning trajectory (10 participants). The second category corresponds to those answers in which a change is mentioned, either a gradual change (10 participants) or an indeterminate change (three participants). The third category groups together those answers that contained a reference to an experience that was easily identified by the participants as a turning point. As seen in Table 7.1, the majority of participants (108, that is, 85.7%) mentioned a critical event that took place in an input-intensive context. Of these, almost half (50) mentioned an experience abroad in an English-speaking country (or in a country where English was used as the

Table 7.1 Answers concerning the existence of a turning point

Categories	N
No turning point	10
Gradual or indeterminate change	13
Input-intensive learning contexts	108
Stay abroad	50
At home intensive formal setting	33
At home intensive informal setting	25
Non input-intensive learning contexts	19
Total	150

lingua franca). It needs to be noted that all but two of the learners who had enjoyed a stay abroad (52 in total) mentioned this experience first. Next, 33 participants mentioned the learning experience during the English-medium degree, and 25 mentioned an intensive informal setting, such as a network of friends. Finally, Table 7.1 shows a total of 150 answers from 142 participants owing to the fact that eight participants mentioned not one but two turning points (for example, an experience abroad and engaging in an informal network of English-speaking friends once returned).

The answers given by the participants illustrate their perceptions regarding the existence of a turning point and its characteristics. The thematic analysis revealed four salient themes, with the two most frequent being agency and practice. Also recurrent was the reference to language progress, either as general improvement or with a focus on a specific area (such as fluency or comprehension). A fourth theme that emerged in these answers on several occasions was linguistic assimilation. Table 7.2 shows the frequency of the themes, as well as a brief description of them.[1] Sometimes participants made reference to more than one of those topics in their answer, and sometimes their answer was too imprecise to identify a specific theme.

One of the previous questions in the interview had asked participants about the factors that had been most influential in their English language learning,[2] and hence it may have paved the way to the answers we examine here. A comparison of the answers to the two questions revealed that in slightly more than one-fifth of cases (23.7%), there existed a close relationship between the two. For example, one of the participants stated that watching undubbed films with English subtitles had motivated her a lot; later she identified a turning point as the time when she watched and fully understood an undubbed film without subtitles (a film she liked and knew from having watched it previously in Spanish).

Table 7.2 Thematic content of answers

Themes	Brief description	N
Agency	Awareness or control of own learning process, intentionality, taking actions, applying effort, creation of learning opportunities, engagement, confidence, pride when meeting with success	63
Practice	Constant use of language, immersion	54
Language improvement	General language progress Specific language areas or skills	38
Linguistic assimilation	Language dominance, unconscious language choice	7

Participants' accounts

As mentioned above, the main theme in these participants' accounts is agency. Agency is defined by Duff (2012: 6) as 'people's ability to make choices, take control, self-regulate, and thereby pursue their goals as individuals leading, potentially, to personal or social transformation'. Agency is recognized as an important factor in language learning that is connected with identity and power (e.g. Duff *et al.*, 2010; Huang, 2011). It also has a close connection with the construct of autonomy, defined as 'the feeling of being the agent of one's own actions' (Van Lier, 1997: 48) or 'the capacity to take control of one's own learning' (Benson, 2001: 47). From a sociocultural perspective, Ahearn (2011: 112) defines agency as 'the socioculturally mediated capacity to act'. Along those lines, Malcom (2011: 198) notes that, rather than being an inherent capacity, agency can be achieved only in transaction with a particular situation, and can only be understood retroactively. The fact that participants in the current study were asked to remember a critical event in their trajectories may have enhanced their learning self-awareness and their sense of agency.

The participants in this study reflected their agency in different ways: expressing awareness of their learning process; expressing engagement; recalling the steps they took and the effort they applied towards learning English; and conveying the emotions felt when meeting with success. In Excerpt 1, the participant identifies a turning point in her trajectory as the moment in which she took control of her own learning:

Excerpt 1
It was that crucial moment that I started self learning I don't know how to call it it's yeah the moment I took books and actually listened to English and how to pronounce them and practice it myself.[3]

Excerpt 2 comes from a learner who identifies a turning point as the moment in which she realized she was pursuing her goals in an institutional intensive setting; she remarks that her self-esteem increased with that realization.

Excerpt 2
I didn't have difficulties to pass my exams my written essays were better and my self-esteem increased a lot because I realized that everything was right and I was getting my aim my goal.

A large number of participants related how they created and sustained language learning opportunities. This is also noted by Duff *et al.* (2010), who identified agency as a major theme in the narratives of Canadian learners of Chinese as an additional language. According to these authors, 'taking ... steps toward creating or sustaining language learning opportunities and engaging meaningfully with the language can also foster the conditions for future successes', which in turn led to growing confidence and autonomy as learners (Duff *et al.*, 2010: 25). In the current study, participants related how they took positive actions and steps towards creating English language environments in informal settings that provided them with plenty of exposure and contact with the target language. Excerpt 3 illustrates this active creation of opportunities for learning and practising the FL: the account makes explicit mention of taking a decision. It also references the boyfriend/girlfriend factor, which appears in a handful of accounts (see below), as well as to the nature of FL improvement (gains in fluency).

Excerpt 3
I decided well this [Barcelona] is a very cosmopolitan city this is not the case like Buenos Aires but here it is so I started to have language exchanges with people from America England Canada whatever so that was a really big turning point because although I never got to live in an English-speaking country I'm always relating to English-speaking people and that makes such a big difference and I also dated a Canadian for a year and so now my English is more fluent because of that because I spent a lot of time with him.

In Excerpt 4, the participant recalls the effort she put into learning in a domestic setting and how she created her own English language environment. This excerpt as the previous one also contains a reference to constant productive or receptive language use.

Excerpt 4
I put such a big effort that it made me improve a lot because I was immersed I created my own immersion in English I always saw films in English so I listened to the radio in English and I only read in English.

Owing to the nature of the question posed to participants concerning a qualitatively distinct change in their learning progress, many participants recounted an experience of success that made them feel proud of themselves and improved their self-confidence. Participants commonly expressed their satisfaction with the remembered successful experience, such as the participant in Excerpt 5, who considered it 'cool'. This account is also concerned with the nature of the linguistic improvement experienced in a study-abroad experience, in this case gains in oral skills, comprehension of another English accent and lexicon.

Excerpt 5
I was an Erasmus student last year in Ireland and before I went I thought yeah my English is pretty good and when I talked to people over there

they said to me your English is really good you know and sometimes people told me are you English? it was like there talking to people and all that I really see myself that I have improved a lot especially when I speak you know [...] when I was there I thought yes I'm able to understand another accent you know that it's quite difficult to understand and I could well and I even used the words that they used you know I thought wow that's really cool so when I was back I saw the big difference.

The participant in Excerpt 6, in a non-intensive exposure setting, felt 'happy' for having outperformed other learners. The encouragement participants felt might have motivated them and sustained their efforts and confidence to continue learning English.

Excerpt 6
Maybe when we took the first certificate exam because we got an A and we were very happy because it was a way to know about your level in relation to other people and to the standard measure system I don't know that there was a turning point it was a way of being aware of how we were doing so far.

However, in a few cases, agency follows from an experience of failure. In Excerpt 7, taking control is a reaction to a negative experience of (unfair) failure in an exam. This experience triggers this participant's 'obsession' with learning English and immersing herself in an English environment. In this case the unsuccessful experience is converted into motivation to learn. The account makes explicit mention of 'taking a decision', and the steps taken to learn as much English as possible in an autonomous way.

Excerpt 7
When I was sixteen because at the age of fifteen I took the (...) the fifth level and I failed it (...) when I was just fifteen because I got like a very difficult topic in the oral part precisely I was told to talk about how I would save a language that is dying out and at the age of fifteen I didn't have the maturity or nor the knowledge to speak about it and it was not because of my English but because of the topic so they failed me and that's it and then I that made me very angry so I decided to get a very good grade next year and that's what I did and when I was sixteen I passed the test with an 88 (...) I became obsessed with English everything I didn't know every word I searched I looked it up in the dictionary I started to talk to many people in English in chat rooms I watched movies in the original version everything in English I got really obsessed for that whole year I wrote many essays everything.

Similarly, the participant in Excerpt 8 alludes to her realization of lack of progress and the actions she took (going abroad, socializing in English) in order to improve her English.

Excerpt 8
When I felt I started to stuck up and really not learning more here in Spain I moved to Dublin and I spent there like a couple of months or so and when I came back I said well I really have learnt English. I think it was basically because I was in a real English speaking environment not only in English courses but going to a bar meeting people learning how they speak basically that was a turning point living there.

Language practice, that is, constant use of the target language, is a prevalent theme in these participants' answers, and is closely related to their intensive exposure experiences. In Excerpt 9 the participant alludes to the constant use of the target language during a stay abroad.

Excerpt 9
I think that the turning point was when I went to England and stood there for summer period and when I came back I noticed that my English had improved a lot because there I had to live every day at every moment in English from the beginning of the day till the end so even in order I had to use it to communicate to ask things and then I saw that at this stage my English had improved.

Practice overlaps with other themes, as can be seen in many of the excerpts above. Sustaining language learning opportunities that give them constant practice with the target language, participants also exert their agency. Among these opportunities, the following are mentioned: chats, music (listening and composing songs), Internet forums, YouTube, videogames, series, films, television, reading, summer camps and job-related tasks. Excerpts 10–12 illustrate some of these activities in which learners engage, which allow them to be immersed in English in a domestic setting and that are perceived by them as turning points in their learning trajectory. In these excerpts we can also observe how learners' affiliation to different communities of practice has enhanced their motivation to learn English (Sade, 2011). In a number of participants' accounts it is English culture, especially music and literature, that is a source of motivation for learning and practicing English.

Excerpt 10
Basically the best input I got from English learning was because I discovered this website where people wrote their stories and it was an American website so everything was in English and I started reading and I read the

stories for months and then I started writing my own stories in English which were obviously kind of bad compared to Americans.

Excerpt 11
Recently actually because I have gone into internet and there are these chats where you go and you practice your English in fact with I mean you sort of teach English whatever you know no matter what you can be the teacher for half an hour or two hours or whatever you want and then everybody forty people are listening to you are following your examples and your exercises and things.

Excerpt 12
When I was playing these games I had a friend who is Spanish Catalan like me but we started joking and speaking in English one day we were like that every day of our lives we were talking in English between us in real life in high school ... it just started like a joke I'm making jokes in English and then because every day we were talking about this game and always in English we started talking in English and I said yeah I know English now.

A few participants mentioned an English-speaking boyfriend (no girl-friends were mentioned but there were few male participants; see also Excerpt 3). This type of personal relationship provided not only intensive language use, but often greater engagement with the language in order to fully understand and express feelings. In Excerpt 13 the participant (P) is able to explain to the researcher (R) why having a boyfriend (while abroad) produces a significant change in one's FL ability, stretching one's competence through negotiation of meaning (Long, 1996) and personal involvement.

Excerpt 13
P: ... I had a boyfriend and I think is the best teacher you can have you can't avoid the subject with the boyfriend you know so you need to find
R: to make things clear
P: yeah to make things clear yeah to find the exact words. With friends is different because sometimes is like if I have to explain this I explain another thing but [with a boyfriend] you need to okay say a word that means all that because it's different and the predisposition
R: ... how interested you are in getting yourself understood
P: yeah, understand the other what you are saying.

Another recurrent theme is the characteristics of participants' language improvement. Some participants comment on their language progress in general while others refer to the specific gains experienced (for example, in comprehension or in vocabulary). Fluency is most frequently mentioned by participants who have stayed abroad (Excerpt 14; see also Excerpt 3 above).

Excerpt 14
Yes I think a couple of months I thought oh well my English is very very good now it was not my English that had improved it was my fluency because they don't have another chance you know or speaking English or starve you know.

Finally, a theme that appeared only in intensive learning contexts, and mostly in reference to a stay abroad, was linguistic assimilation. The reflection in Excerpt 15 is an illustration: the participant realizes that during a stay abroad the second language is permeating her thoughts. The participant in Excerpt 16 vividly expresses her lack of control over this process of language assimilation. Pavlenko (2011) remarks that a common theme in immigrant memoirs and bilinguals' autobiographies is linguistic assimilation involving shifts to 'thinking' in the L2.

Excerpt 15
Yes one summer I think it was in Edinburgh I wake up and I thought oh Gemma you have to have a shower or have breakfast or something like this and I was like astonished because I said oh you haven't thought in Catalan but in English.

Excerpt 16
I'm not sure about it I don't know I remember I started thinking in English when I was living in Blackpool for a month or two [...] it's a habit I have I don't know why it's just that my head is so confused my mind is like flowing.

Excerpt 17 illustrates how an intensive instructional setting may also result in linguistic assimilation, infiltrating learners' dreams.

Excerpt 17
Not the first day but when I was maybe for the second month here (the University) because the most important thing was that I was here maybe four hours per day and on these four hours I was listening all the time the teachers and the classmates speaking in English you know and for me this is new absolutely at the first I thought oh my God I cannot resist this but step by step I was learning a lot and it was fantastic and sometimes I dream in English.

This section has illustrated four salient themes in accounts that identify turning points in intensive contexts, abroad or at home, in formal settings or in informal settings, as well as in non-intensive contexts. However, not all settings evoke all themes with the same frequency. Specifically, participants who identify a stay abroad as a scenario of a turning point in their language-learning history mention the importance of practice as well as the phenomenon of linguistic assimilation much more often than the other participants; those whose turning point is experienced in an intensive formal or informal setting refer to agency and practice very frequently; and those whose turning point is experienced in a non-intensive formal setting mention agency and language improvement, in this order, with high frequency.

Conversely, themes are not similarly distributed across settings. Agency appears more frequently in accounts relating turning points in intensive informal and formal settings, and less to stay-abroad settings. Practice seems more predominant in accounts that relate turning points in stay-abroad settings particularly, and also in intensive informal settings. Language improvement is more relatively salient in accounts relating turning points to non-intensive formal settings. Finally, linguistic assimilation is mentioned most frequently by participants whose turning point took place in a stay-abroad setting.

Final Discussion and Conclusions

The analysis of the participants' accounts of turning points in their language-learning histories has yielded some interesting findings. In relation to the first research question, the current study has found that an intensive learning context was indicated most frequently as the setting of a qualitative change in participants' learning histories (85.7%). For the majority of these participants a stay abroad brought about the change. Indeed, all but two of those who had stayed abroad recognized that experience as the scenario of a turning point. In other words, the more intensive and extensive the exposure to the target language (i.e. stay abroad) is, the greater the opportunities for learners to experience a qualitative change in their learning history. In Ushioda's (2007) terms, study-abroad experiences act as 'optimal challenges' that stretch learners' L2 abilities and bolster their confidence in their use. Research using learners' narratives converges to show such experiences as crucial for learners' L2 development (e.g. Chik & Breidbach, 2011). The partial immersion of an English-medium degree provided the second best scenario for a qualitative significant change in these participants' L2 development. This finding complements previous findings that show superior gains in study-abroad situations and in immersion programmes at home (e.g. Freed *et al.*, 2004).

The present study has also revealed that learners may create their own immersion environment at home, increasing hours of input and output of all skill types, and this may be the scenario for a turning point in their language learning histories. Coincidentally, Doughty (2006) reports a study with highly motivated and advanced FL learners who were asked about the most important and effective factors in success. The learners identified, first, the amount of time learning and using the foreign language, and second, creating a speaking environment – seeking or generating opportunities to use the language with native speakers. Moreover, in the case of English particularly, it seems that classroom-based learning is less and less the sole path followed for learning the language and that out-of-class exposure offers increased learning opportunities. In the current study, we have seen how students seek complementary paths to speed up their proficiency, most of them internet-based (online communities, webs and films) or related to English language popular culture (see, e.g. Murray, 2008).

These findings also confirm the limitations of traditional FL provision, as shown by research (e.g. Freed *et al.*, 2004; Rifkin, 2005) and confirmed by learners' dissatisfaction with the amount of learning accomplished in such an environment (e.g. Amunzie & Winke, 2009: 373). The reasons may lie in both the paucity of input and the extremely small number of hours of exposure, as well as in the lack of intensity (Serrano, 2011).

The second research question was concerned with the nature of the experience identified by participants as a turning point in their learning histories. The analysis unveiled the importance of agency for participants' language learning, and adds the perspectives of language learners in FL contexts to the evidence already accumulated in recent years (see Norton & Toohey, 2001). As in previous studies, agency may be seen to be related to other constructs such as autonomy, motivation and self-efficacy (Ehrman, 1996; Sade, 2011). When participants exercise their agency – their capacity for autonomy – making conscious decisions and choices about their learning, their motivation is enhanced (see Murphy, 2011). At the same time, motivation has led many participants in this study to create and sustain opportunities for learning, particularly those in domestic formal and informal intensive settings. This engagement with learning is, for Little (2007), one of the principles for language learning autonomy and success. When meeting with success, participants also improve their perception of self-confidence, especially when they have experienced a stay abroad. This is likely to have an effect on their self-efficacy beliefs, in line with previous studies that have documented changes in language learners' beliefs as a result of study abroad. For example, Amuzie and Winke (2009) found that study-abroad experiences brought about a belief that improvement depended more on the learner's own efforts than the teachers' efforts, hence increasing learners' independence. Similarly, Tanaka and Ellis (2003) claim that stays abroad have the strongest effect on self-efficacy and confidence, seen as major achievement of stay abroad.

Constant language use and practice have also often been chosen as instrumental in the change experienced, particularly by those who have experienced a stay abroad. The combination of intensive learning environments and practice seems fundamental for learners' perceptions of progress. In many cases, learners exert their agency by controlling input, providing for themselves intensive input and interaction opportunities (see Ushioda, 2009). The reflections of these expert learners have also focused on the nature of the language development experienced, particularly those who identify a turning point within their regular non-intensive learning process. Whereas participants in domestic settings have referred to improvement in vocabulary and other language areas, participants who have experienced a stay abroad often refer to gains in fluency. The learners' perception of improvement in fluency is in line with the findings from stay-abroad studies as well (see Llanes, this volume). As observed by DeKeyser (2007), learning the L2 abroad provides opportunities for practice in real-life situations and thus automatization of L2 (see Schmidt, 1992).

Finally, linguistic assimilation also appears in these participants' accounts. It is interesting to observe that immersion begins to influence the thought process of participants relatively early, contrary to Pavlenko's remark: 'Only when speakers move to the country where the language is spoken ... this language begins to exert influence on their thinking, and even then the influence is not immediately apparent' (Pavlenko, 2011: 5). The evidence from the participants in the current study seems to indicate that this influence may appear even after just a few weeks of immersion in some cases, which may be explained by their generally high proficiency on arrival.

A final comment on the particular question that was used to elicit learners' voices is in order here, since, to my knowledge, no previous study has used it before. However, when reading through learners' language learning histories or the researchers' reflections on them, turning points emerge in many narratives. For example, Menezes (2011: 66, my emphasis) points out from the perspective of complexity theory that new initial conditions *for a new phase in an SLA process*, such as living or studying abroad or being hired by a hotel, 'change the route of the systems as they offer opportunities for interactions in authentic linguistic social practices'. The present study has focused precisely on the nature of the experience that opens the gate to a new productive and meaningful phase for FL learners.

To finish, this study has a number of limitations. First of all, participants' gender is not balanced since the majority of students are females, as in modern language departments in general. Although no gender-related differences were observed in the participants' answers to the question, these accounts may be more representative of female students than male students. Likewise, the participants in this study have specific characteristics as experienced plurilingual students of language(s), and it could well be that their language learning awareness is higher than that of other learners.

Going back to the research that motivated the present study, it can be concluded that intensive experience with the L2 is both significantly related to outcomes and significant for learners themselves. To conclude with Ushioda's (2011: 188) words:

> The mutually constitutive relationship between learner and context seems crystallized in particular in the dynamics of L2 input, since how learners deal with input, orient to it, attend to it, respond to it, and how they engage with and relate to the people who produce the input, will necessarily affect the content, amount, relevance and quality of further input to which they are exposed in the communication process.

Acknowledgements

Thanks are due to the MICINN for funding for the project FFI2010-21478, to AGAUR (2009SGR137) and to ICREA Acadèmia. My most sincere appreciation is expressed to Colleen Hamilton for her valuable help and critical comments, to Elsa Tragant, and the GRAL research group.

Notes

(1) P. Duff's work was an important source of inspiration in the analysis. I thank her for kindly sharing her work with me.
(2) The question was worded in the following way: what were some of the most important factors that influenced your learning of English?
(3) Extracts from the interviews are transcribed as they were spoken by participants, including their (grammatical) inaccuracies in English.

References

Ahearn, L.M. (2001) Language and agency. *Annual Review of Anthropology* 30, 109–137.
Amuzie, G.L. and Winke, P. (2009) Changes in language learning beliefs as a result of study abroad. *System* 37, 366–379.
Benson, P. (2001) *Teaching and Researching Autonomy in Language Learning*. Harlow: Pearson Education.
Chik, A. and Breidbach, S. (2011) Identity, motivation and autonomy: A tale of two cities. In G. Murray, X. Gao and T. Lamb (eds) *Identity, Motivation and Autonomy in Language Learning* (pp. 145–159). Bristol: Multilingual Matters.
Collins, L. and White, J. (2011) An intensive look at intensity and language learning. *TESOL Quarterly* 45 (1), 106–133.
DeKeyser, R. (2000) The robustness of critical period effects in second language acquisition. *Studies in Second Language Acquisition* 22 (4), 499–533.
DeKeyser, R. (2007) Study abroad as foreign language practice. In R. DeKeyser (ed.) *Practice in a Second Language: Perspectives from Applied Linguistics and Cognitive Psychology* (pp. 208–226). Cambridge: Cambridge University Press.
DeKeyser, R. and Larson-Hall, J. (2005) What does the critical period really mean? In J.F. Kroll and A.M.D. De Groot (eds) *Handbook of Bilingualism: Psycholinguistic Approaches*. Oxford: Oxford University Press.
Derwing, T.M. and Munro, M.J. (2012) The development of L2 oral language skills in two L1 groups: A seven-year study. *Language Learning* (in press).

Doughty, C. (2006) *Pathways to High-Level Success in Foreign Language Learning*. Technical Report, Vol. 1. College Park, MD: University of Maryland, Center for Advanced Study of Language.

Duff, P. (2012) Identity, agency, and SLA. In A. Mackey and S. Gass (eds) *Handbook of Second Language Acquisition* (pp. 410–426). London: Routledge.

Duff, P., Anderson, T., Ilinyckyj, R., Lester, E., Wang, R. and Yates, E. (2010) Learning Chinese as an additional language: Investigating learners' identities, communities, and trajectories. Paper at *AAAL*, Atlanta, GA, 7 March.

Ehrman, M.E. (1996) *Understanding Second Language Learning Difficulties*. London: Sage.

Flege, J. (2009) Give input a chance! In T. Piske and M. Young-Scholten (eds) *Input Matters in SLA* (pp. 175–190). Bristol: Multilingual Matters.

Flege, J. and Liu, S. (2001) The effect of experience on adults' acquisition of a second language. *Studies in Second Language Acquisition* 23(4): 527–552.

Freed, B.F., Segalowitz, N. and Dewey, D.P. (2004) Context of learning and second language fluency in French: Comparing regular classroom, study abroad, and intensive domestic immersion programs. *Studies in Second Language Acquisition* 26, 275–301.

García Mayo, M.P. and García Lecumberri, M.L. (eds) (2003) *Age and the Acquisition of English as a Foreign Language: Theoretical Issues and Field Work*. Clevedon: Multilingual Matters.

Huang, J. (2011) A Dynamic account of autonomy, agency and identity in (T)EFL learning. In G. Murray, X. Gao and T. Lamb (eds) *Identity, Motivation and Autonomy in Language Learning* (pp. 229–246). Bristol: Multilingual Matters.

Jia, G. and Aaronson, D. (2003) A longitudinal study of Chinese children and adolescents learning English in the United States. *Applied Psycholinguistics* 24, 131–161.

Kinginger, C. (2008) *Language Learning in Study Abroad: Case Histories of Americans in France*. Modern Language Journal Monograph Series 1.

Krashen, S.D., Long, M.H. and Scarcella, R.C. (1979) Age, rate, and eventual attainment in second language acquisition. *TESOL Quarterly* 13 (4), 573–582.

Little, D. (2007) Language learner autonomy: Some fundamental considerations revisited. *International Journal of Innovation in Language Learning and Teaching* 1 (1), 14–29.

Llanes, À. and Muñoz, C. (forthcoming) Age effects in a study abroad context: Children and adults studying abroad and at home. *Language Learning* 63 (1).

Long, M.H. (1996) The role of the linguistic environment in second language acquisition. In W.C. Ritchie and T.J. Bhatia (eds) *Handbook of Second Language Acquisition* (pp. 413–468). New York: Academic Press.

Malcolm, D. (2011) 'Failing' to achieve autonomy in English for medical purposes. In G. Murray, X. Gao and T. Lamb (eds) *Identity, Motivation and Autonomy in Language Learning* (pp. 195–211). Bristol: Multilingual Matters.

Menezes, V. (2011) Identity, motivation and autonomy in second language acquisition from the perspective of complex adaptive systems. In G. Murray, X. Gao and T. Lamb (eds) *Identity, Motivation and Autonomy in Language Learning* (pp. 57–72). Bristol: Multilingual Matters.

Moyer, A. (2004) *Age, Accent and Experience in Second Language Acquisition. An Integrated Approach to Critical Period Inquiry*. Clevedon: Multilingual Matters.

Moyer, A. (2009) Input as a critical means to an end: Quantity and quality of experience in L2 phonological attainment. In T. Piske and M. Young-Scholten (eds) *Input Matters in SLA* (pp. 159–174). Bristol: Multilingual Matters.

Muñoz, C. (ed.) (2006a) *Age and the Rate of Foreign Language Learning*. Clevedon: Multilingual Matters.

Muñoz, C. (2006b) The effects of age on foreign language learning: The BAF Project. In C. Muñoz (ed.) *Age and the Rate of Foreign Language Learning* (pp. 1–40). Clevedon: Multilingual Matters.

Muñoz, C. (2008) Symmetries and asymmetries of age effects in naturalistic and instructed L2 learning. *Applied Linguistics* 24 (4), 578–596.
Muñoz, C. (2009) Input and long-term effects of early learning in a formal setting. In M. Nikolov (ed.) *Contextualizing the Age Factor: Issues in Early Foreign Language Learning* (pp. 141–160). Berlin: Mouton de Gruyter.
Muñoz, C. (2011) Is input more significant than starting age in foreign language acquisition? *International Review of Applied Linguistics* 49 (2), 113–133.
Murphy, L. (2011) 'Why am I doing this?' Maintaining motivation in distance language learning. In G. Murray, X. Gao and T. Lamb (eds) *Identity, Motivation and Autonomy in Language Learning* (pp. 107–124). Bristol: Multilingual Matters.
Murray, G. (2008) Pop culture and language learning: Learners' stories informing EFL. *Innovation in Language Learning and Teaching* 2, 1–16.
Norton, B. and Toohey, K. (2001) Changing perspectives on good language learners. *TESOL Quarterly* 35 (2), 307–322.
Pavlenko, A. (2011) Introduction: Bilingualism and thought in the 20th century. In A. Pavlenko (ed.) *Thinking and Speaking in Two Languages* (pp. 1–28). Clevedon: Multilingual Matters.
Piske, T. (2007) Implications of James E. Flege's research for the foreign language classroom. In O-S. Bohn and M.J. Munro (eds) *Language Experience in Second Language Speech Learning. In Honor of James Emil Flege* (pp. 301–314). Amsterdam: John Benjamins.
Ranta, L. and Meckelborg, A. (2002) *Development of the Language Activity Lo.* Edmonton: Department of Educational Psychology, University of Alberta.
Ranta, L. and Meckelborg, A. (2009) How much exposure do international graduate students really get? Measuring language use in a naturalistic setting. Unpublished manuscript.
Rifkin, B. (2005) A ceiling effect in traditional classroom foreign language instruction: Data from Russian. *The Modern Language Journal* 89 (1), 3–18.
Sade, L.A. (2011) Emerging selves, language learning and motivation through the lens of chaos. In G. Murray, X. Gao and T. Lamb (eds) *Identity, Motivation and Autonomy in Language Learning* (pp. 42–56). Bristol: Multilingual Matters.
Schmidt, R. (1992) Psychological mechanisms underlying second language fluency. *Studies in Second Language Acquisition* 14, 357–385.
Serrano, R. (2011) The time factor in EFL classroom practice. *Language Learning* 61, 117–143.
Serrano, R. and Muñoz, C. (2007) Same hours, different time distribution: Any difference in EFL? *System* 35, 305–321.
Serrano, R., Llanes, À. and Tragant, E. (2011) Analyzing the effect of context of second language learning: Domestic intensive and semi-intensive courses vs. study abroad in Europe. *System* 39, 133–143.
Singleton, D. (1995) A critical look at the Critical Period Hypothesis in second language acquisition research. In D. Singleton and Z. Lengyel (eds) *The Age Factor in Second Language Acquisition* (pp. 1–29). Clevedon: Multilingual Matters.
Singleton, D. and Muñoz, C. (2011) Around and beyond the Critical Period Hypothesis. In E. Hinkel (ed.) *Handbook of Research In Second Language Teaching and Learning* (Vol. II), (pp. 407–426). New York: Routledge.
Snow, C. and Hoefnagel-Höhle, M. (1978) The critical period for language acquisition: Evidence from second language learning. *Child Development* 49 (4), 1114–1128.
Spada, N. and Lightbown, P.M. (1989) Intensive ESL programs in Quebec primary schools. *TESL Canada Journal* 7, 11–32.
Tanaka, K. and Ellis, R. (2003) Study-abroad, language proficiency, and learner beliefs about language learning. *JALT Journal* 25 (1), 63–85.

Ushioda, E. (2007) Motivation, autonomy and sociocultural theory. In P. Benson (ed.) *Learner Autonomy 8: Teacher and Learner Perspectives* (pp. 5–24). Dublin: Authentik.

Ushioda, E. (2009) A person-in-context relational view of emergent motivation, self and identity. In Z. Dörnyei and E. Ushioda (eds) *Motivation, Language Identity and the L2 Self* (pp. 1–8). Bristol: Multilingual Matters.

Ushioda, E. (2011) Context matters: A brief commentary on the papers by Housen et al. and Muñoz. *International Review of Applied Linguistics* 49 (2), 187–189.

Van Lier L. (1997) Action-based teaching, autonomy and identity. *Innovation in Language Learning and Teaching* 1 (1), 46–65.

8 Change or Stability in Learners' Perceptions as a Result of Study Abroad

Elsa Tragant

Most people acknowledge the importance of study abroad in achieving fluency in a foreign language. How necessary this experience is to becoming fully proficient in a second language would be a matter of debate among second language (L2) experts, but few would probably deny that an extended stay abroad should render great opportunities for language learning. More specifically, a stay abroad (hereafter referred to as 'study abroad', SA) seems to be an ideal context for language learning since it involves L2 use both in the authentic target culture and in classroom situations. The intensity of exposure to the L2 that the SA setting affords led Churchill and Dufon (2006: 1) to state that there are few contexts that are as rich in potential and daunting in complexity. Several other authors (Dörnyei et al., 2004; Freed et al., 2004; Isabelli-García, 2006; Kinginger, 2008) have highlighted the complex nature of the acquisition of the second language in the context of SA. This complexity is in part owing to individual factors (personality, initial level of competence, gender, etc.) as well as factors that come into play during the stay (living arrangements, social network, type of instruction, etc.). Complexity also relates to the fact that the SA experience can impact a wide range of learner dimensions including not only linguistic gains but also language-related psychological, cognitive and cultural domains. The impact of the SA experience as reported by students will be the topic of investigation in the present study, which seeks to investigate their perceptions of linguistic and personal gains as well as changes in language-related beliefs and attitudes. First, studies dealing with self-perceived linguistic and personal growth are reviewed, followed by a synthesis of research that deals with other language-related domains like beliefs, motivations and strategies. Qualitative work in these areas will precede the review of quantitative, mostly survey-based, studies.

Self-perceived Linguistic and Personal Growth in SA

Views on the amount of language learning accomplished as a result of a SA experience tend to vary among students and they seem to be related to their opportunities to interact. In Jackson's study (2006, 2008) involving Chinese students, those who were most satisfied with their language improvement were the ones who had made an effort to seek exchanges with both locals and international students and who had been more active in building a relationship with their host family. On the other hand, in Amuzie and Winke's study (2009) involving mostly Korean and Chinese students in the USA, those who were less satisfied tended to be students with an initial expectation that success would automatically come by studying abroad. These feelings of dissatisfaction could be related to students' unexpected difficulty in finding opportunities to interact with native speakers in some SA contexts.

Gains in personal growth attributes owing to SA seem to be more uniform than self-perceived linguistic gains and have been reported in both short and longer study-abroad periods. According to a large-scale survey including 3723 alumni in the USA (Dwyer, 2004), the changes in these attributes, which Dwyer qualified as 'dramatic', (p. 159) were particularly strong in the areas of increased self-confidence, tolerance of ambiguity, maturation and world view. The impact of the experience was impressive regardless of term length, although gains were higher for full-year students. When comparing these students' reports with how they valued their academic experience abroad or its impact on later academic attainment, their assessments were more moderate. In the case of Erasmus students, the assessment of the academic value of the study period abroad was also more cautious than the cultural, personal and foreign language learning experience (Teichler, 2004). Personal growth was also reported on a five-week sojourn by a group of university students in the UK (Jackson, 2006). These students, most of whom had not been away from home before, reported gains in independence and self-confidence by the end of their study period.

Psychological, Cognitive and Cultural Gains in SA

In addition to the linguistic and personal growth gains that an SA experience is likely to bring about, this learning context has also been shown to trigger changes in language-related psychological, cognitive and cultural domains. These changes have been investigated from different theoretical and methodological perspectives, including sociocultural, phenomenological and activity theories. For example, the sociocultural approach guided Yang and Kim's (2011) and Gao's (2006) studies on language learning beliefs and learning strategies, respectively. In the former, the two Korean learners under analysis were found to have changed their L2 beliefs over the course of their time abroad. In the latter, the 14 Chinese learners' accounts about their sojourn in the UK showed that the different assessment methods and the new mediating agents that students were exposed to in the new context (i.e. supporting English-speakers' communities) caused learners to adopt different strategies. In both studies, students' L2 communicative participation is shown to interact in an important way with individual motivational profiles and changes.

Kinginger (2008) reaches a similar conclusion in a study also guided by sociocultural theory. The study, involving American students in various one-semester programs in France, highlights the fact that, nowadays, students' experiences abroad are deeply influenced by the process of globalization. More specifically, she concludes that L2 communicative participation and ultimately linguistic achievement are heavily influenced by students' abilities or willingness to overcome the difficulties posed by a globalized SA experience, in terms of access to telecommunications technology and challenges to students' national identity, among others. The challenges in terms of national identity, however, may be dependent on the cultural distance between the home and the host countries and can also be affected by international sociopolitical tensions. That would probably explain why national identity was shown to constitute a refuge in American students at a time of sociopolitical tensions between the USA and Europe (Kinginger, 2009: 199), but has not been shown to constitute an issue with European students abroad. In fact, the study of European student mobility by Murphy-Lejeune (2002) showed that these students did not tend to blame the host country in the process of adaptation. Instead, they seemed better prepared than American students to anticipate the difficulties of adaptation and to embody a pan-European identity. Following a phenomenological perspective, Murphy-Lejeune's study examined the experiences of 50 participants who were studying abroad in other European countries for one year or more and belonged to a *migratory elite*.

Learners' sense of identity as L2 users and their perceived sense of security is at the heart of Pellegrino's work (2005), a study that offers one of the most insightful emic accounts of the study-abroad experience. Drawing from the fields of psychology, sociology and social psychology, she provides compelling evidence of the effects of interactions with others on learners' sense of security or self-presentation. Primarily based on six American learners in Russia, Pellegrino concludes that her participants generally underwent a gradual improvement in their perceived sense of security, which was progressively less affected by unfavorable social conditions and behaviors of interlocutors. Instead, learners tended to draw more on themselves for their sense of security over time (Pellegrino, 2005: 124).

By also considering individual differences as dynamic in nature, Isabelli-García (2006) made use of social networks as a primary approach to studying the connection between motivation, target language interaction, cultural adjustment and second language acquisition during the SA experience. Similarly to Yang and Kim (2001), Gao (2006) and Kinginger (2008), this study confirms the important role of interactions in shaping students' experiences, motivations and attitudes towards the host culture. Through case studies, Isabelli-García shows how some American students on SA in Argentina changed from one motivational orientation type to another depending on their social relations. Diary entries also evidence how some learners who demonstrated positive or neutral attitudes at the start of their sojourn had changed to negative attitudes five months later. Differences in students' nonlinguistic changes also emerged in Allen (2010), who followed an activity theory perspective. The study focused on six American university students on a six-week SA program in France and showed different patterns of change between students who had linguistically driven motives and those who had pragmatic and non-linguistic motives. Students who were linguistically driven tended to be able to articulate more concrete subgoals during their stay abroad. They also grew more motivated to continue studying or using French personally through SA than the students who viewed the SA primarily as a cultural and travel experience.

Despite the different perspectives taken by the studies reviewed thus far, the ability to become a participating member of the host community emerges as a crucial factor in the student populations under study. Thus this ability, which numerous researchers have found to be an important predictor of language improvement and awareness in an SA context (see for example, Aguilar Stewart, 2010; Hernández, 2010; Juan-Garau & Pérez-Vidal, 2007; Yager, 1998), seems to have a mediating effect on students' perceptions and experiences as well.

Quantitative Studies of Learners' Perceptions

Apart from the studies mentioned above that address students' perceptions with qualitative data, few studies have followed a pre-/post-test design to quantitatively document changes in learners' perceptions. Adams (2006) used the Strategic Inventory for Language Learning (Oxford, 1990) to evaluate learning strategy development in American students enrolled in two- and four-month programs in various countries. Comparison of pre- and post-Strategic Inventory for Language Learning scores showed that students' self-reported gains in overall proficiency were related to cognitive strategy development. Also, increased reported use of communicative strategies was related to students who had traveled less with the study group and therefore had more chances of interacting with native speakers. However, the association between gains in overall proficiency and metacognitive strategy development was difficult to interpret, and study group travel was not ultimately related to language learning strategy development.

Other pre-/post-test design studies have been published that deal with learners' beliefs related to stay abroad. In Tanaka and Ellis' work (2003) with Japanese students on a 15-week program in the USA, comparisons of the Learner Belief Questionnaire prior to and after their stay showed that there were statistical differences in the three factors under analysis (Experiential Learning, Analytic Learning, and Self-efficacy and Confidence). The items in the Self-efficacy and Confidence factor underwent the greatest changes concerning students' increased satisfaction with their progress in English and their decreased concern about making mistakes. The item that demonstrated the least change concerned the belief that they could learn well by living in an English-speaking country. In the more recent study on beliefs by Amuzie and Winke (2009), two groups of learners with different lengths of stay demonstrated the importance of that difference: for two of the three factors under analysis (teacher's role and self-efficacy), changes between responses prior to and after stay were only significant for the group of students whose mean length of residence was 14 months, but not the other group (mean of four months). Students' comments in a later interview showed that some students' initial expectations about opportunities to communicate with native speakers and about amount of language learning had not been fulfilled.

The above review clarifies that learners' perceptions of their SA experience have been investigated from a range of theoretical and methodological approaches which all view learners' perceptions as dynamic mental representations that are sensible to external experiences and learning contexts. Generally speaking, qualitative studies have been better able to capture learners' individual differences while quantitative studies indicate that not all aspects of learners' perceptions may change to the same extent as a result of a learning experience abroad. Nevertheless, both qualitative and quantitative studies highlight the relevance of learners' ability to use the second language with people outside their study group as a mediator of students' developing perceptions during their academic sojourn.

Research Questions

The present study is based on a group of Spanish students who spent one or part of one academic year as Erasmus students in the UK. Earlier research on these students after one semester (Llanes et al., 2011) showed that their expectations of future achievement in English as well as some of their orientations to the learning of English were related to their linguistic gains. Also, students' perceptions of progress in English were found to be related to language development. Research on the students who stayed for two semesters (Serrano et al., 2012) showed that some of their beliefs towards English people and the English language could partially explain linguistic gains in some areas.

Unlike these two studies that examined the effect of individual differences on language learning, the present study focuses on the changes in learners' perceptions during an extended intensive experience abroad. For students coming from a country like Spain, where exposure to English outside the classroom is limited (Muñoz, 2000), and language teaching at primary and secondary school is characterized by a 'drip-feed' approach (Spada & Lightbown, 1989), the Erasmus program offers considerable potential for the development of students' linguistic abilities as well as language-related attitudes and motivations. In particular, the following questions are examined in this piece of research:

(1) Do students' beliefs about the English language and themselves as language learners change during their study-abroad experience?
(2) Do students' attitudes towards English people and orientations towards learning English change as a result of an academic stay?
(3) What linguistic and non-linguistic development do students perceive as a result of their Erasmus experience?

Method

Participants

A total of 24 students ranging in age from 19 to 24 participated in the present investigation (seven males and 17 females). Participants were all Spanish undergraduates, learners of English as an L2, who were studying at the same British university in the southwest of England as part of the Erasmus program (the most popular mobility program for studying abroad in Europe). This university was chosen because it was ideal in the sense that it traditionally hosts quite a large number of Spanish Erasmus students and has a well-structured Erasmus program.

All students had studied English for at least 13 years as part of the school curriculum at the time this study was carried out. Ten of them had taken extra English lessons outside school for several years; six of them had received some extra English lessons for less than three years; and eight had never taken extra lessons. Out of the students who held a degree in English, this was at the A2/B1 levels (according to the *Common European Framework of Reference for Languages*, 2001) for two students and at the B2/C1 levels for nine students. The remaining 13 students had no degree in English. Out of the 24 students, 10 of them had been to the UK previously on a stay of more than two weeks.

Nine of the participants were studying English philology, six were pursuing a degree in translation, three were studying other arts degrees (i.e. history) and six were pursuing degrees in the sciences (i.e. mathematics and engineering). Except for four students who were writing a research project as part of their undergraduate degree, most of them attended classes for 8–14 hours a week, with some students ($n = 18$) attending an English language course (2–3 hours/week). Regarding accommodation, 14 students lived in apartments with other undergraduates, five in residence halls and five other students with a host family. Out of the 24 students, 10 of them stayed for one semester (Semester 1) and the other 14 for the two semesters (Semesters 1 and 2). Five of the students staying for a semester were studying in the UK out of a requirement from their home university.

Instrument and analysis

The questionnaire included six items related to attitudes towards English people and three items related to students' beliefs about the English language. Semantic differential five-level scales were used for the nine items. The questionnaire also included two items about students' beliefs about themselves as language learners and 11 items covering different reasons for wanting to learn English (hereafter referred to as *orientations*). All of these items were based on a six-point Likert-type scale. The beliefs scale ranged from *I strongly agree* to *I strongly disagree* and the orientation scale ranged from *very important* to *definitely not important*. Self-perceptions of linguistic development were also elicited with a six-point Likert-type scale ranging from *very much* to *hardly any* prompted by the question: 'To what extent do you think you have made any progress in your English proficiency?' Students were asked to respond to this question in reference to different skills and language areas. In addition, students were asked to rate their level of overall satisfaction (from 1 to 10) with their Erasmus experience and explain.

Students' language learning history and different aspects of their stay abroad such as language contact were also elicited in order to be able to provide the necessary background for this investigation. Because questionnaires were administered by the researcher at the host university to students individually or in pairs, there was also an opportunity to chat informally with them and record the relevant exchanges as fieldnotes. A research log was also used to record significant exchanges with the Erasmus coordinator and one faculty teacher at the School of Humanities, where most of the participants were studying.

Questionnaire data was processed with the Statistical Package for the Social Sciences (SPSS) and analyses included non-parametric tests for two related samples (Wilcoxon test).

Procedure

Data were elicited in writing with a self-reported questionnaire in the students' first language. All students filled in a questionnaire at the beginning of their stay in September (Time 1, hereafter referred to as T1) and towards the end of Semester 1 in December (Time 2, hereafter referred to as T2).

Questionnaires at T1 and T2 are reproduced in Appendices 1 and 2 respectively. Students who were staying over for Semester 2 ($n = 14$) completed a questionnaire a third time (see Appendix 3) towards the end of Semester 2 in May (Time 3, hereafter referred to as T3). At each data collection time, samples of students' oral and written production were also elicited but are not part of the present study.

Results

This section starts with some information about students' lives during their stay at the British university. This information will provide the necessary context to understand the sections that follow on students' beliefs, attitudes and perceptions, in answer to the three research questions of the study.

Students' lives during SA

This section first presents information about students' motivations for participating in the Erasmus program and then reports students' social contact and free time activities.

At the start of their stay (T1), students' motivations to participate in the Erasmus program were multiple. For all of them ($n = 24$) improving their level of English was *important* or *very important* and for a majority of them personal (*'Personal development'*, *'To enjoy and have fun'*, *'To travel'*) and cultural motives (*'To meet people from other countries'*, *'To get to know a different country'*, *'To meet English people'*) were also a priority.

Contact with compatriots and other foreign students was more common than with native English speakers, both in Semesters 1 and 2. At T2 ($n = 24$), when students were asked to list up to five people that they had the most contact with (irrespective of context), figures show that on average 42.6% of their contacts were with compatriots, 34.1% with international students and 23.3% with native-English speakers. For 17 out of these 24 students, contact with compatriots was strengthened by the fact that they had a close friend with whom they interacted most of the time. When students were asked to list up to four people they had most contact with while at the university at T3, eight out of 14 did not make any reference to native speakers of English. A member of the faculty commented on the fact that British students in general tended not to be too active in seeking contact with international students, an impression that was also related by a few students. Also, the fact that students in the Humanities had a restricted number of courses from which to choose resulted in Spanish students enrolling in the same courses and, therefore, meeting regularly in class.

In addition, all students had regular contact via information and communications technology with their family and friends back home. The amount of time spent on these contacts varied from student to student. While seven students spent on average less than 30 minutes per day, the rest spent more than that (11 students spent from 30 minutes to one hour and the remaining six more than one hour), with a tendency to spend more time in Semester 2.

Three items in the questionnaire addressed students' free-time activities, one related to reading, another related to extramural activities and a third related to vacation periods. Students' responses show that exposure to written English in their free time was limited. As regards reading novels, there were two students (out of 24) who had read two or more books during Semester 1. In Semester 2, there were also two students (out of 14) who had also read two or more books. In both semesters there were some students who had not read any book for pleasure (10 out of 24 at T2 and 8 out of 14 at T3). As regards newspaper reading in English (either online or in print), most students did not have this habit during their stay. At T2 there were three students (out of 24) who reported reading newspapers three or more days a week. At T3 there was only one student (out of 14) who reported this habit.

Most students did not participate in any scheduled activity outside the university. In Semester 1 there were 14 students (out of 24) who reported no extramural activity and, except for one student who sporadically worked as a part-time waiter, the other students practiced individual sports (i.e. jogging, gym), which entailed little social contact. The picture in Semester 2 is similar, with only three students (out of 14) carrying out some type of regular group or social activity (i.e. playing tennis).

Students had two vacation periods (Christmas and Spring) of 6 weeks total. These school breaks allowed Erasmus students to spend considerable time outside the UK during their academic year abroad. In the case of the 14 students in the study who stayed for two semesters, they had spent a mean of 5.4 weeks outside the UK by the beginning of May.

In sum, these students' experiences abroad were mainly centered around university life with limited exposure to written English and little social contact outside the university environment. For a majority of students, their daily lives were marked by limited contact with native speakers of English, even though learning English during their stay abroad was a priority for all students.

Beliefs about the English language and themselves

Students' beliefs about the English language were elicited at three points in time (T1, T2 and T3). These included three bipolar adjectives: *simple/complex, beautiful/ugly, pleasant/not pleasant sounding*. Students' perceptions about themselves as language learners were also elicited at T1, T2 and T3, and they made reference to self-efficacy beliefs, more specifically to general

L2 aptitude (*I am good at English*) and expected future achievement (*I will never know enough to be able to understand original version movies*).

Results concerning the English language show a tendency for both one- and two-semester students to think of the L2 as more pleasant sounding as time goes by. This tendency is almost significant when comparing answers between T1 and T2 ($n = 24$, $Z = -1.9$, significance $= 0.06$). Table 8.1 includes students' answers to this question in frequencies and percentages. Results also show a tendency in students who stayed for two semesters to view English as a more beautiful language by T3. This tendency was also close to being significant ($n = 14$, $Z = -1.89$, significance $= 0.06$), as shown in Table 8.2. Appendix 4 (Tables 8.6 and 8.7) reproduces students' answers more thoroughly.

In contrast, students' perception of general L2 aptitude remained stable between T1 and T2 and between T1 and T3. While there was a tendency for beliefs about expected future achievement to obtain a higher value at T2 than at T1 ($n = 24$, $Z = -1.83$, significance $= 0.07$), this was not confirmed in comparing T1 and T3. Appendix 4 (Tables 8.8 and 8.9) reproduces students' answers to these two items. However, the only students whose ratings of expected future achievement in listening were lower at T2 and T3 than at T1 were among those with high percentages of contact with Spanish speakers (ranging from 60 to 73%). They were also among the students who reported doing almost everything with a close Spanish friend.

Table 8.1 Students' answers to: *The English language sounds pleasant/unpleasant* ($n=24$)

	Not pleasant sounding			Pleasant sounding	
	1	2	3	4	5
Time 1	0	3 (12.5)	7 (29.2)	6 (25)	8 (33.3)
Time 2	0	0	8 (33.3)	7 (29.2)	9 (37.5)

Percentages are reported in parentheses

Table 8.2 Students' answers to: *The English language is beautiful/ugly* ($n=14$)

	Ugly				Beautiful
	1	2	3	4	5
Time 1	0	0	6 (42.9)	4 (28.6)	4 (28.6)
Time 3	0	0	3 (21.4)	5 (35.7)	6 (42.9)

Percentages are reported in parentheses

Attitudes towards English people and language learning orientations

Attitudes towards English people were elicited three times (T1, T2 and T3) and included the following six bipolar traits: *sociable/reserved, friendly/unfriendly, open/narrow minded, humble/snobby, honest/false* and *reliable/unreliable*. Orientations to learn English were elicited twice (T1 and T3) from students who stayed for the two semesters. Items covered a variety of reasons for wanting to learn English, ranging from those related to L2 comprehension (*To read books, To understand movies*), to interpersonal motives (*To meet people from other countries, To meet English people*), cultural reasons (*To know more about other countries, To know more about England, To learn about Anglo-Saxon culture*) and various pragmatic reasons (*To travel, For pleasure, To have better job prospects*).

Regarding attitudes towards English people, students' responses tended to be quite neutral and comparisons from T1 to T2 and T1 to T3 yielded no significant differences. These results show that there was no clear group trend in the data, with some students' attitudes remaining stable while others showed a change towards more positive or negative attitudes over time. Appendix 4 (Tables 8.10 and 8.11) reproduces students' answers to these items. Similarly, regarding students' orientations, there was no clear group trend in students' responses in 10 out of the 11 orientations under analysis between T1 and T3, although responses to most items showed a high level of motivation on the part of the students. It was only in the item related to wanting to learn English *To know more about England* (see Table 8.3) where students reported significantly lower levels of interest at T3 than at T1 ($n = 14$, $Z = -1.99$, significance $= 0.046$). There was also a ceiling effect in the answers to two items related to instrumental motivation (*Because it's useful for my degree; To have better job prospects*). Table 8.12 (in Appendix 4) reports students' answers to the 11 items.

Perceptions of linguistic and non-linguistic development

Students' perceptions of linguistic gains in English were elicited towards the end of Semester 1 (T2) and made reference to four skills (reading, speaking, listening and writing) and four linguistic areas (vocabulary, grammar,

Table 8.3 Students' orientation: *To know more about England* ($n=14$)

	Definitely not important	Not important	Not very important	Somewhat important	Important	Very important
Time 1	—	1 (7.1)	1 (7.1)	2 (14.3)	5 (35.7)	5 (35.7)
Time 3	—	—	5 (35.7)	6 (42.9)	2 (14.3)	1 (7.1)

Percentages are reported in parentheses

pronunciation and accent). Students' level of satisfaction with their overall Erasmus experience was also elicited with two open questions about their academic and personal experience abroad.

When students were asked about how much English they thought they had learned (linguistic gains), their answers were mostly positive regarding listening, speaking, reading, vocabulary and pronunciation, and moderately positive for writing, grammar and accent. See Table 8.4 for students' answers to linguistics aspects and Table 8.5 for students' answers to the four skills. The four students who reported highest progress in oral skills (a variable that was created by aggregating the values in speaking, listening, pronunciation and accent) had low percentages of contact with Spanish speakers (ranging from 0 to 27%).

When students were asked about their level of satisfaction with their overall experience abroad, their responses were highly positive. From an academic point of view, students on average rated their experience with a 7.8 (on a 10-point scale). Their most recurrent comments (a total of 14) made reference to their English and the chances they had to practice the language (linguistic development). One student commented on the fact that she was now more aware of her real level of English (student 15, T2). Except for one student, the other 13 were mainly satisfied with the progress they noticed. Here are the comments from three articulate students:

> I have learned to use a lot of the grammar that I had learned but did not really use. I am now more at ease when speaking in English. I understand

Table 8.4 Students' self-ratings of linguistic progress at T2 ($n=24$)

	Hardly any	Little	Some	Considerable	Much	Very much
Vocabulary	—	—	6 (25)	12 (50)	4 (16.7)	2 (8.3)
Grammar	—	11 (45.8)	4 (16.7)	7 (29.2)	2 (8.3)	—
Pronunciation	—	1 (4.2)	11 (45.8)	6 (25)	6 (25)	—
Accent	2 (8.3)	5 (20.8)	5 (20.8)	9 (37.5)	2 (8.3)	1 (4.2)

Percentages are reported in parentheses

Table 8.5 Students' self-ratings of progress in the four skills at T2 ($n=24$)

	Hardly any	Little	Some	Considerable	Much	Very much
Listening	—	—	5 (20.8)	6 (25)	13 (54.2)	—
Speaking	—	1 (4.2)	3 (12.5)	13 (54.2)	7 (29.2)	—
Reading	—	1 (4.2)	8 (33.3)	11 (45.8)	3 (12.5)	1 (4.2)
Writing	—	5 (20.8)	8 (33.3)	8 (33.3)	3 (12.5)	—

Percentages are reported in parentheses

> much more but I still need to become more fluent and improve my knowledge with native speakers. (Student 3, T2)

> I am now less shy when I speak in English. Because I have become friends with English people, I have been able to learn many linguistic aspects that are not learned in English lessons. (Student 12, T2)

> I think my oral English has improved and also my understanding and writing. I have improved in fluency and with the papers, (I have also improved) my expression in writing. (Student 11, T2)

Several students ($n = 9$) also mentioned aspects in teaching approach or course contents at the host university. Five of these comments were positive (e.g. 'Teachers pay more attention to students and they value your work during the semester, not only the exam') and four were negative (e.g. 'There are no exams, so you can forget what you learn in class').

In response to the open question about personal experience, students gave an average rating of 8.9 (on a 10-point scale). Their most recurrent comments referenced the people they had met (interpersonal development, 14 comments), the experience of learning to live independently (intrapersonal development, 11 comments) and the experience of learning about a different culture (intercultural development, 13 comments). As regards interpersonal development, all comments were positive and students tended to mention the large number of people they had met, often referring to the fact that they were from different nationalities, and/or the fact of having made friends ('I have made some friends I would not like to lose' (Student 8, T2), 'I came alone and go back with friends and knowledge' (Student 1, T2)). With regard to intrapersonal development, all students' comments were positive and they mentioned learning to live independently (i.e. managing a house, money, time) and solve problems on their own, and becoming more mature persons. The following are comments from two students:

> You learn to rely on yourself in a foreign country, to know about your own limits and capabilities and also your real level of English. (Student 15, T2)

> I am much more independent now and I have learned to carry out tasks that are completely necessary in everyday life. (Student 16, T2)

Finally and regarding intercultural development, most comments (10 out of 13) were positive and they tended to reference gaining knowledge about another country, a different living style and a new culture or a diversity of cultures. A few students also commented on the fact that they felt integrated or well-adapted in the new environment or that they felt they had become more open-minded.

Discussion

The present study had the objective of identifying changes in Spanish students' perceptions over several aspects related to their academic stay at a British university. Data were collected through questionnaires that were administered before and after one and two semesters. The questionnaires included three types of questions: (1) closed questions for the researchers to later compare students' answers; (2) closed questions where students were themselves asked to rate their level of change towards the end of a semester; and (3) open questions where students were asked to evaluate and discuss their experience.

Most of the items in the questionnaires belonged to type 1 questions and dealt with students' beliefs about the English language, self-efficacy beliefs, attitudes towards English people and orientations to learning English (research questions 1 and 2). Comparison of students' answers across different data collection times failed to capture statistically significant patterns of change in most of the aspects analyzed, with only a tendency for students to become fonder of the English language and more optimistic about expected future achievement in listening. A significant difference was also found showing less interest in knowing about England. The fact that more convergent results between this and the study of Amuzie and Winke regarding self-efficacy beliefs were not obtained might be explained by considerable differences in the mean lengths of stay of the two studies. Also, these results can be partly affected by methodological aspects of the study, like the small sample size or the levels of the semantic differential and Likert scales employed. Our scales included between five and six levels and are narrower than those employed in other studies like Amuzie and Winke (2009), who used 10 levels. Also, features of the SA program under analysis, like the few hours of instruction per week and the difficulty of access to native speakers (both in class and at home), probably contributed to the stability of answers that were obtained over time. The ease of contact with compatriots both at the university and back home (through ICT and during vacation periods) may have had a similar effect. How these social factors can impede linguistic and self-development as well as cultural adaptation has been thoroughly documented in the literature, especially through case studies (Dörnyei *et al.*, 2004; Isabelli-García, 2006; Kinginger, 2008; Yang & Kim, 2011). Finally, the fact that this study, unlike most of the reviewed investigations, involved European students studying in a different European country with less need for sociocultural adaptation than if they had moved to a different continent might also help explain the lack of changes in students' perceptions.

Type 2 and 3 questions yielded richer information about changes in students' perceptions of linguistic and non-linguistic development (research question 3). When asked to rate their level of linguistic progress, an overwhelming majority of students reported having noticed from 'some' to 'much' change as regards their productive (speaking, pronunciation) and receptive skills (listening and reading) as well as vocabulary development. Students felt less satisfied with their progress in grammar, writing and accent. These students' differentiated perceptions for different areas of language are in line with the literature that suggests that SA does not affect all aspects of a learner's competence in the same way, with less development in grammatical than in oral abilities like fluency in one-semester to one-year stays (for a review see Collentine, 2009). The effects of SA on writing skills have yielded less clear results with a few studies finding some gains (Pérez-Vidal & Juan-Garau, 2009; Sasaki, 2007), and others failing to find any significant progress (i.e. Freed *et al.*, 2003).

When asked to evaluate their academic experience in general, 14 out of the 24 students mentioned the English they had learned or used during their stay abroad and not what they had learned in their fields of study. This should not come as a surprise since for these students learning English was rated very high in their initial motivations to participate in the Erasmus program, the same as in Teichler's report (2004) on Erasmus students. In addition, in the present study students' evaluation of their personal experience was rated higher than their academic experience. Students in similar proportions referred to gains in interpersonal and intercultural development but also to intrapersonal development. The fact that Spain is one of the European countries where young adults tend to stay longer with their parents may explain students' perceptions of intrapersonal growth when away from their family.

According to Pellegrino (2005), interpersonal growth progressively leads to the learners' development of the self, the establishment of higher degrees of personal security and a sense of identity in social interactions. The qualities of SA in terms of both the intensity and duration of the experience offer great potential for this type of development. However, the intensity of the experience may vary widely among individual students in the same program and across SA programs and seems to be a central mediator of students' self-development.

Conclusions

The present study set out to identify changes in Spanish students' perceptions as a result of a study-abroad experience in the UK over the course of one and two semesters. Results show that students are able to perceive some type of linguistic development by the end of Semester 1, mainly associated with oral production and receptive skills. There is also evidence in the data of students' interpersonal, intrapersonal and intercultural development over time. A tendency for more positive beliefs about the English language and expected future achievement has also been identified as well as a significant loss of interest in wanting to learn English to learn more about England by the end of Semester 2. No other group trend was found to be significant regarding attitudes towards English people or other language learning orientations and self-efficacy beliefs. This could partially be explained by methodological aspects of this study as well as some of the features of the program and the type of life students led during their sojourn, with little contact outside the university environment.

Acknowlegments

This research was supported by grants FFI2010-18006 (Ministry of Science and Innovation, Spain), and 2006BE-200339 and SGR 137 (Generalitat de Catalunya).

References

Adams, R. (2006) Language learning strategies in the study abroad context. In M. Dufon and E. Churchill (eds) *Language Learners in Study Abroad Contexts* (pp. 259–293). Clevedon: Multilingual Matters.
Aguilar Stewart, J. (2010) Using e-journals to assess students' language awareness and social identity during study abroad. *Foreign Language Annals* 43 (1), 138–159.
Allen, H.W. (2010) Language-learning motivation during short-term study abroad: An activity theory perspective. *Foreign Language Annals* 43 (1), 27–49.
Amuzie, G. and Winke, P. (2009) Changes in language learning beliefs as a result of study abroad. *System* 37, 366–379.
Churchill, E. and DuFon, M. (2006) Evolving threats in study abroad research. In M. Dufon and E. Churchill (eds) *Language Learners in Study Abroad Contexts* (pp. 1–30). Clevedon: Multilingual Matters.
Collentine, J. (2009) Study abroad research: Findings, implications and future directions. In M.H. Long and C.J. Doughty (eds) *The Handbook of Language Teaching* (pp. 218–233). Chichester: Wiley-Blackwell.
Common European Framework of Reference for Languages (2001) Cambridge: Cambridge University Press.
Dörnyei, Z., Durow, V. and Zahran, K. (2004) Individual differences and their effects on formulaic sequence acquisition In N. Schmitt (ed.) *Formulaic Sequences* (pp. 87–106). Amsterdam: Benjamins.
Dwyer, M. (2004) More if better: The impact of study abroad program duration. *Frontiers* 10, 151–163.
Freed, B.F., So, S. and Lazar, N.A. (2003) Language learning abroad: How do gains in written fluency compare with oral fluency in French as a second language? *ADFL Bulletin* 34 (3), 34–40.
Freed, B.F., Dewey, D., Segalowitz, N. and Halter, R. (2004) The language contact profile. *Studies in Second Language Acquisition* 26, 349–356.
Gao, X. (2006) Understanding changes in Chinese students' uses of learning strategies in China and Britain: A socio-cultural re-interpretation. *System* 34, 55–67.
Hernández, T.A. (2010) The relationship among motivation, interaction, and the development of second language oral proficiency in a study-abroad context. *The Modern Language Journal* 94 (4), 600–617.
Isabelli-García, C. (2006) Study abroad social networks, motivation and attitudes: Implications for second language acquisition. In M. Dufont and E. Churchill (eds)

Language Learner in Study Abroad Contexts (pp. 232–258). Clevedon: Multilingual Matters.

Jackson, J. (2006) Ethnographic pedagogy and evaluation in short-term study abroad. In M. Byram and A. Feng (eds) *Living and Studying Abroad. Research and Practice* (pp. 134–156). Clevedon: Multilingual Matters.

Jackson, J. (2008) *Language, Identity and Study Abroad: Sociocultural Perspectives*. London: Equinox.

Juan-Garau, M. and Pérez-Vidal, C. (2007). The effect of context and contact on oral performance in students who go on a stay abroad. *Vigo International Journal of Applied Linguistics* 4, 117–134.

Kinginger, C. (2008) Language learning in study abroad: Case studies of Americans in France. [Monograph.] *Modern Language Journal* 92, 1–131.

Kinginger, C. (2009) *Language Learning and Study Abroad: A Critical Reading of Research*. Basingstoke: Palgrave Macmillan.

Llanes, À., Tragant, E. and Serrano, R. (2011) The role of individual differences in a study abroad experience: The case of Erasmus students. *International Journal of Multilingualism* (doi: 10.1080/14790718.2011.620614).

Muñoz, C. (2000) Bilingualism and trilingualism in school students in Catalonia. In M. Cenoz and U. Jessner (eds) *English in Europe: The Acquisition of a Third Language* (pp. 157–178). Clevedon: Multilingual Matters.

Murphy-Lejeune, E. (2002) *Student Mobility and Narrative in Europe*. London: Routledge.

Oxford, R. (1990) *Language Learning Strategies: What Every Teacher Should Know*. New York: Newbury House.

Pellegrino, V. (2005) *Study Abroad and Second Language Use. Constructing the Self*. Cambridge: Cambridge University Press.

Pérez-Vidal, C. and Juan-Garau, M. (2009) The effect of study abroad on written performance. *EUROSLA Yearbook* 9 (1), 269–295.

Sasaki, M. (2007) Effects of study-abroad experiences on EFL writers: A multiple-data analysis. *Modern Language Journal* 91 (iv), 602–620.

Serrano, R., Tragant, E. and Llanes, À. (2012) A longitudinal analysis of the effects of one year abroad. *The Canadian Modern Language Review/La Revue canadienne des langues vivantes* 68 (2), 138–163.

Spada, N. and Lightbown, P.M. (1989) Intensive ESL programs in Québec primary schools. *TESL Canadian Journal* 7 (1), 11–32.

Tanaka, K. and Ellis, R. (2003) Study-abroad, language proficiency, and learner beliefs about language learning. *JALT Journal* 25 (19), 63–85.

Teichler, U. (2004) Temporary study abroad: the life of ERASMUS students. *European Journal of Education* 39 (4), 395–408.

Yager, K. (1998) Learning Spanish in Mexico: The effect of informal contact and student attitudes on language gains. *Hispania* 81 (4), 898–913.

Yang, J. and Kim, T. (2011) Sociocultural analysis of second language learner beliefs: A qualitative case study of two study-abroad ESL learners. *System* 39, 324–334.

Appendix 1: Questionnaire at T1

Name and surnames .... Age ....
Major (in Spain) ....
Language(s) spoken at home ....
What study period are you in right now?
- Undergraduate (fist cycle) - Undergradute (second cycle)
- Undergraduate (final project) - Master's degree - PhD studies - Other: ....

Evaluate your level of English according to the following scale: (1) elementary, (2) low intermediate, (3) intermediate, (4) upper intermediate, (5) advanced

listening	speaking	reading	writing

Write a brief account of how you have learned English up to now (age of start, trips, language schools, etc.).

When did you last take an English class? Where was it? Specify start and end dates.

Do you hold any degrees in English? If so, specify which.

Date of arrival at the universty in England ....
Approximate date of final departure ....
Contact phone during your stay ....
E-mail during your stay ....

In general, what is your opinion about English people?

sociable	___ ___ ___ ___ ___	reserved
friendly	___ ___ ___ ___ ___	unfriendly
open minded	___ ___ ___ ___ ___	narrow minded
humble	___ ___ ___ ___ ___	snobby
honest	___ ___ ___ ___ ___	false
reliable	___ ___ ___ ___ ___	unreliable

And about the English language?

simple	___ ___ ___ ___ ___	complex
beautiful	___ ___ ___ ___ ___	ugly
pleasant sounding	___ ___ ___ ___ ___	no pleasant sounding

Next you will find some opinions about the learning of English. Choose the option that best approximates your position. Choose one and make a cross.
(FD = I strongly disagree; D= I disagree; PA= I hardly agree; MA= I moderately agree; A= I agree; FA= I strongly agree)

	SD	D	HA	MA	A	SA
I like studying English.						
One day I would like to be able speak English with native-speaker fluency.						
In general I find English lessons boring.						
I really want to learn English.						
In general, I am good at English.						
I think I will never know enough to be able to understand original version movies.						

What motivated you to participate in the Erasmus program? Note down how important (1-6) the followings reasons are for you.
(1= definitely not important, 2 = not important, 3 = not very important, 4 = a little important, 5 = important, 6 = very important)

	1	2	3	4	5	6
To improve my level of English						
Personal development						
To have a good academic experience						
To meet people from other countries						
To get to know a different coutnr.y						
To trave.l						
To enjoy and have fun.						
To have a better cv.						
To meet English people.						
To get to know Englan.d						
To be able to study my major in a foreign institution.						
Other:						

Why are you interested in becoming proficient in English?

(1= definitely not important, 2 = not important, 3 = not very important, 4 = a little important, 5 = important, 6 = very important)

	1	2	3	4	5	6
To understand TV, movies, etc. without difficulty.						
Because it's useful for my degree.						
To meet English people.						
To read books, journals, etc. for my degree.						
To meet people from other countries.						
To travel.						
For pleasure.						
To have better job prospects.						
To learn about Anglo-Saxon culture.						
To know more about other countries.						
To know more about England.						
Other:						

Appendix 2: Questionnaire at T2

Name and surnames ....

What courses are you currently enrolled in?

How many hours a week do you have class?

So far, approximately how many times have you met with your teacher(s)/tutor?

Are you enrolled in any English class? If so, write down the course title, weekly hours of tuition and your level of attendance.

Do you do any activity outside your classes at the university (sports, theatre, etc.)? If so, what?

Where are you staying?
- Single room in residence hall
- Shared room in residence hall
- Flat shared with other students
- Rented room in private home

How would you qualify your academic experience in England so far?
Write a number from 1 to 10 according to this scale: 1 = extremely negative, 10 = extremely positive. ☐

Why?

How would you qualify your personal experience in England so far?
Write a number from 1 to 10 according to this scale: 1 = extremely negative, 10 = extremely positive. ☐

Why?

To what extent do you think you have made any progress in your English proficiency? Fill in the following boxes according to this scale:
(1) hardly any (2) little (3) some (4) considerable (5) much (6) very much

listening	speaking	reading	writing	vocabulary	grammar	pronounciation	accent

In general, what is your opinion about English people?

sociable	___ ___ ___ ___ ___	reserved
friendly	___ ___ ___ ___ ___	unfriendly
open minded	___ ___ ___ ___ ___	narrow minded

humble   ___ ___ ___ ___ ___   snobby
honest   ___ ___ ___ ___ ___   false
reliable ___ ___ ___ ___ ___   unreliable

And about the English language?
simple   ___ ___ ___ ___ ___   complex
beautiful   ___ ___ ___ ___ ___   ugly
pleasant sounding ___ ___ ___ ___ ___   no pleasant sounding

Read the following statements and qualify them from 1–10 as they reflect your attitude (1= I strongly disagree; 10 = I strongly agree).
  I like studying English. ☐
  One day I would like to be able speak English with native-speaker fluency. ☐
  I really want to learn English. ☐

Cross the option that best reflects your opinion:
(FD = I strongly disagree; D= I disagree; HA= I hardly agree; MA= I moderately agree; A= I agree; FA= I strongly agree)

	SD	D	HA	MA	A	SA
In general, I am good at English.						
I think I will never know enough to be able to understand original version movies.						

Indicate the five people with which you have had more contact with so far (at home, at the university or during weekends).

Relationship (classmate, friends, flatmate, etc.)	How much contact have you had? A little/ some/much	Nationality	Most common language of communication

From these five people, is there anyone with which you have done everything or almost everything with together? If so, draw a cross in the appropriate box in the table above.

About how many movies have you watched during your stay in England so far?

Have you read or are you reading any novel in English so far? Yes/No.

If so, how many?

How often do you usually read a newspaper in English (in print or online)?
- ☐ Everyday or almost everyday
- ☐ Between three and five days a week
- ☐ One or two days a week
- ☐ Hardly ever or never

On average, how much time a week do you spend watching TV?...................

Do you follow some TV series? Yes/No How many? ....

On average how much time do you estimate you have spent on virtual communication in your mother tongue with friends and/or family (e-mail, telephone, Skype, etc.)?...........................

Appendix 3: Questionnaire at T3

Name and surnames ....

How old were you when you started learning English? ....

About how many days have you been outside the UK from the time when you arrived at the university in September?

In general, what is your opinion about English people?

sociable	_____ _____ _____ _____ _____	reserved
friendly	_____ _____ _____ _____ _____	unfriendly
open minded	_____ _____ _____ _____ _____	narrow minded
humble	_____ _____ _____ _____ _____	snobby
honest	_____ _____ _____ _____ _____	false
reliable	_____ _____ _____ _____ _____	unreliable

And about the English language?

simple	_____ _____ _____ _____ _____	complex
beautiful	_____ _____ _____ _____ _____	ugly
pleasant sounding	_____ _____ _____ _____ _____	no pleasant sounding

Cross the option that best reflects your opinion:
(FD = I strongly disagree; D= I disagree; HA= I hardly agree; MA= I moderately agree; A= I agree; FA= I strongly agree)

	SD	D	HA	MA	A	SA
In general, I am good at English.						
I think I will never know enough to be able to understand original version movies.						

At the moment, why are you interested in becoming proficient in English?
(1= definitely not important, 2 = not important, 3 = not very important, 4 = a little important, 5 = important, 6 = very important)

	1	2	3	4	5	6
To understand TV, movies, etc. without difficulty.						
Because it's useful for my degree.						
To meet English people.						
To read books, journals, etc. for my degree.						
To meet people from other countries.						

To travel.					
For pleasure.					
To have better job prospects.					
To learn about Anglo-Saxon culture.					
To know more about other countries.					
To know more about England.					
Other:					

About how many movies have you watched (at home or at the cinema) during your stay in England since January?

Have you read or are you reading any novel in English since January? Yes/No.

If so, how many?

How often do you usually read a newspaper in English (in print or online)?

- ☐ Everyday or almost everyday
- ☐ Between three and five days a week
- ☐ One or two days a week
- ☐ Hardly ever or never

On average, how much time a week do you spend watching TV............................

Do you follow some TV series? Yes/No How many? ....

On average how much time do you estimate you have spent on virtual communication in your mother tongue with friends and/or family (e-mail, telephone, Skype, etc.)?

What courses are you currently enrolled in this semester?

How many hours a week do you have class? (excluding English lessons)

Since January, approximately how many times have you met with your teacher(s)/tutor?

Are you enrolled in any English class? If so, write down the course title, weekly hours of tuition and your level of attendance.

Do you do any activity outside your classes at the university (sports, theatre, etc.)? If so, what?

Where are you living this semester?

- Residence hall
- Student flat
- Host family

Indicate the following information about a maximum of 4 people with which you have more contact with when you are *'at home'*.

NAME	How much contact have you had: a little/some/much	Nationality	Language of communication

Indicate the following information about a maximum of 4 people with which you have more contact with when you are *'at the university'* (and *'at work'* if you are working)

NAME	Contact: a little/some/much	Nationality	Language of communication

Indicate the following information about a maximum of 4 people with which you have more contact *'during weekends'*.

NAME	Contact: a little/some/much	Nationality	Language of communication

Appendix 4

Table 8.6 Beliefs about the English language T1–T2 ($n = 24$)

		Answers to differential scales					T1–T2 compared		
		1 (–)	2	3	4	5 (+)	Lower value at T2	Same value	Higher value at T2
(–) Complex/	T1	0	3	7	12	2	6	10	8
(+) simple	T2	0	3	7	11	3			
(–) Ugly/	T1	0	0	10	8	6	2	19	3
(+) beautiful	T2	0	0	10	7	7			
(–) Not pleasant/	T1	0	3	7	6	8	2	13	9
(+) pleasant sounding	T2	0	0	8	7	9			

Table 8.7 Beliefs about the English language T1–T3 ($n = 14$)

		Answers to differential scales					T1–T3 compared		
		1 (–)	2	3	4	5 (+)	Lower value at T3	Same value	Higher value at T3
(–) Complex/	T1	0	1	4	7	2	4	9	1
(+) simple	T3	0	3	3	7	1			
(–) Ugly/	T1	0	0	6	4	4	0	10	4
(+) beautiful	T3	0	0	3	5	6			
(–) Not pleasant/	T1	0	2	4	2	6	1	10	3
(+) pleasant sounding	T3	0	0	4	3	7			

Table 8.8 Self-efficacy beliefs T1–T2 ($n = 24$)

		Answers to Likert scales						T1–T2 compared		
		1 (–)	2	3	4	5	6 (+)	Lower value at T2	Same value	Higher value at T2
I am good at English	T1	0	3	0	10	9	2	2	18	4
	T2	0	0	1	12	8	3			
I will never know enough to understand movies*	T1	1	0	1	6	9	7	3	10	11
	T2	0	1	0	2	11	10			

*reversed values

Table 8.9 Self-efficacy beliefs T1–T3 (n = 14)

		Answers to Likert scales						T1-T3 compared		
		1 (−)	2	3	4	5	6 (+)	Lower value at T3	Same value	Higher value at T3
I am good at English	T1	0	2	0	5	5	3	2	8	4
	T3	0	0	2	5	2	5			
I will never know enough to understand movies*	T1	0	0	1	3	5	5	3	7	4
	T3	0	0	0	3	7	4			

*reversed values

Table 8.10 Attitudes towards English people T1–T2 (n = 24)

		Answers to differential scales					T1-T2 compared		
		1 (−)	2	3	4	5 (+)	Lower value at T2	Same value	Higher value at T2
(−) Reserved/ (+) sociable	T1	1	10	8	3	2	6	10	8
	T2	3	5	9	4	3			
(−) Unfriendly/ (+) friendly	T1	0	2	13	4	5	5	12	7
	T2	0	1	10	10	3			
(−) Narrow/ (+) open minded	T1	0	7	10	6	1	5	11	8
	T2	1	5	10	6	2			
(−) Humble/ (+)snobby	T1	1	2	15	6	0	7	11	6
	T2	0	6	12	5	1			
(−) Honest/ (+) false	T1	0	3	13	6	2	6	14	4
	T2	0	5	11	6	2			
(−) Unreliable/ (+) reliable	T1	0	2	6	8	8	4	15	5
	T2	0	0	8	8	8			

Table 8.11 Attitudes towards English people T1–T3 (*n* = 14)

		\multicolumn{5}{c}{Answers to differential scales}	\multicolumn{3}{c}{T1–T3 compared}
		1 (−)	2	3	4	5 (+)	Lower value at T3	Same value	Higher value at T3
(−) Reserved/	T1	1	5	4	3	1	4	5	5
(+) sociable	T3	3	2	2	7	0			
(−) Unfriendly/	T1	0	0	8	3	3	5	4	5
(+) friendly	T3	0	3	2	7	2			
(−) Narrow/	T1	0	4	5	4	1	5	2	7
(+) open minded	T3	1	1	3	7	2			
(−) Humble/ (+)snobby	T1	0	1	10	3	0	7	4	3
	T3	1	4	7	1	1			
(−) Honest/ (+) false	T1	0	2	6	4	2	3	9	2
	T3	1	1	6	5	1			
(−) Unreliable/	T1	0	1	3	5	5	3	8	3
(+) reliable	T3	0	0	2	8	4			

Table 8.12 Language learning orientations T1–T3 (*n* = 14)

		\multicolumn{6}{c}{Answers to Likert scales}	\multicolumn{3}{c}{T1–T3 compared}
		1 (−)	2	3	4	5	6 (+)	Lower value at T3	Same value	Higher value at T3
To understand TV, movies, etc. without difficulty.	T1	1	0	4	1	5	3	3	6	5
	T3	0	1	4	2	2	5			
Because it's useful for my degree.	T1	0	0	0	2	2	10	1	11	2
	T3	0	0	0	2	1	11			
To meet English people.	T1	0	1	2	2	6	3	6	3	5
	T3	0	1	2	5	3	3			
To read books, journals, etc. for my degree.	T1	0	0	1	2	4	7	3	7	4
	T3	0	0	0	3	5	6			
To meet people from other countries.	T1	0	0	0	3	5	6	1	8	5
	T3	0	0	0	0	7	7			
To travel.	T1	0	0	1	1	6	6	2	9	3
	T3	0	0	0	0	9	5			

For pleasure.	T1	0	0	4	2	3	5	6	2	6
	T3	0	1	3	0	7	3			
To have better job prospects.	T1	0	0	0	1	3	10	1	11	2
	T3	0	0	1	0	2	11			
To learn about Anglo-Saxon culture.	T1	0	2	2	2	3	5	7	2	5
	T3	0	1	3	1	7	2			
To know more about other countries.	T1	0	0	1	1	7	5	6	3	5
	T3	0	0	0	2	7	5			
To know more about England.	T1	0	1	1	2	5	5	10	1	3
	T3	0	0	5	6	2	1			

Part 4
Naturalistic Immersion

9 The Impact of Study Abroad and Age on Second Language Accuracy Development

Àngels Llanes

Introduction

The effects of learning context on second language (L2) development is a topic of growing interest in second language acquisition (Collentine, 2009; Freed, 1995; Llanes, 2011). Most of the research on study abroad (SA) has focused on documenting the progress of an L2 as a result of the experience abroad and has sometimes compared such development across other learning contexts such as an at-home (AH) institution or an immersion (IM) setting. These three learning contexts differ in several aspects, of which the intensity of exposure to the L2 and the opportunities participants have to practice the L2 are probably the most remarkable ones. However, most of the SA research has focused on the effects of learning context on L2 development in adult participants. To date, only one study has examined the effects of learning context on L2 development in a population other than adults, namely children (Llanes & Muñoz, forthcoming), and the results seem to indicate that children benefit from the opportunities that the SA context provides them. Additionally, most SA research has focused on documenting the effects of said learning context on the participants' oral fluency, and although several SA articles have reported the effects of learning context on L2 accuracy, most have done so by taking one or two general measures of accuracy rather than providing a more detailed analysis. The present study addresses this lacuna in the fields of SA and age.

Literature Review

Study abroad

Although several L2 domains have been investigated in relation to SA, most research has concerned oral fluency (Freed, 1995; Lennon, 1990;

Llanes & Muñoz, 2009, 2012; Segalowitz & Freed, 2004). Those studies with no control group have concluded that spending some time abroad has a positive impact on the participants' oral skills, and those comparing the SA context with another one have mostly concluded that the SA context is superior to the AH context, although not to the IM or intensive AH programs (Freed *et al.*, 2004a; Serrano *et al.*, 2011). Vocabulary growth as a result of an SA experience has also been investigated and has corroborated the efficiency of the SA context, regardless of whether research has compared the SA context with other learning settings (Dewey, 2008; Foster, 2009) or not (Ife *et al.*, 2000; Milton & Meara, 1995). Although there is little research examining the L2 development in relation to the participants' listening skills, these few studies also support the efficiency of the SA context (Cubillos *et al.*, 2008; Dyson, 1988; Llanes & Muñoz, 2009).

However, the effectiveness of the SA context on other areas, such as pronunciation, reading, writing and grammar development, is still unclear. Regarding pronunciation, Díaz-Campos (2004) and Mora (2008) showed that pronunciation patterns did not improve after spending four or three months abroad, respectively. This clear lack of superiority of the SA contexts is also attested concerning reading ability in an L2; Dewey (2004) compared the reading development of participants in an SA and an IM setting, and found that the SA participants differed from the IM participants only in that they felt more confident when reading in the L2. As for the development of the writing skills, whereas some authors claim that the SA context is conducive to the improvement of the participants' oral skills but not for their written ones (Freed *et al.*, 2003; Llanes & Muñoz, forthcoming), other investigators have found that a period abroad plays an important role in the improvement of writing skills (Pérez-Vidal & Juan-Garau, 2009; Sasaki, 2004, 2009). However, as Llanes (2011) suggests, this controversy could lie on the differences in background of the participants as well as on the differences in the type of measures used in these studies.

Controversy also dominates the investigation of SA effects on grammar and accuracy. Collentine (2004), for example, compared the grammatical abilities of participants learning the L2 in two different contexts: AH ($N = 20$) and SA ($N = 26$). After exhaustively analyzing the 17 measures of accuracy of the speech samples of the participants (related to gender, number, person, mood and tense accuracy), Collentine concluded that the AH context fostered the development of grammatical abilities more than the SA setting since the AH group showed the greatest improvement on the five variables that turned out to be statistically significant (subordinate-clause count, plural-verb accuracy, coordinate-clause count, past-tense accuracy and feminine-pronoun accuracy).

The SA context does not automatically favor grammatical development either, as shown by DeKeyser (1991). This study compared the oral production of copula in Spanish (*ser* and *estar*) of a group of participants learning the L2 in an AH context ($N = 5$) with the oral production of another group of students learning Spanish in an SA setting ($N = 7$) and did not find any differences between the two groups. Another study that documents the lack of superiority of the SA context over the AH one regarding grammatical development is that by O'Donnell (2004), who examined the relationship of 37 undergraduate students' self-reported perceptions of their learning experiences in two learning contexts (AH and SA), with their performance in oral fluency, grammar, pronunciation, vocabulary, communicative ability and cognitive ability. O'Donnell concluded that differences between the two contexts were evident in that the AH learners were minimally exposed to native speakers outside the classroom and attributed their L2 learning to their L2 classes, whereas the SA group enjoyed a great deal of exposure and attributed their L2 learning to their social interactions while abroad. However, according to O'Donnell, this contact with the L2 was only related to gains in their ability to communicate orally, and seemed to have negatively affected the learners' ability to produce grammatical forms. Another study that failed to document the benefits of the SA context regarding L2 accuracy development is that of Juan-Garau and Pérez-Vidal (2007). These authors investigated the lexical and grammatical errors of a group of L1 Catalan–Spanish bilinguals who engaged in a three-month SA experience and found that participants did not significantly improve in any of the accuracy measures examined.

Notwithstanding, other studies that have examined the effects of the SA context on L2 grammar and accuracy have found positive results. Llanes and Muñoz (2009), for example, analyzed the oral accuracy production of a group of Catalan–Spanish bilingual participants who engaged in a 3–4 week SA experience. The authors found that, even after this short period of time abroad, participants significantly reduced the ratio of average errors per clause and produced significantly more error-free clauses. Furthermore, the ratios of morphological errors, syntactic errors and lexical errors were also significantly reduced in the post-test. Further evidence of the efficacy of the SA context on L2 grammar comes from studies conducted by Howard (2005, 2006). Howard (2005) examined the effects of learning context on past tense marking in French and concluded that the SA context was superior to the AH one for past tense reference. Likewise, Howard (2006) explored the effects of learning context on number agreement in the L2 and found that SA participants were more accurate in terms of using number agreement in French than AH participants. Similarly, Regan *et al.* (2009) provide empirical evidence on the effectiveness of the SA context on accuracy in several areas such as specific grammar items (namely future temporal reference) as well as pragmatics, phonology and sociolinguistic competence.

Finally, Llanes and Muñoz (forthcoming) confirmed the efficiency of the SA context related to improved accuracy in an L2. The authors investigated the effects of learning context (AH vs SA) and age (children vs adults) on L2 development by examining several measures, among which one stood for accuracy: the average number of errors per *T*-unit.[1] With respect to accuracy, the authors found that child SA participants experienced greater gains than their AH peers and that SA children experienced the greatest gains in accuracy.

Age

The role of age has largely been debated in the field of SLA. However, this debate has mainly focused on two learning contexts (naturalistic L2 learning and foreign language learning) and on different issues according to the learning context of the participants. Whereas studies in a naturalistic setting have mainly focused on ultimate attainment, studies in foreign language settings have focused on rate of acquisition (Muñoz, 2008a).

Research on the role of age in a naturalistic setting often aims to confirm or falsify the Critical Period Hypothesis (CPH), which claims that there is a period of time beyond which a language cannot be learned with native-like results. This research has been conducted in several L2 domains such as morphosyntax (Ervin-Tripp, 1974), pronunciation (Birdsong, 1992; Flege *et al.*, 1995, 1999; Moyer, 1999) and global L2 learning (Ekstrand, 1976).

A study that seems to support the CPH is that of Johnson and Newport (1989), who examined the grammatical level of 46 Korean immigrants who had resided in the USA for at least five years and who had immigrated at different ages. Results revealed that participants who had immigrated before age seven performed in the native-speaker range, whereas participants who had immigrated at an older age performed in a way that was negatively correlated with their arrival age in the target language country. Further evidence of the CPH comes from Hyltenstam (1992), who analyzed the errors in Swedish of participants who had immigrated to Sweden before puberty and found that the number of grammatical and lexical errors made by participants who arrived in Sweden before age seven was very similar to the number of errors made by native speakers of Swedish.

Studies that compare younger learners with older learners in a naturalistic context usually support the generalizations that Krashen *et al.* (1979) made based on all previous research. The authors state that older learners have a faster rate of L2 acquisition than younger learners, that older children acquire an L2 faster than younger children, and that those who are exposed to the L2 during childhood usually achieve a higher L2 proficiency level than those who are not exposed to the L2 until adulthood.

On the other hand, research regarding the effects of age in a foreign language setting has either compared groups of participants that have started learning the L2 at different ages but that have received the same amount of exposure to the L2, or compared groups of the same age but with different amount of exposure (see Muñoz, 2008b). Regardless of the type of comparison made, the overarching conclusion is that older participants have a faster rate of acquisition. These findings apply to different L2 domains such as oral comprehension (Asher & Price, 1967; Muñoz, 2003), phonetics (Fullana, 2006), oral fluency (Mora, 2006), vocabulary (Miralpeix, 2006) and writing (Celaya & Navés, 2009; Lasagabaster & Doiz, 2003). Studies assessing participants' global L2 proficiency have also shown that, in general, older participants have a faster rate of acquisition (Burstall et al., 1974; Cenoz, 2003; García-Mayo, 2003; Muñoz, 2006; Oller & Nagato, 1974). When comparing groups of participants with different amounts of exposure to the L2, advantages for younger starters with more exposure have been found in a handful of cases, such as Kuo (2003) for listening comprehension, and Domínguez and Pessoa (2005) for listening comprehension, speaking and writing.

In the previously mentioned study, Llanes and Muñoz (forthcoming) found that adults outscored children in all measures examined. However, when the authors looked at the interaction between age and learning context, they found advantages for different groups depending on the L2 domain under analysis: SA children's gains were higher than those of the rest of the groups in oral fluency and accuracy, whereas SA adults' gains were higher than those of the rest of the groups in oral lexical complexity, and AH adults' gains were higher than those of the remaining groups in written fluency and grammatical complexity.

The Present Study

The data used in this investigation come from the study reported on above (Llanes & Muñoz, forthcoming), in which the authors found a positive effect of learning context on a general measure of accuracy (number of errors per T-unit). This superiority of the participants in the SA context was partly attributed to the effects of the intensive input to which they were exposed. The authors also found that the SA context was particularly beneficial for children in that SA children made higher gains in oral accuracy than the rest of the groups. However, as seen above, not all SA studies have shown that engaging in an SA experience has a positive impact on accuracy. Given this controversy, the findings merit a more in-depth analysis of accuracy that looks at the patterns of improvement of different types of errors in the two age populations and the two learning contexts.

The following general research question and specific subquestions were formulated in this study:

(1) To what extent do learning context (AH vs SA) and age (children vs adults) affect oral and written accuracy, measured in terms of syntactic errors (serr), morphological errors (merr), lexical errors (lexerr), spelling errors (sperr) and errors per T-unit (Err/TU)?

(a) Which learning context is more effective for reducing the oral and written types of errors in English as an L2, measured in terms of serr, merr, lexerr, sperr and Err/TU?
(b) Which age group benefits the most, in terms of error reduction, from each learning context?
(c) Which kind of error is most reduced in each learning context?

Method

Participants

A total of 139 students participated in the present study, distributed as follows: 34 AH children (30 males and four females), 39 SA children (35 males and four females), 20 AH adults (three males and 17 females) and 46 SA adults (12 males and 34 females).

Child participants were aged 10–11 and came from three different private schools in the area of Barcelona. These participants attended English classes four hours a week and science classes in English two hours a week; thus they were exposed to English six hours a week. In the second term, some of the participants were given the opportunity to engage in an SA program in Ireland for two or three months. Children who undertook the SA experience were placed in regular Irish schools with no other Catalan–Spanish classmates. These students attended classes six hours a day, and after classes the Catalan teacher that accompanied them taught them Catalan and Spanish. The selection of the SA children depended on their school. One of the schools selected their participants on the basis of their academic records and their behavior, whereas the other ones let the children's parents choose whether to enroll their children in the SA program or not. Therefore, approximately 40% of the children who enrolled in an SA exchange program were chosen for having good marks and being responsible students, whereas the remaining 60% of the child participants who went abroad did so because their parents made this decision.

AH adult participants were aged 19+ and were studying English Philology at the Universitat de Barcelona. These participants attended classes in English for an average of 15 hours a week. SA adult participants were awarded an Erasmus scholarship to study in Ireland or the UK for a term (for some of the participants the post-test was carried out two months after their arrival in the L2 country; since no differences were found between those participants spending two and three months abroad, they were grouped together in the present investigation). The number of hours that SA Erasmus students attended classes varied according to their needs. Given the lack of demand for Erasmus scholarships at the time this study was carried out, there was no selection for this group of participants.

All participants had studied English for at least five years at the time this investigation was carried out. All were Catalan–Spanish bilinguals, with the exception of 8% of adult SA students who did not speak Catalan.

Procedure

This study has a pre/post-test design. For most of the AH and SA participants, the pre-test was administered the week prior to the SA participants' departure for the L2 country and the post-test was administered the week after their arrival from the host country. Both the pre-test and the post-test were mostly administered at the participants' AH institution. However, for 28 out of the 39 SA child participants the post-test was collected in their school in the host country, and for 25 out of the 46 Erasmus students data were collected in their SA university at both testing times. For the adult participants, the oral and written tests were administered on the same day, but for children this data collection was carried out on two separate days at the request of the schools and because of time constraints.

Instruments

The instrumentation consisted of a written composition, a picture-elicited narrative task and a questionnaire. Written data were collected first and gathered by means of a composition entitled 'My life: past, present and future expectations', in which participants were asked to write a minimum of seven lines within 15 minutes. This topic was chosen because it had previously been used with participants of different ages with satisfactory results (Muñoz, 2006).

Oral data were gathered by means of an interview in which participants answered several biographical questions and several questions regarding their experience as L2 learners. This semi-structured interview served as a warm-up and led to a picture-elicited narrative task. Participants were shown a series of pictures and then described what they saw in those pictures. Participants were given 1 minute to look at the story and plan their utterances.

Finally, participants filled out a questionnaire that was an adaptation of the Language Contact Profile (Freed *et al.*, 2004a, 2004b). This questionnaire elicited some biographical information as well as information regarding the amount and type of L2 contact that participants experienced. For participants who went abroad, this questionnaire also asked questions regarding the accommodation type and the type and frequency of interaction they engaged in. The researchers helped children fill out this questionnaire to ensure that they understood the questions well and to help them calculate the amount of hours they interacted in English. Of the 46 Erasmus students, 25 did not return the questionnaire. Therefore, the information regarding L2 exposure of the SA adults comes from 21 Erasmus participants only.

Measures

A total of nine accuracy measures were calculated in the present investigation, five for the written data and four for the oral data. First of all, following Bardovi-Harlig and Bofman (1989), oral and written errors were classified as morphological, syntactic and lexical. Morphological errors (merr) referred to errors in nominal morphology, verbal morphology, determiners, articles, prepositions and derivational morphology. Syntactic errors (serr) concerned errors regarding word order, absence of constituents, combining sentences or verb complementation. Finally, lexical errors (lexerr) referred to idiomatic expressions or words. Additionally, two other accuracy measures were computed in the present investigation: spelling errors (sperr) and the average number of errors per *T*-unit (Err/TU). The former referred to any words that were not written properly, whereas the latter was a general measure of accuracy that took into account all the errors that participants made, regardless of type. The measure Err/TU was chosen because it is among the most reliable measures of accuracy according to Wolfe-Quintero *et al.* (1998), and in the previous study (Llanes & Muñoz, forthcoming) it proved to be sensitive to accuracy gains.

Once all the errors were classified, the ratios of errors per *T*-unit were computed by dividing the total number of each type of error by the total number of *T*-units. The average errors per *T*-unit were calculated by dividing the total number of errors (morphological errors + syntactic errors + lexical errors + spelling errors) by the number of *T*-units. Next, intra- and inter-rater reliabilities were computed, reaching 95.4 and 92.4% respectively.

Results

Tables 9.1 and 9.2 display the descriptive statistics of all the measures for each group of participants (means and standard deviations in parentheses).

In order to answer the specific questions concerning which learning context was more effective for reducing the oral and written ratios of errors in English as an L2, and which age group benefitted the most (in terms of error reduction) from SA experiences, multivariate analysis of covariance

Table 9.1 Descriptive statistics for each of the groups in the pre-test

	Serr	Merr	Lexerr	Sperr	Err/TU
Oral					
AH CHI	0.03 (0.03)	0.10 (0.04)	0.16 (0.15)		2.4 (1.27)
SA CHI	0.05 (0.07)	0.11 (0.05)	0.15 (0.14)		2.24 (1.09)
AH AD	0.01 (0.01)	0.04 (0.04)	0.01 (0.01)		0.81 (0.61)
SA AD	0.00 (0.01)	0.04 (0.03)	0.01 (0.01)		0.73 (0.53)
Written					
AH CHI	0.03 (0.03)	0.08 (0.06)	0.03 (0.03)	0.07 (0.05)	1.44 (1.17)
SA CHI	0.02 (0.02)	0.07 (0.05)	0.03 (0.03)	0.06 (0.06)	1.42 (0.77)
AH AD	0.01 (0.01)	0.03 (0.01)	0.02 (0.01)	0.00 (0.01)	1.09 (0.46)
SA AD	0.00 (0.00)	0.02 (0.02)	0.01 (0.01)	0.00 (0.00)	0.48 (0.32)

SA, Study abroad; AH, at home; CHI, children; AD, adults

Table 9.2 Descriptive statistics for each of the groups in the post-test

	Serr	Merr	Lexerr	Sperr	Err/TU
Oral					
AH CHI	0.03 (0.02)	0.12 (0.05)	0.14 (0.14)		2.44 (1.18)
SA CHI	0.03 (0.02)	0.07 (0.04)	0.04 (0.04)		1.43 (0.88)
AH AD	0.00 (0.01)	0.04 (0.02)	0.01 (0.01)		0.68 (0.43)
SA AD	0.00 (0.00)	0.03 (0.03)	0.01 (0.00)		0.66 (0.39)
Written					
AH CHI	0.03 (0.05)	0.08 (0.05)	0.03 (0.03)	0.06 (0.05)	1.45 (0.80)
SA CHI	0.01 (0.01)	0.05 (0.03)	0.01 (0.02)	0.04 (0.04)	1.02 (0.63)
AH AD	0.00 (0.00)	0.02 (0.03)	0.01 (0.01)	0.00 (0.01)	0.74 (0.69)
SA AD	0.00 (0.01)	0.02 (0.01)	0.01 (0.00)	0.00 (0.00)	0.54 (0.35)

SA, Study abroad; AH, at home; CHI, children

(MANCOVA) tests were employed. MANCOVA tests were chosen because they allow the exploration of differences between groups while controlling for an additional variable that might influence the scores of the dependent variable; in this case, age was strongly and positively correlated with all the measures examined, showing that adults had a higher proficiency level. MANCOVA tests were run separately for the oral and written variables. The MANCOVA tests regarding oral variables were significant for learning context ($F(4, 122) = 8.727$, $p = 0.000$, Wilks's $\lambda = 0.778$), age ($F(4, 122) = 3.132$, $p = 0.017$, Wilks's $\lambda = 0.907$) and the interaction between learning context and age ($F(4, 122) = 7.610$, $p = 0.000$, Wilks's $\lambda = 0.800$). The tests also showed statistically significant results for writing skills (learning context: $F(5, 122) = 2.967$, $p = 0.015$, Wilks's $\lambda = 0.892$; age: $F(5, 122) = 6.248$, $p = 0.000$, Wilks's $\lambda = 0.796$); and interaction between learning context and age: $F(5, 122) = 3.147$, $p = 0.010$, Wilks's $\lambda = 0.886$). Therefore, the follow-up analyses were carried out.

These follow-up analyses showed that the SA learning context was statistically significant for the improvement of the following ratios concerning oral measures (see Table 9.1): morphological errors ($F(1, 125) = 16, 904$, $p = 0.000$, $\eta^2 = 0.119$), lexical errors ($F(1, 125) = 23, 559$, $p = 0.000$, $\eta^2 = 0.159$) and errors per T-unit ($F(1, 125) = 24, 424$, $p = 0.000$, $\eta^2 = 0.163$). The SA setting was also found to be statistically significant for the improvement of the following ratios regarding the written measures: morphological errors ($F(1, 126) = 7, 685$, $p = 0.006$, $\eta^2 = 0.057$), lexical errors ($F(1, 126) = 3, 957$, $p = 0.049$, $\eta^2 = 0.030$) and errors per T-unit ($F(1, 126) = 4, 920$, $p = 0.028$, $\eta^2 = 0.038$).

As far as age is concerned, the follow-up analyses indicated that adults experienced significantly greater gains than children in the four measures that turned out to be significant: oral morphological errors ($F(1) = 10, 372$, $p = 0.002$, $\eta^2 = 0.077$), oral errors per T-unit ($F(1) = 5, 083, p = 0.026, \eta^2 = 0.039$), written morphological errors ($F(1) = 8, 288, p = 0.006, \eta^2 = 0.062$) and written spelling errors ($F(1) = 8, 204, p = 0.005, \eta^2 = 0.061$).

Finally, MANCOVA tests also revealed that the interaction between learning context and age was especially significant regarding oral measures because three out of the four oral measures examined turned out to be statistically significant. Namely, it was found that SA adults experienced significantly greater gains than the rest of the groups regarding oral morphological errors ($F(1) = 12, 816, p = 0.000, \eta^2 = 0.093$), followed by the group of AH adults, SA children and AH children, respectively. However, for oral lexical errors it was the group of SA children whose gains were higher than those of other groups ($F(1, 125) = 22, 252, p = 0.000, \eta^2 = 0.151$), followed by the group of SA adults, who experienced almost the same gains as the group of AH adults. AH children showed the fewest gains. The same was true for oral errors per T-unit ($F(1, 125) = 23, 268, p = 0.000, \eta^2 = 0.157$), in which SA children's gains surpassed SA adults, AH adults and AH children, respectively.

As for the effects of the interaction between the two independent variables – learning context and age – on the written measures, only one statistically significant value was found. Morphological errors ($F(1, 126) = 4.680, p = 0.032, \eta^2 = 0.452$) showed improvement for the group of SA adults, followed by AH adults, SA children and AH children. Table 9.3 displays the results of the MANCOVA tests (p-level) with an indication of which groups had the highest scores.

In order to further address the second subquestion and answer the third one, concerning the age group that makes the most of SA and the kind of

Table 9.3 Summary of the MANCOVA results

Measures	Learning context (LC)	Age (A)	LC × Age
O. Serr	0.330	0.671	0.367
O. Merr	0.000* SA	0.002* AD	0.000* SA AD
O. Lexerr	0.000* SA	0.097	0.000* SA CHI
O. Err/TU	0.000* SA	0.026* AD	0.000* SA CHI
W. Serr	0.122	0.321	0.230
W. Merr	0.006* SA	0.005* AD	0.032* SA AD
W. Lexerr	0.049* SA	0.107	0.081
W. Sperr	0.222	0.005* AD	0.233
W. Err/TU	0.028* SA	0.034	0.225

SA, Study abroad; AH, at home; CHI, children; AD, adults; O, oral; W, written. * Statistically significant at $p < 0.05$

Table 9.4 Summary of the paired samples *T*-tests results

Measures	AH CHI	SA CHI	AH AD	SA AD
O. Serr	0.655	0.015*	0.185	0.948
O. Merr	0.141	0.000*	0.947	0.276
O. Lexerr	0.928	0.000*	0.484	0.021*
O. Err/TU	0.690	0.039*	0.573	0.092
W. Serr	0.815	0.002*	0.247	0.347
W. Merr	0.638	0.007*	0.081	0.144
W. Lexerr	0.384	0.030*	0.808	0.253
W. Sperr	0.655	0.015*	0.185	0.948
W. Err/TU	0.141	0.000*	0.947	0.276

SA, Study abroad; AH, at home; CHI, children; AD, adults; O, oral; W, written. * Statistically significant at $p < 0.05$

error that is most reduced in each learning context, respectively, paired samples *T*-tests were carried out separately for each of the groups of participants (see Table 9.4 with the *p* level of the results). It was found that none of the AH groups experienced significant gains from pre- to post-test; in other words, none of the accuracy ratios were significantly reduced in the post-test. This was not the case for the groups of SA participants, especially for the group of children, whose accuracy ratios were significantly reduced from pre- to post-test and therefore showed an improvement in accuracy: O. Serr, $t(37) = 2, 552, p = 0.015$; O. Merr, $t(37) = 4, 054, p = 0.000$; O. Lexerr, $t(37) = 5, 536, p = 0.000$; W. Serr, $t(38) = 2, 135, p = 0.039$; W. Merr, $t(38) = 3, 303, p = 0.002$; W. Lexerr, $t(38) = 2, 845, p = 0.007$; and W. Sperr, $t(38) = 2, 264, p = 0.030$.

Although the AH groups did not reduce any of the ratios significantly, the group of AH children reduced their written spelling errors the most, whereas the group of adults reduced their written morphological errors the most. As seen in Table 9.4, the two SA groups improved significantly in lexical errors.

Discussion

The main purpose of the current study was to determine to what extent learning context and age affect L2 accuracy as measured by type and frequency of errors. More specifically, the first subquestion asked about the learning context that is most effective to reduce learners' errors, and it was found that the SA context was more effective than the AH one. This finding is in line with previous research that shows the superiority of the SA context over the AH context for accuracy improvement (Howard, 2001, 2005, 2006; Llanes & Muñoz, forthcoming), but it runs counter to previous findings that did not find differences concerning accuracy between groups of participants studying abroad and at home (Collentine, 2004; DeKeyser, 1986, 1991). This discrepancy may be at least partly explained by the fact that the latter studies examined discrete grammatical points that accounted for accuracy (i.e. the use of Spanish copula *ser* before a predicate noun), while the measures used in the present study were probably more sensitive to general improvement. Additionally, the lack of improvement found in certain studies could be due to the participants' characteristics, which are different in many aspects (age, L2 initial proficiency level, degree of bilingualism/multilingualism, etc.) from the participants in the present study (Llanes, 2011).

The SA superiority could be explained by the role of input and interaction. The information extracted from the questionnaire showed that SA participants were exposed to the L2 much more than AH participants and that SA participants interacted in the L2 more and more often than AH participants (see Appendix). Besides the intensity of the input, the quality of the input to which SA participants abroad are exposed is also relevant as it is usually richer and more varied. Participants abroad had the opportunity to interact with different interlocutors and probably in different registers, whereas most AH participants were limited to interacting with their teacher during the language class. This is in line with the predictions of the Comprehensible Output Hypothesis (Swain, 1985) and the Interaction Hypothesis (Long, 1981), which could also explain the superiority of the SA context since they highlight the importance of L2 production and being active learners to learn the L2 efficiently. The data from the questionnaire attest that SA participants spoke and interacted in the L2 more often than their AH counterparts. In addition, the superiority of the SA context over the AH context for L2 accuracy improvement could also be explained by the role of practice (Anderson, 1983, 1992; DeKeyser, 2007) in that participants may have practiced the L2 extensively, a fact that is possible in an L2 context, and after so many hours of practice, they may have automatized certain aspects of the L2. This would explain error reduction in general.

The second subquestion asked about the age group (children or adults) that benefitted the most from the SA experience in terms of error reduction, and the answer is not simple. In terms of absolute gains, that is to say, when adults and children were compared, it was found that adults experienced greater significant gains than children in four out of the nine measures analyzed (oral merr and Err/TU, and written merr and sperr) after two to three months abroad. This finding is in line with previous research conducted in foreign language settings, which claims that, initially, older learners show a faster rate of acquisition (García-Mayo & García-Lecumberri, 2003; Muñoz, 2006).

However, in terms of relative gains, that is to say, when SA children were compared with AH children, and SA adults were compared with their AH counterparts, it was found that SA children experience higher relative gains than SA adults. It was found that SA children significantly improved in all the measures examined relative to AH children, whereas SA adults significantly improved in only one measure relative to AH adults. None of the AH groups experienced any significant gains. This finding complements the previous analysis of these data, in which adults' gains outscored children's in oral lexical complexity, and written fluency, lexical complexity and grammatical complexity.

MANCOVA tests also showed an effect in the interaction between learning context and age, which indicated that participants in both age groups equally benefitted from SA experiences: in two out of these four statistically significant values it was the group of SA adults whose gains surpassed those of the rest of the groups, whereas in the other two, it was the group of SA children whose gains surpassed the remaining groups. These interaction effects revealed that SA experiences seem to be more favorable for children for the improvement of oral skills, since the gains of the group of SA children were higher than those of the rest of the groups regarding oral lexical errors and oral errors per T-unit. However, SA adults' gains were superior to those of all other groups regarding oral and written morphological error gains. Additionally, T-tests revealed that SA children experienced greater gains than AH children in all measures and that SA adults experienced greater gains than their AH counterparts in only one measure. Therefore, children seem to benefit more than adults from the SA context, although these differences seem to be limited to within-groups comparisons.

This finding reflects the more general analysis in Llanes and Muñoz (forthcoming), as cited above, and could be attributed to the more intensive input and output provided by the SA context as well as to the greater practice that SA children experienced. The fact that SA children's gains were higher than those of SA adults in oral skills could be due to their greater oral practice of as well as to the greater intensity and quality of the input they received. Additionally, it could also be explained by the type of learning mechanisms that characterize children (implicit learning) and that seem to be fostered in contexts that provide students with the opportunity to be immersed in the L2, such as naturalistic and SA settings (DeKeyser, 2003). As seen above, the only variables in which children who went abroad show superiority over adults are two oral variables, which compared with written skills are believed to tap more into implicit knowledge rather than explicit knowledge (Ellis, 2005). Therefore, the fact that SA children surpassed the remaining groups of participants in gains in two oral measures might be due to the use of more implicit learning mechanisms by children; in contrast, adults' learning is characterized by the use of more explicit mechanisms, which results in less efficient and slower performance because it requires some previous thinking prior to speaking (Ellis, 2004; Mathews et al., 1989). The fact that SA adults (as opposed to children) reduced morphological errors more than the other groups shows that they are probably formally aware of morphology. This could be related to the fact that adults have received L2 grammar classes (mostly explicit instruction) for more years than children. If this hypothesis were confirmed, this would in turn provide evidence for the claim that adults use more explicit mechanisms (DeKeyser, 2010). Possibly, adults' explicit learning mechanisms help them focus on form.

Finally, the last subquestion enquired about the kind of error that is most reduced in each learning context, and it was found that all SA participants significantly reduced oral lexical errors the most. Although AH participants did not experience any statistically significant reduction, AH children reduced spelling mistakes the most, whereas AH adults reduced written morphological errors. These findings seem to suggest that the SA setting fosters implicit learning or automatization of the L2 more than the AH setting, since SA participants all experienced a significant reduction of an oral measure. The fact that AH adults reduced written morphological errors the most adds further evidence to the implicit and explicit hypothesis discussed above because AH adults received instruction in the L2 that was mainly focused on L2 grammar rules.

Additionally, the facts that AH participants improved their written errors most and that SA participants reduced their oral errors the most could be related to the type of L2 practice experienced. Thus, whereas SA participants spoke in the L2 for many hours a week, AH participants practiced their written skills more than their oral ones. Further, reduction of this type of error could be related to the type of instruction that participants received: AH adults read and wrote frequently in the L2 and were penalized for the mistakes they made, so this would explain why they reduced their morphological written errors the most; AH children were asked to correct and recopy their spelling mistakes several times, so they may have focused especially on spelling and this would explain why they reduced their spelling errors the most.

Conclusion and Limitations

Three conclusions are drawn from this study. Firstly, SA participants improved accuracy significantly more than AH participants, who did not improve significantly in any of the measures examined. Secondly, adults experienced greater gains than children in terms of absolute gains, but children experienced greater gains than adults in terms of relative gains; that is to say, SA children experienced higher gains than AH children, whereas SA adults did not experience as many significant gains compared to their AH counterparts. Thirdly, as for the type of errors that were reduced in the different learning contexts, it was found that the SA context helped learners to improve in lexical accuracy, whereas the AH context did not seem to benefit the reduction of any specific type of error. This study also suggests that the intensity and quality of input and the type of learning mechanisms employed could be mediated by participants' age and learning context. Specifically, children, who experienced a more intensive exposure to the L2, probably made use of their implicit learning mechanisms more than adults, who did not practice the L2 as intensively as children. As for the learning context, the SA setting probably leads to more implicit learning than the AH context.

The results of this study add to the discussion about accuracy improvement in the area of SA research and age-related studies, but it has some limitations. Firstly, the information extracted through the questionnaire is self-reported and therefore there are questions concerning the validity of these data; secondly, not all SA adult participants returned the questionnaire, so these self-reported data regarding the amount and type of interaction among SA adults come from only half of the participants. Further research should both attempt to design a more reliable instrument for gathering L2 contact data and try to include the information extracted from a larger number of participants and therefore have more generalizable results.

Acknowledgments

This research was supported by grants FFI2010-18006 and SGR 137. I would like to thank Carmen Muñoz for her insightful suggestions for improvement of this chapter.

Note

(1) A second measure, error-free *T*-units per *T*-unit, was not sensitive to accuracy gains.

References

Anderson, J. (ed.) (1983) *The Architecture of Cognition*. Cambridge, MA: Cambridge University Press.
Anderson, J. (1992) Automaticity and the ACT* Theory. *American Journal of Psychology* 105 (2), 165–180.
Asher, J.J. and Price, B.S. (1967) The learning strategy of the total physical response: Some age differences. *Child Development* 38 (4), 1219–1227.
Bardovi-Harlig, K. and Bofman, T. (1989) Attainment of syntactic and morphological accuracy by advanced language learners. *Studies in Second Language Acquisition* 11, 17–34.
Birdsong, D. (1992) Ultimate attainment in second language acquisition. *Language* 68 (4), 706–755.
Burstall, C., Jamieson, M., Cohen, S. and Hardgreaves, M. (eds) (1974) *Primary French in the Balance*. Windsor: NFER.
Celaya, M.L. and Navés, T. (2009) Age-related differences and associated factors in foreign language writing. Implications for L2 writing theory and school curricula. In R. Manchón (ed.) *Writing in Foreign Language Contexts: Learning, Teaching, and Research* (pp. 130–155). Bristol: Multilingual Matters.
Cenoz, J. (2003) The influence of age on the acquisition of English: General proficiency, attitudes and code mixing. In M.P. García-Mayo and M.L. García-Lecumberri (eds) *Age and the Acquisition of English as a Foreign Language* (pp. 77–93). Clevedon: Multilingual Matters.

Collentine, J. (2004) The effects of learning contexts on morphosyntactic and lexical development. *Studies in Second Language Acquisition* 26, 227–248.

Collentine, J. (2009) Study abroad research: Findings, implications and future directions. In C. Doughty and M. Long (eds) *Handbook of Language Teaching* (pp. 218–233). Malden, MA: Blackwell.

Cubillos, J.H., Chieffo, L. and Fan, C., (2008) The impact of short-term study abroad programs on L2 listening comprehension skills. *Foreign Language Annals* 41 (1), 157–185.

DeKeyser, R.M. (1986) From learning to acquisition? Foreign language development in a U.S. classroom and during a semester abroad. PhD thesis, Stanford University.

DeKeyser, R.M. (1991) Foreign language development during a semester abroad. In B.F. Freed (ed.) *Foreign Language Acquisition Research and the Classroom* (pp. 104–119). Lexington, MA: D.C. Heath.

DeKeyser, R.M. (2003) Implicit and explicit learning. In C. Doughty and M.H. Long (eds) *The Handbook of Second Language Acquisition* (pp. 313–348). Oxford: Blackwell.

DeKeyser, R.M. (ed.) (2007) *Practice in a Second Language. Perspectives from Applied Linguistics and Cognitive Psychology.* New York: Cambridge University Press.

DeKeyser, R. (2010) Monitoring processes in Spanish as a second language during a study abroad program. *Foreign Language Annals* 43 (1), 80–92.

Dewey, D.P. (2004) A comparison of reading development by learners of Japanese in intensive and domestic Immersion and Study Abroad contexts. *Studies in Second Language Acquisition* 26, 303–327.

Dewey, D.P. (2008) Japanese vocabulary acquisition by learners in three contexts. *Frontiers: The Interdisciplinary Journal of Study Abroad* XV, 127–148.

Díaz-Campos, M. (2004) Context of learning in the acquisition of Spanish second language phonology. *Studies in Second Language Acquisition* 26, 249–273.

Domínguez, R. and Pessoa, S. (2005) Early versus late start in foreign language education: Documenting achievements. *Foreign Language Annals* 38 (4), 473–483.

Dyson, P. (1988) *The Year Abroad. Report for the Central Bureau for Educational Visits and Exchanges.* Oxford: Oxford University Language Teaching Centre.

Ekstrand, L. (1976) Adjustment among immigrant pupils in Sweden. *International Review of Applied Psychology* 25 (3), 167–188.

Ellis, R. (2004) The definition and measurement of L2 explicit knowledge. *Language Learning* 54, 227–275.

Ellis, R. (2005) Measuring implicit and explicit knowledge of a second language: A psychometric study. *Studies in Second Language Acquisition* 27, 141–172.

Ervin-Tripp, S. (1974) Is second language learning like first? *TESOL Quarterly* 8 (2), 111–127.

Flege, J.E., Munro, M.J. and MacKay, I.R.A. (1995) Factors affecting degree of perceived foreign accent in a second language. *Journal of the Acoustical Society of America* 97, 3125–3134.

Flege, J., Yeni-Komshian, G. and Liu, S. (1999) Age constraints on second-language acquisition. *Journal of Memory and Language* 41, 78–104.

Foster, P. (2009) Lexical diversity and native-like selection: The bonus of studying abroad. In B. Richards, M. Daller, D. Malvern, P. Meara, J. Milton and J. Treffers-Daller (eds) *Vocabulary Studies in First and Second Language Acquisition* (pp. 91–106). Basingstoke: Palgrave Macmillan.

Freed, B.F. (1995) What makes us think that students who study abroad become fluent? In B.F. Freed (ed.) *Second Language Acquisition in a Study Abroad Context* (pp. 123–148). Amsterdam: John Benjamins.

Freed, B.F., So, S. and Lazar, N.A. (2003) Language learning abroad: How do gains in written fluency compare with gains in oral fluency in french as a second language? *ADFL Bulletin* 34 (3), 34–40.

Freed, B.F., Segalowitz, N. and Dewey D.P. (2004a) Context of learning and second language fluency in French: Comparing regular classroom, study abroad, and intensive domestic immersion programs. *Studies in Second Language Acquisition* 26, 275–301.

Freed, B.F., Dewey, D.P., Segalowitz, N. and Halter, R. (2004b) The language contact profile. *Studies in Second Language Acquisition* 26, 349–356.

Fullana, N. (2006) The development of English (FL) perception and production skills. In C. Muñoz (ed.) *Age and the Rate of Foreign Language Learning* (pp. 41–64). Clevedon: Multilingual Matters.

García-Mayo, M.P. (2003) Age, length of exposure and grammaticality judgements in the acquisition of English as a foreign language. In M.P. García-Mayo and M.L. García-Lecumberri (eds) *Age and the Acquisition of English as a Foreign Language* (pp. 94–114). Clevedon: Multilingual Matters.

García-Mayo, M.P. and García-Lecumberri, M.L. (eds) (2003) *Age and the Acquisition of English as a Foreign Language*. Clevedon: Multilingual Matters.

Howard, M. (2001) The effects of study abroad on the L2 learner's structural skills: Evidence from advanced learners of French. *Eurosla Yearbook* 1, 123–141.

Howard, M. (2005) On the role of context in the development of learner language: Insights from study abroad research. *ITL International Journal of Applied Linguistics* 148, 1–20.

Howard, M. (2006) The expression of number and person through verb morphology in French interlanguage. *International Review of Applied Linguistics* 44 (1), 1–22.

Hyltenstam, K. (1992) Non-native features of near-native speakers: On the ultimate attainment of childhood L2 learners (pp. 351–368). In R.J. Harris (ed.) *Cognitive Processing in Bilinguals*. Amsterdam: Elsevier Science.

Ife, A., Vives, G. and Meara, P. (2000) The impact of study abroad on the vocabulary development of different proficiency groups. *Spanish Applied Linguistics* 4 (1), 55–84.

Johnson, J.S. and Newport, E.L. (1989) Critical period effects in second language learning: The influence of maturational state on the acquisition of English as a second language. *Cognitive Psychology* 21, 60–99.

Juan-Garau, M. and Pérez-Vidal, C. (2007) The effect of context and contact on oral performance in students who go on a stay abroad. *VIAL* 4, 117–134.

Krashen, S.D., Long, M.H. and Scarcella, R.C. (1979) Age, rate and eventual attainment in second language acquisition. *TESOL Quarterly* 13 (4), 573–582.

Kuo, Y. (2003) The effects of age on Taiwanese EFL learners' long-term English proficiency. PhD thesis, University of Kansas.

Lasagabaster, D. and Doiz, A. (2003) Maturational constraints on foreign language written production. In M.P. García-Mayo and M.L. García-Lecumberri (eds) *Age and the Acquisition of English as a Foreign Language* (pp. 136–160). Clevedon: Multilingual Matters.

Lennon, P. (1990) Investigating fluency in EFL: A quantitative approach. *Language Learning* 40, 387–417.

Llanes, À. (2011) The many faces of study abroad: An update on L2 gains emerged during a study abroad experience. *International Journal of Multilingualism* 3, 189–215.

Llanes, À. and Muñoz, C. (2009) A short stay abroad: Does it make a difference? *System* 37 (3), 353–365.

Llanes, À and Muñoz, C. (forthcoming) Age effects in a study abroad context: Children and adults studying abroad and at home. *Language Learning* 63 (1).

Long, M.H. (1981) Input, interaction and second language acquisition. *Annals of the New York Academy of Sciences* 379, 259–278.

Mathews, R.C., Buss, R.R., Stanley, W.B., Blanchart-Fields, F., Cho, J.R. and Druhan, B. (1989) Role of implicit and explicit processes in learning from examples: A synergistic effect. *Journal of Experimental Psychology*, 1083–1100.

Milton, I. and Meara, P. (1995) How periods abroad affect vocabulary growth in a foreign language. *ITL Review of Applied Linguistics* 107 (8), 17–34.

Miralpeix, I. (2006) Age and vocabulary acquisition in English as a foreign language. In C. Muñoz (ed.) *Age and the Rate of Foreign Language Learning* (pp. 89–106). Clevedon: Multilingual Matters.

Mora, J.C. (2006) Age effects on oral fluency development. In C. Muñoz (ed.) *Age and the Rate of Foreign Language Learning* (pp. 65–88). Clevedon: Multilingual Matters.

Mora, J.C. (2008) Learning context effects on the acquisition of a second language phonology. In C. Pérez-Vidal (Coord.), M. Juan-Garau and A. Bel (eds) *A Portrait of the Young in the New Multilingual Spain* (pp. 241–263). Clevedon: Multilingual Matters.

Moyer, A. (1999) Ultimate attainment in L2 phonology. *Studies in Second Language Acquisition* 21, 81–108.

Muñoz, C. (2003) Variation in oral skills development and age of onset. In M.P. García-Mayo and M.L. García-Lecumberri (eds) *Age and the Acquisition of English as a Foreign Language* (pp. 161–181). Clevedon: Multilingual Matters.

Muñoz, C. (ed.) (2006) *Age and the Rate of Foreign Language Learning*. Clevedon: Multilingual Matters.

Muñoz, C. (2008a) Symmetries and asymmetries of age effects in naturalistic and instructed L2 learning. *Applied Linguistics* 29 (4), 578–596.

Muñoz, C. (2008b) Age-related differences in foreign language learning. Revising the empirical evidence. *International Review of Applied Linguistics* 46 (3), 197–220.

O'Donnell, K. (2004) Student perceptions of language learning in two contexts: At home and study abroad. PhD thesis, Carnegie Mellon University.

Oller, J.W. and Nagato, N. (1974) The long-term effect of FLES: An experiment. *The Modern Language Journal* 58, 15–19.

Pérez-Vidal, C. and Juan-Garau, M (2009) The effect of study abroad on written performance. *Eurosla Yearbook 9*, 269–295.

Regan, V., Howard, M. and Lemée, I. (eds) (2009) *The Acquisition of Sociolinguistic Competence in a Study Abroad Context*. Bristol: Multilingual Matters.

Sasaki, M. (2004) A multiple-data analysis of the 3.5-year development of EFL student writers. *Language Learning* 54 (3), 525–582.

Sasaki, M. (2009) Changes in English as a foreign language students' writing over 3.5 years: A sociocognitive account. In R. Manchón (ed.) *Writing in Foreign Language Contexts: Learning, Teaching, and Research* (pp. 49–76). Bristol: Multilingual Matters.

Segalowitz, N. and Freed, F.B. (2004) Context, contact, and cognition in oral fluency acquisition: Learning Spanish in at home and study abroad contexts. *Studies in Second Language Acquisition* 26, 173–199.

Serrano, R., Llanes, À. and Tragant, E. (2011) Analyzing the effect of context of second language learning: Domestic intensive and semi-intensive courses vs. study abroad in Europe. *System* 39 (2), 133–143.

Swain, M. (1985) Bilingual education for the English-speaking Canadian. In J. Atlantis and J. Staczek (eds) *Perspectives on Bilingualism and Bilingual Education* (pp. 385–398). Washington, DC: Georgetown University Press.

Wolfe-Quintero, K., Inagaki, S. and Kim, H.Y. (eds) (1998) *Second Language Development in Writing: Measure of Fluency, Accuracy and Complexity. Technical Report 17*. Manoa, HI: University of Hawai'i Press.

Appendix: Information Extracted from the Questionnaire

Table 9.5 Information about the number of extra English lessons taken (if any), the time devoted to extra English lessons, the number of hours a week of class, the number of hours spent using a language other than English, the age of onset and the context in which English was used the most

		Extra English (%)	Extra English time (hours per week)	Class (hours per week)	Other language (hours per week)	Age of onset (in years)	Context (%)
SA CHI	No: 44.2		$M = 1.15$ (1.14)	$M = 30$ (3.29)	$M = 9.6$ (6.28)	4.39 (1.43)	Family: 80.4 School: 17.6
	Yes: 55.7						Friends: 1.6
AH CHI	No: 75.6		$M = 0.37$ (0.8)	$M = 6$ (0.93)	—	5.09 (1.14)	School: 100
	Yes: 24.4						
SA AD	No: 90		$M = 0.76$ (2.14)	$M = 11.67$ (8.24)	$M = 12.62$ (11.53)	8.5 (2.39)	University: 11.1 Friends: 39.7 Family members or roommates: 49.2
	Yes: 10						
AH AD	No: 60		$M = 2.95$ (4.33)	$M = 15$ (0.000)	—	8.35 (2.39)	University: 100
	Yes: 40						

SA, Study abroad; AH, at home; CHI, children; AD, adults; M, mean; standard deviations in parentheses

Table 9.6 Information about the type of accommodations, the amount of time devoted to interacting with the participants' roommates, the family member with whom they interacted the most (only for participants who lived with a home-stay family) and the amount of time spent interacting with native speakers (NSs) and non-native speakers (NNSs)

	SA CHI	AH CHI	SA AD	AH AD
Accommodation type (%)	Family: 100	—	Family: 4.8 Dormitory: 38.1 Apartment alone: 4.8 Apartment with English or fluent people: 28.6 Apartment with non-fluent people: 23.8	—
Time at accommodation (in hours per week)	$M = 28.07\ (6.56)$	—	$M = 6.9\ (10.91)$	—
Family member interacted with most (%)	Siblings: 56.4 Mother: 29.1 Father 4.5	—	—	—
Interaction with NSs and NNSs (in hours a week)	NSs $M = 28.19\ (9.94)$ NNSs $M = 1.97\ (0.57)$	NSs $M = 0\ (0)$ NNSs $M = 4.2\ (2.28)$	NSs $M = 6.95\ (4.64)$ NNSs $M = 15.62\ (8.53)$	NSs $M = 3.32\ (1.15)$ NNSs $M = 6.13\ (4.28)$

SA, Study abroad; AH, at home; CHI, children; AD, adults; M, mean; standard deviations in parentheses

10 Oral and Written Development in Formal Instruction and Study Abroad: Differential Effects of Learning Context

Carmen Pérez-Vidal, Maria Juan-Garau, Joan C. Mora and Margalida Valls-Ferrer

Introduction

In a recent study focusing on the effects of a sojourn abroad on learners' linguistic progress, an attempt was made to characterize study abroad (SA) periods in terms of the potential intensity of exposure to the target language (TL) and the practice opportunities they offer as well as the linguistic progress learners can achieve through them (Pérez-Vidal & Juan-Garau, 2011). The following three dimensions were identified: the architecture of SA programmes; micro-level features; and macro-level features. In the present study, these elements are used to contrast SA and formal instruction (FI) contexts of learning, generally characterized by affording learners a lower intensity of exposure to the TL and hence potentially fewer opportunities for substantial linguistic improvement. The objective of our study is to describe the differential impact that an SA and an FI context of learning have on learners' progress in oral and written abilities, as a result of the different opportunities for practice each context provides. In order to do so, we will begin by characterizing both contexts as distinct language acquisition environments.

Study abroad and formal instruction contexts

In this section a summary of the three main dimensions proposed for a characterization of SA is presented. Regarding the SA programmes' architecture, eight context variables allow for a comprehensive description of SA programmes: length of SA programme, SA living conditions, opportunities for finding employment, pre-departure level, pre-departure preparation, point in the academic career at which the SA takes place, academic work assignments abroad, and re-entry conditions. They can be used as a standard protocol for the description of SA programmes. As for their micro-level features, they represent the individual variables that come into play and condition the degree to which learners avail themselves of the opportunities for establishing contact with native speakers (NSs) while living in the host country, and hence for increasing the intensity of input exposure and opportunities for interacting in the TL. Variation in learners' ability to establish contact with the TL is found not only in SA settings, but also in FI and immersion contexts. Such ability has been characterized by Dörnyei and Skehan (2006: 611–612) as a 'multidimensional construct, including cognitive, metacognitive, motivational, behavioural and environmental processes that learners can use to enhance academic achievement'.

Finally, the macro-level features of SA programmes revolve around two axes, the sociolinguistic and the language acquisition axes. Along the former axis, an SA context has been characterized as one in which massive amounts of TL input can be obtained, in a variety of situations, while taking part in different speech events and assuming different social roles, within myriad human relationships and social domains (Kasper & Rose, 2002). Along the language acquisition axis, cognitive mechanisms and processes are to be considered; for instance, those processes activated while interacting in meaning-oriented communication through conversation, as is typical in natural contexts such as SA, are seen to give way to incidental learning, without consciousness or awareness (Ellis, 1994; Gass, 2006; Hulstijn, 2006; Schmidt, 1994). In radical contrast, in FI contexts, language exposure and interaction, although often happening exclusively through the medium of the TL, tend to be sociolinguistically circumscribed to the contact hours included in the educational programme that learners happen to follow, unless virtual environments and other extra materials in the TL are used by learners. Moreover, in FI classrooms, input and output are fashioned by teachers so that learners attend mostly to form with the ultimate objective of improving their linguistic expertise. In sum, it is the interface between macro and micro features that allows certain learners to make greater progress. Finally, a well-constructed SA programme should give the best opportunities to make such effort efficient and long-lasting.

At this point it is worth noting that FI and SA have not only been described as opposing contexts; it has also been claimed that an SA context may facilitate automatization of the linguistic competence practised, whose proceduralization might have begun in an FI context (DeKeyser, 2007). These are processes that, to some degree, involve implicit and explicit cognitive mechanisms being activated either separately or at once. Furthermore, there can be a transfer of knowledge from the practice conducted in one context to another context so that knowledge acquired in one setting can be activated in another. In an attempt to pursue DeKeyser's view, Pérez-Vidal (2011) has stressed the interest of investigating the complementariness of different learning contexts. If it is the case, as it would seem, that the skills most practised in one learning context do not coincide with those most practised in another, different contexts may complement one another from the point of view of learning opportunities.[1] Thus, a sequential combination of all contexts might offer the ideal formula for greater linguistic progress. In short, putting both views together, it may be argued that different learning contexts may have a complementary impact on learners' skill development. It is to the role of practice of different linguistic skills in diverse learning contexts that the following subsection is devoted.

Contexts of learning, practice opportunities and skill development

It is worth focusing on the concept of practice in relation to different contexts of learning in more detail. The differences in the type and amount of practice that students can avail themselves of in the learning contexts in this study, SA and FI, have already been stressed. Indeed, the features that characterize each context result in particular patterns of learner behaviour and language skills practised.

When we apply this view in contrasting SA and FI contexts, what we find is that the acquisition of a foreign language in a formal instructional setting typically involves large amounts of declarative knowledge focusing on form, very limited exposure to authentic L2 input and few opportunities for meaningful interaction in the L2. Moreover, as is typical in academic contexts, FI typically revolves around writing and/or receptive rather than productive oral skills. In contrast, the SA context as described above allows learners to focus on meaning-oriented communication and substantial practice in oral skills. As previously mentioned, DeKeyser's (2007) view that it is the experience accumulated in FI that may play a role in the relative benefits of a subsequent period spent abroad explains such an apparent contrast as a continuity effect instead. Indeed, the SA input features and practice opportunities represent the kind of intensive language practice that may enhance the proceduralization – and ultimately automatization – of knowledge previously acquired in declarative form in FI. We will now turn to research on oral and written skills development.

Research on oral and written skills development during SA

Study abroad research has mainly focused on the development of oral skills, particularly speaking, This is also reflected in expectations for gains in this domain on the basis of the skill that is supposed to be most practised this context. Results have confirmed this view and overall oral proficiency has been found to yield considerable gains abroad (Isabelli-García, 2003; Lindseth, 2010; Segalowitz & Freed, 2004). Oral fluency has been examined with respect to various temporal and hesitation phenomena, revealing that SA learners increase the length and rate of their fluent speech runs, while reducing their pauses and dysfluencies (Freed *et al.*, 2004; Isabelli-García, 2003; Segalowitz & Freed, 2004; Mora & Valls-Ferrer, 2012; Towell *et al.*, 1996; Valls-Ferrer, 2011). However, contrary to what might have been expected, results are mixed in the area of pronunciation. Findings have not consistently supported the hypothesis that the SA context enhances L2 speech pronunciation and perception (Díaz-Campos, 2004; Mora, 2008; Valls-Ferrer, 2011).

In comparison with the oral skills, very few studies have focused on the acquisition of literacy and writing. The scant literature in this area offers some evidence that SA can enhance this skill (Kinginger, 2009), although comparative studies have not established a clear advantage for the SA context over FI settings at home (AH) in this respect. Thus, Freed *et al.* (2003) find more progress in written fluency AH than after SA, although SA participants are considered more ambitious in writing than their FI counterparts. In a similar vein, Sasaki (2004, 2007) shows that both groups, the AH participants in Japan and the group on SA (four to nine months), improved their written quality/fluency, but the SA group's motivation to write increased. Pérez-Vidal and Juan-Garau (2009) also report some benefits of the SA period on writing, particularly in the domains of fluency and lexical complexity, which register more gains abroad, while accuracy improves similarly in both learning contexts.

On the basis of what has been discussed so far, the present chapter investigates the impact of skill-specific intensity of exposure in SLA on the linguistic development of advanced undergraduate English as a foreign language (EFL) learners. The study focuses on linguistic progress in both written and oral skills as a differential effect of practice in two learning contexts, an SA and an FI context. Based on data from the Study Abroad and Language Acquisition (SALA) project (see Pérez-Vidal, 2011 for further information), this chapter seeks to add evidence to the existing body of research into SA effects on SLA. We now turn to the presentation of the study.

The Present Study

The study presented in this chapter analyses an SA period experienced by advanced EFL undergraduates as a result of a compulsory three-month

Erasmus–Socrates exchange following a period of FI in their home university (88% of participants travel to the UK and Ireland). This allows for a relevant comparison of the impact of an SA context and an FI instruction context. It deals with two of the linguistic competence areas covered by the SALA project, oral and written competence, elicited by means of two different tasks.

Research questions

The study addresses three different research questions in relation to intensity of exposure and oral and written practice opportunities for which evidence is either scarce or contradictory:

(1) How do the abilities of a group of non-native speakers (NNSs) of English compare with those of a group of NSs, who provide baseline data?
(2) What progress is made in those skills over three data collection times in two different learning contexts, SA and FI?
(3) To what extent is the linguistic progress made by NNSs in oral and written communication skills similar or different as a function of learning context?

Participants

The subjects analysed were a group of 29 undergraduates with an advanced level of English (NNSs). Their ages ranged between 17 and 25. They were bilingual in Catalan and Spanish and had English as an L3.

The sample was largely made up of females (91.9%), representing the largest part of the student body at the Translation and Interpreting College in Barcelona, Spain. In their four-year degree, they additionally study a second foreign language, either French or German, and some of them reportedly learn other languages, such as Arabic, Chinese, Italian or Portuguese, outside university. According to curricular recommendations, they should have a linguistic competence in English at a B2 CEFR level upon entrance. Their curriculum also includes the three-month compulsory SA period in an English-speaking country that is the main focus of our study.

These NNSs' performance was compared with that of 10 NSs. The NS baseline group included undergraduates from the UK and the USA following an SA exchange programme at a different Spanish university. They were 20 years old on average at the time of data collection. The NS group afforded highly comparable data that were used to operationalize language proficiency.

Design

Table 10.1 displays the different periods under study and the different data collection times within the SALA project design. The NNS group was followed longitudinally over the course of the first two academic years of

Table 10.1 SALA project: Treatment and data collection times

		Years					
		2005/2006			2006/2007		
Term	1	2	3	1	2	3
	FI	FI			FI	FI
Treatment	↓ (40 h)	(40 h) ↓	—	SA ↓	(40 h)	(40 h)
Data collection	T1		T2		T2	T3

their degree and measured at three data collection times. The baseline group of NSs was tested once.

For the NNS group the organization of the degree established a continuum with an initial block of FI, followed by the SA period, and then another block of FI.[2] Data collection times were placed along this continuum at the beginning and end of each block. Thus, T1 was the pre-test that takes place upon entry to the degree. T2 took place after 80 hours of formal instruction distributed between two 40 hour English subjects. T3 took place after their SA programme. T1 was thus a pre-test, while T2 was both a post-test for T1 and a pre-test for T3. In turn, T3 was a post-test.

The conditions of both the FI and the SA contexts of acquisition were as follows. During the autumn and winter terms in which participants learn English in an FI context in Barcelona, before SA, they follow two 40 hour courses in which English is the medium of instruction. Students additionally follow a preparatory module to help them cope with their SA programme and benefit from it as much as possible. They are also instructed to complete an optional piece of work, a written personal diary. There is no FI during the third term of the first year. During the SA period taking place in the first term of the second academic year, students attend mostly content courses on subjects related to their field of study as explained below.

Treatment and intensity of exposure

The exchange framework in which the SALA Project participants were involved is quite conventional from the Western Europe exchange perspective, taking advantage of the European Union's Erasmus scheme, which guarantees free tuition in a partner institution. Consequently, this is the kind of SA programme that combines the benefits of living in the country where the TL is spoken and attending content courses in which it is the language of instruction. The programme is not sheltered in that no tutor accompanies the students to their university destinations abroad.

Participants in this study were individually tutored in their home institutions before enrolling in a minimum of four academic subjects at their exchange university destination. The host institutions offered two different streams – either in an Applied Modern Languages department or a more traditional Philology department – and the students' programmes of study were tailored to meet their academic requirements and interests as much as possible. Generally speaking, the four subjects included one English language module, one bi-directional Translation module, one module in the students' second foreign language (German or French), and one elective module. Students were also encouraged to take advantage of language learning facilities available to them. The formal instruction described amounted at least to eight hours of in-class instruction per week.

During the FI period preceding their term abroad, participants follow two subsequent 40 hour English language subjects, each totalling four contact hours per week and four hours of homework. In the AH setting, courses mainly focus on language forms, semantics and discourse. Students also receive some practice in written skills through discrete point exercises as well as written essays and compositions. However consistently English might be used by teachers and students at the university, it is not spoken in the environment outside of the classroom. The sociolinguistic situation in the city of Barcelona is one where, except for circumstances where tourists may be encountered, little English is heard in the media or in the public sphere.

Socially speaking, students travel to their SA destinations in groups of three to five. They tend to live in residences, sometimes in flats, and less frequently with host families. They occasionally find a job and they travel around as much as possible.

Data collection and analysis

Two tasks were used for data collection in this study. For development in oral communication, a semi-guided interview was used to gather oral data from paired subjects. Participants were provided with a set of seven questions each on the topic *University Life* and they were then asked to act as both interviewers and interviewees. First, the participant acting as interviewer asked the questions one at a time and the interviewee responded to each question before proceeding to the next. Subsequently, they switched roles. The analyses were performed solely on the answers to the interview questions. Measures of oral fluency, accuracy and complexity were used to track development in oral competence following Freed *et al.* (2004); Segalowitz and Freed (2004) and Mora and Valls-Ferrer (2012).

For the analysis of written development a composition was used. Participants were allowed 30 minutes to write on the following topic: *Someone who moves to a foreign country should always adopt the customs and way of life of his/her new country*. Written development was measured quantitatively in the conventional domains of fluency, accuracy and complexity – both grammatical and lexical (see Celaya *et al.*, 2001; Polio, 2001; Polio & Gass, 1997; Torras *et al.*, 2006; Wolfe-Quintero *et al.*, 1998).

Compositions were transcribed following Computerized Language Analysis (CLAN) conventions with the help of research assistants. The interviews were recorded, digitalized and computer-edited for subsequent orthographic transcriptions with CLAN. Differences between the performances of NSs and NNSs were explored through independent-samples *t*-tests. Then, development in written and oral competence across data collection times was assessed through one-way repeated measures analysis of variation (ANOVA) and T1–T2 (FI) and T2–T3 (SA) *post-hoc* contrasts. Differences in the size of gains obtained during the FI and SA learning contexts, as well as differences between written and oral competence gains (NGains), were compared through paired-samples *t*-tests.

Learners' development of language production skills was assessed by means of two measures per domain (fluency, accuracy and complexity) within each language production mode (oral and written) across the three data collection times (see Table 10.2).

At this point some clarification is needed. Although written and oral measures tap into the same set of linguistic production dimensions (fluency, accuracy and complexity) and these might be related in the two production modes, they are not directly comparable. The tasks used to elicit written and oral data are different in nature and consequently the measures capture different underlying processes in language production. In order to make the comparison feasible between the FI and the SA learning contexts, gains obtained at T2 and T3 as a proportion of the total score obtained at the previous data collection time (T1 and T2, respectively) were calculated for each measure. This provided us with a comparable measure of 'amount of improvement' or normalized gains (NGain) between data collection times and across written and oral performance, which allowed us to assess the differential effects of learning contexts on linguistic gains as a function of the type of production modality (written vs oral). We also checked the extent to which the amount of language produced by learners in the written and oral modalities was different. Learners produced an average of 8.4 words per minute at T1 (range 3.6–15.1) when writing a composition for which they were given 30 minutes, and

Table 10.2 Measures used per domain

	Measures	
Fluency	Words per clause (W/C)	W/C
	Words per minute (W/M)	W/M
Accuracy	Errors per clause (E/CL)	E/CL
	Errors per word (× 10) (E/W)	E/W
Complexity	Guiraud index (GuirIndx)	GuirIndx
	Clause per sentence (CL/S) (written)	CL/S
	Clause per Analysis of Speech (AS) unit (CL/AS) (oral)	CL/AS

Table 10.3 Mean total number of words produced in the written and oral task (standard deviation, SD, in parentheses) and results of *t*-tests comparing total number of words produced in the written and oral tasks

Words	Data collection times		
	T1	T2	T3
Written	252.4 (99.4)	203.1 (50.9)	249.2 (62.5)
Oral Word count	252.2 (118.4)	227.6 (78.3)	248.2 (107.3)
Total time (seconds)	123.4 (57.6)	110.9 (39.3)	108.3 (53.04)
t-Tests (paired)	$t(28) = 0.007$, $p = 0.994$	$t(28) = -1.33$, $p = 0.194$	$t(28) = 0.007$, $p = 0.994$

produced an average of 252.4 words (range 110–453), whereas in the oral elicitation task learners talked for an average of 2.05 minutes or 123.4 seconds (range 1.01–5.45) to produce 252.2 words (range 100–696). Thus, although the time taken to complete the written (30 minutes) and oral (2.05 minutes) tasks was very different, the amount of language produced (measured in total number of words) was almost the same in the written and oral tasks at all three data collection times, which further ensured the comparability of the measures between the two production modes (see Table 10.3).

Having presented the study, in the following section the outcomes of our comparative analyses are reported and discussed.

Results and Discussion

The results for the three research questions addressed in this chapter are presented below. Firstly, the performance of NNS was contrasted with that of NSs as baseline data. Secondly, developmental progress over time, after a period spent abroad following FI, was measured for both linguistic modalities, written and oral, independently and across skills. Thirdly, the study analysed how gains in written and oral performance differed from each other as a function of learning context (FI vs SA).

Non-native vs native speaker performance

When comparing NNSs and NSs, the results of the analysis show contrasting findings according to linguistic modality. On the one hand, despite the improvement of NNSs between T1 and T3, *t*-test analyses of the oral task showed that the NS group significantly outperformed NNSs in all but one measure (W/C) at all data collection times, as expected, indicating that NSs produced more fluent, complex and accurate language in the oral interview than NNSs. On the other hand, interestingly, this was not the case in the writing task, where already at T1 NSs only outperformed NNSs significantly

Table 10.4 Mean fluency, accuracy and complexity scores at T1, T2 and T3 for NNSs (n = 29) and NSs (n = 10) (SD in parentheses). Bold values indicate significant NNS–NS differences

		Written production				Oral production			
		T1	T2	T3	**NSs**	T1	T2	T3	**NSs**
Fluency	W/C	7.36	7.03	6.98	6.71	6.05	6.11	6.35	6.97
		(1.39)	(3.13)	(1.81)	(1.21)	(0.58)	(0.60)	(0.60)	(3.27)
	W/M	8.41	**6.77**	8.31	9.11	**124.1**	**125.4**	**142.1**	182.9
		(3.31)	**(1.69)**	(2.08)	(1.96)	**(23.1)**	**(23.8)**	**(24.7)**	(23.5)
Accuracy	E/CL	**0.44**	**0.36**	**0.28**	0.004	**0.24**	**0.21**	**0.17**	0.04
		(0.29)	**(0.36)**	**(0.20)**	(0.009)	**(0.13)**	**(0.14)**	**(0.11)**	(0.01)
	E/W	**0.62**	**0.52**	**0.42**	0.007	**0.39**	**0.34**	**0.26**	0.01
		(0.44)	**(0.47)**	**(0.30)**	(0.001)	**(0.22)**	**(0.22)**	**(0.18)**	(0.03)
Complexity	GuirIndx	7.98	**7.46**	7.96	8.34	**6.72**	**6.85**	**6.92**	7.85
		(0.96)	**(0.93)**	(0.72)	(0.96)	**(0.86)**	**(0.66)**	**(0.74)**	(0.80)
	CL/S–CL/AS	3.61	3.76	3.69	3.66	**1.61**	**1.58**	**1.62**	1.85
		(0.98)	(1.17)	(1.25)	(1.66)	**(0.21)**	**(0.21)**	**(0.25)**	(0.27)

in accuracy, suggesting that the written performances of NNSs and NSs do not differ substantially in either fluency or lexical and syntactic complexity. Table 10.4 displays the means and standard deviations of the contrasts, for both oral and written performance, between NNS and NS production at the three data collection times.

Table 10.5, in turn, offers an account of the comparisons between the different NNS data collection times and NS performance, as calculated through independent-samples *t*-tests.

Given these results, there are two possible interpretations that are worth mentioning here, one on purely linguistic grounds and another on methodological grounds. It could be argued that written abilities are more amenable to progress through adequate treatment than oral abilities. Hence, our participants, specializing in Translation, have a command of written English acquired through EFL teaching that places them at (near) native-like levels of competence. A more plausible explanation, however, is that the measures used to assess learners' fluency and complexity in writing fail to capture underlying NS–NNS differences. Research in progress within the SALA project is exploring new ways of capturing such differences between first and second language written development.[3] We will now turn to the second set of comparisons.

Progress in written and oral production

This section tackles the second research question concerning NNSs' oral and written progress over the span of 14 months, encompassing an SA

Table 10.5 Independent-samples t-tests comparing the performances of NSs and NNSs T1, T2 and T3 (bold values indicate significance)

		T1		T2		T3	
		$t\,(38)$	p	$t\,(38)$	p	$t\,(38)$	p
Written production							
Fluency	W/C	1.30	0.200	0.311	0.758	0.424	0.674
	W/M	−0.625	0.536	−3.61	**0.001**	−1.06	0.294
Accuracy	E/CL	4.64	**<0.001**	3.16	**0.003**	4.43	**<0.001**
	E/W	4.37	**<0.001**	3.41	**0.002**	4.33	**<0.001**
Complexity	GuirIndx	−1.02	0.311	−2.54	**0.015**	−1.32	0.193
	CL/S–CL/AS	−0.110	0.913	0.204	0.839	−0.54	0.957
Oral production							
Fluency	W/C	−1.47	0.150	−1.37	0.178	−0.988	0.330
	W/M	−6.90	**<0.001**	−6.59	**<0.001**	−4.56	**<0.001**
Accuracy	E/CL	5.31	**<0.001**	4.68	**<0.001**	4.49	**<0.001**
	E/W	5.21	**<0.001**	4.65	**<0.001**	4.38	**<0.001**
Complexity	GuirIndx	−3.61	**0.001**	−3.92	**<0.001**	−3.35	**0.002**
	CL/S–CL/AS	−2.61	**0.013**	−2.88	**0.006**	−2.18	**0.035**

context of acquisition preceded by an FI context. More specifically, for both the written and the oral modalities independently, three issues in the participants' linguistic development were examined by means of the following three subquestions: (a) whether progress occurred over time (T1–T3); (b) whether progress made over time was due to gains obtained during SA (T2–T3), during FI (T1–T2) or both; and (c) whether gains obtained during SA (T2–T3) and FI (T1–T2) were significantly different.

Regarding subquestion (a), that is, progress made between T1, T2 and T3 in each of the modalities, written and oral, the overall pattern of development that emerges is displayed in Table 10.4. In writing, fluency does not show a consistent trend toward improvement. Whereas W/C decreased at T2 and remained stable through SA, W/M decreased drastically at T2 and then increased to the initial T1 level at T3. As regards accuracy, measures improved over time, that is, learners gradually reduced the number of errors they made when writing. Finally, lexical complexity decreased at T2 and increased to its T1 level at T3, whereas grammatical complexity increased at T2 and then decreased slightly at T3. These results indicate that, after FI, but not after SA, learners' written productions were shorter on average, consisted of shorter clauses and used a more limited vocabulary range (these results are in accordance with Pérez-Vidal & Juan-Garau, 2009; Pérez-Vidal et al., 2011; Sasaki, 2004, 2007). Given the fact that during FI learners received some specific instruction on writing and had to submit several written assignments, the loss in written fluency and complexity could be explained by learners' focus on accuracy, central to the FI curriculum as already explained. This trade-off hypothesis, however, is not supported by the Pearson *r* correlation analysis conducted between accuracy scores and fluency and complexity scores, which did not produce significant negative correlations for any of the measures at either T1 or T2. Another possible interpretation of these results might be, along the lines of DeKeyser's (2007) view referred to above, that the improvement made during SA may also be explained by the fact that learners were attending courses, submitting written assignments and, for many of them, writing their SA diaries in an academic environment comparable to that of the home university, only much richer in terms of the intensity of exposure and varied opportunities for meaningful communication. This might have enhanced the learners' communicative abilities in the written modality already practised during FI.

In oral production, fluency, complexity (both lexical and grammatical) and accuracy all show a consistent trend of improvement across the three data collection times, particularly after the SA period, thus corroborating previous research findings (Freed *et al.*, 2004; Isabelli-García, 2003; Llanes & Muñoz, 2009; Llanes, 2010; Mora & Valls-Ferrer, 2012; Pérez-Vidal *et al.*, 2011; Segalowitz & Freed, 2004).

In order to test for the significance of the changes across the three data collection times in written and oral production described above, fluency, accuracy and complexity scores were submitted to a series of repeated measures ANOVAs with *time* (T1, T2, T3) as the within-subjects factor (Table 10.6). In writing, overall significant changes as a function of data collection time were found for one fluency measure (W/M), accuracy (E/CL and E/W) and lexical complexity (GuirIndx). However, the statistically significant changes over time in fluency and complexity were due to a decrease in W/M and GuirIndx at T2 followed by an increase of both measures at T3 to reach T1 values. In oral production, however, both fluency (W/M) and accuracy (E/CL and E/W) obtained significant gains over time, whereas changes in complexity turned out to be non-significant.

Regarding subquestion (b), that is, whether progress made over time was due to gains obtained during SA, during FI, or both, the results indicate differences as a function of modality and linguistic dimension (Table 10.6). In writing, as already mentioned above, there was a decrease in fluency and lexical complexity at T2 that was compensated for by significant gains occurring during SA. Accuracy changed over time, reflecting a gradual improvement across all three data collection times that could not be exclusively attributed to either the FI or the SA learning contexts, whereas grammatical complexity did not significantly improve over time. In oral production, the significant improvement in fluency (W/M) and accuracy (E/CL and E/W) over time was mainly due to substantial gains only occurring during SA,

Table 10.6 One-way repeated measures ANOVAs with Time (T1, T2, T3) and T1–T2 (FI) and T2–T3 (SA) contrasts. All values of F = (2, 27) and (1, 28) for the T1–T2 and T2–T3 contrasts (bold values indicate p < 0.0.9, *p < 0.05; + indicates gains)

		T1–T2–T3		T1–T2 (FI)			T2–T3 (SA)		
		F	p	F	Gain	p	F	Gain	p
Written production									
Fluency	W/C	0.474	0.628	0.251	–	0.620	0.022	–	0.844
	W/M	8.85	**0.001***	7.26	–	0.35	0.12	+	**<0.001***
Accuracy	E/CL	7.39	**0.003***	1.23	+	**0.042***	2.67	+	0.087
	E/W	5.88	**0.008***	1.09	+	0.305	2.17	+	0.152
Complexity	GuirIndx	4.72	**0.017***	6.36	–	**0.018***	8.58	+	**0.007***
	CL/S	0.246	0.784	0.498	+	0.486	0.191	–	0.665
Oral production									
Fluency	W/C	3.31	**0.52**	0.172	+	0.681	2.54	+	0.122
	W/M	10.1	**<0.001***	0.111	+	0.742	16.1	+	**<0.001***
Accuracy	E/CL	4.39	**0.022***	1.41	+	0.244	3.69	+	**0.065**
	E/W	5.92	**0.007***	2.07	+	0.161	4.61	+	**0.041***
Complexity	GuirIndx	1.12	0.338	0.999	+	0.326	0.852	+	0.364
	CL/AS	0.430	0.655	0.229	–	0.636	0.832	+	0.369

further confirming the results of previous research (Mora & Valls-Ferrer, 2012). In general, as shown in Table 10.6, positive significant gains (+) occurred more frequently for both written and oral production in the SA context than in the FI context.

In order to further examine the changes over time occurring during SA from the perspective of inter-subject variation, we conducted two correlation analyses (Pearson *r*) for all measures, first between NNSs' scores at T2 and at T3 and then between FI gains (calculated by subtracting T1 from T2 scores) and SA gains (calculated by subtracting T2 from T3 scores). In general, a positive significant correlation between T2–T3 written and oral production scores indicated that participants who had obtained higher scores at T2 also obtained higher scores at T3, that is, inter-subject differences among participants in written and oral production were maintained (Table 10.7). However, all correlations between FI and SA gains, most of which were highly significant, were negative, suggesting that those learners who showed the least improvement during FI improved the most during SA.

Regarding subquestion (c), that is, whether gains obtained during FI and SA were different, we first calculated FI and SA gains. We then ran a series of paired-samples *t*-tests to check for differences between mean results in FI and SA gains. In writing, these tests (Table 10.8) revealed significant differences attributable to learning context in the case of fluency (W/M) and

Table 10.7 Pearson r product–moment correlations between T2 and T3 scores and FI and SA gains (bold values indicate significance)

Pearson		Written (T2–T3 scores)		Oral (T2–T3 scores)		Written (FI–SA gains)		Written (FI–SA gains)	
		r	p	r	p	r	p	r	p
Fluency	W/C	0.792	**<0.001**	0.095	0.624	−0.778	**<0.001**	−0.687	**<0.001**
	W/M	0.398	**0.032**	0.579	**0.001**	−0.274	0.150	−0.417	**0.024**
Accuracy	E/CL	0.681	**<0.001**	0.630	**<0.001**	−0.753	**<0.001**	−0.458	**0.013**
	E/W	0.651	**<0.001**	0.538	**0.003**	−0.739	**<0.001**	−0.469	**0.010**
Complexity	GuirIndx	0.423	**0.022**	0.798	**<0.001**	−0.545	**0.002**	−0.210	0.275
	CL/S – CL/AS	0.743	**<0.001**	0.556	**0.002**	−0.486	**0.007**	−0.268	0.159

Table 10.8 T1–T2 (FI) and T2–T3 (SA) gains and FI–SA paired samples t-tests (bold values indicate significance; − indicates loss, and + indicates gains)

		FI (T1–T2)	SA (T2–T3)	t (28)	p
Written production					
Fluency	W/C	−0.33	−0.05	−0.280	0.781
	W/M	−1.64	+1.53	−3.93	**0.001**
Accuracy	E/CL	−0.07	−0.08	0.027	0.979
	E/W	−0.01	−0.01	−0.046	0.964
Complexity	GuirIndx	−0.51	+0.49	−3.07	**0.005**
	CL/S	+0.14	−0.07	0.680	0.502
Oral production					
Fluency	W/C	+0.06	+0.23	−0.656	0.517
	W/M	+1.31	+16.68	−2.25	**0.032**
Accuracy	E/CL	−0.02	−0.04	0.481	0.634
	E/W	−0.004	−0.007	0.514	0.611
Complexity	GuirIndx	+0.12	+0.07	0.268	0.791
	CL/AS	−0.02	+0.03	−0.855	0.400

lexical complexity (GuirIndx) in favour of the SA context, and in oral production fluency gains (W/M) were significantly larger during SA than during FI. Hence, when FI–SA differences arise, it is always the case that gains are larger during SA than FI (see means and *t*-tests in Table 10.8).

Written and oral development as a function of learning context

Finally, in reply to the third research question that motivated our study, an exploration of how gains in written and oral performance differ from each other as a function of learning context (FI vs SA) is presented in this section. In order to find out whether differences between written and oral modalities were significant, a series of *t*-tests were conducted on the FI and SA normalized gains (NGains, see below). NGains, as opposed to T1–T2 or T2–T3 gains reported in the previous section, is a normalized measure of gains obtained by calculating the percentage of the T1 score the gain at T2 represented for FI, and the percentage of the T2 score the gain at T3 represented for SA. For example, a mean NGain score of 10 in fluency (W/M) in SA represented a 10% increase in the W/M score with respect to the mean T2 score of 6.77 words per minute in writing, that is, a gain of 0.67 words per minute, whereas in oral production the same 10% increase in the W/M score with respect to the mean T2 score of 125.4 words per minute would represent an increase of 12.5 words per minute.

The results of the *t*-tests show that on the NGain measures written and oral development were not significantly different in either FI or SA, except for lexical complexity, where the size of the NGains was greater in oral than in written production in FI and less prominent in oral than in written production after SA (see Table 10.9). From the perspective of practice opportunities, this finding can be interpreted as an effect of teaching methods. It could be argued that practice has not only a quantitative but also a qualitative dimension. That is, whereas an FI context is generally not conducive to practising the oral skills, the teaching methods that prevail at the learners' home university, with English used as the vehicle for communication at all times, seem to have a positive impact on learners' oral lexical development. Conversely, the type of practice accrued in the SA context seems to have an impact on lexical progress in writing. It could also be argued, following Hokanson (2000) that the skills most practised in a particular context are not necessarily the ones to progress the most.

We then analysed differences in the NGain scores between learning contexts (FI vs SA) independently for the written and oral modalities by running a series of paired-samples *t*-tests on the NGain scores (see Table 10.10).

Table 10.9 NGains in written and oral production during FI and SA, and *t*-tests comparing written vs oral production (bold values indicate significance)

		FI				SA			
NGain (% score gain)		Written	Oral	t(28)	p	Written	Oral	t(28)	p
Fluency	W/C	−0.83	1.87	−0.287	0.776	5.50	4.78	0.125	0.902
	W/M	−9.03	2.32	−10.67	0.105	26.8	15.3	1.53	0.135
Accuracy	E/CL	56.8	1.68	1.15	0.275	20.3	2.2	0.616	0.543
	E/W	51.3	1.97	0.99	0.329	15.1	−3.01	0.648	0.523
Complexity	GuirIndx	−5.58	2.54	−2.99	**0.006**	7.71	1.25	2.58	**0.015**
	CL/S	8.22	−0.28	1.27	0.212	−0.19	2.98	−0.74	0.461

Table 10.10 NGains in FI and SA for written and oral production and *t*-tests comparing FI vs SA NGains (bold values indicate significance)

		Written production				Oral production			
NGain (% score gain)		FI	SA	t(28)	p	FI	SA	t(28)	p
Fluency	W/C	−0.83	5.50	−0.500	0.621	1.87	4.78	−0.625	0.537
	W/M	−9.03	26.8	−3.42	**0.002**	2.32	15.3	−2.15	**0.040**
Accuracy	E/CL	56.8	20.3	0.622	0.539	1.68	2.2	−0.006	0.995
	E/W	51.3	15.1	0.698	0.491	1.97	−3.01	0.280	0.782
Complexity	GuirIndx	−5.58	7.71	−3.17	**0.004**	2.54	1.25	0.550	0.586
	CL/S–CL/AS	8.22	−0.19	0.922	0.365	−0.28	2.98	−0.744	0.463

Within written production, NGains in fluency (W/M) and lexical complexity (GuirIndx) were significantly larger after SA than after FI, whereas within oral production NGains were not significantly different in FI and SA, except for the greater fluency (W/M) NGains obtained in FI, something that may be explained along the same lines as the *t*-tests results just discussed.

Finally, we explored the relationship between the written and oral modalities from a within-subjects perspective by running a series of *Pearson r* correlations on subjects' written and oral scores in fluency, accuracy and complexity. The aim of this analysis was to uncover possible relationships between the two modalities. For example, participants using more grammatically complex structures in writing might also be producing more complex sentences when speaking, which would indicate a similar level of competence in grammatical complexity across the two production modalities. No significant correlations between written and oral scores were found, except in the linguistic domain of accuracy. As far as accuracy is concerned, written and oral production scores were significantly correlated at T1 (E/CL, $r = 0.674$, $p < 0.001$; E/W, $r = 0.613$, $p < 0.001$) and T2 (E/CL, $r = 0.723$, $p < 0.001$, E/W: $r = 0.722$, $p < 0.001$), but not at T3, suggesting that at T1 and T2 more accurate learners in writing were also more accurate in speaking, whereas at T3 this relationship was no longer apparent, probably owing to the significant increase in oral accuracy taking place during SA, as indicated by the results of ANOVA analyses in Table 10.6.

Summary and Conclusions

In this chapter we have sought to explore a particular context of learning, study abroad, in which higher intensity of exposure to input can be obtained, in contrast with formal instruction at home. In order to do so we firstly compared the oral and written abilities of a group of non-native speakers of English with those of a group of native speakers, who provide baseline data. We then compared progress in writing skills and progress in oral skills at three different points of development and in two different learning contexts, SA and FI, in the case of the group of NNSs, to our knowledge a contrast seldom made in SA research. Finally we contrasted their written and oral progress while abroad with progress made during an FI period, for which evidence exists but is often contradictory. A summary of the results obtained in the analyses conducted follows.

As a preliminary step, considering that the underlying processes that take place in the written and oral modes are different, we first ensured that the linguistic dimensions measured were comparable as regards amount of language produced (in terms of raw word counts) in the written and oral tasks at all three data collection times. After that, our first research question explored the gains obtained by our NNS participants in two different learning contexts in contrast with NS baseline production.

The results of the analyses revealed that learners' oral performance, despite considerable improvement after SA, remained very different from NSs' oral performance in all linguistic domains. In contrast, no such differences could be found in writing except in the domain of accuracy. In fact, already at T1, NNSs were not significantly different from NSs for the remaining domains of written linguistic competence. With these findings in mind, we tackled our second research question in order to verify whether progress was made by NNSs after a sojourn abroad subsequent to FI, measuring the impact of each context separately. Our data show that written accuracy as well as oral fluency and accuracy improved over time, although gain sizes were always larger after SA, and significantly so in oral production. We then finally tackled our third research question, regarding the differences between written vs oral development as a function of learning context. Firstly, the analyses show that the amount of improvement in written and oral development was not significantly different after FI nor after SA, except for lexical complexity. For this dimension, the gains obtained in FI were significantly larger in speaking than in writing, whereas in SA the gains were significantly larger in writing than in speaking. This is because written lexical complexity decreased significantly at T2 and increased significantly at T3, whereas in oral lexical complexity improvement occurred both during FI and SA but was significantly larger in FI. Secondly, both in written production and in oral production, the amount of improvement obtained in fluency (W/M) was significantly larger in SA than in FI. Thirdly, the fact that in fluency and complexity written and oral scores were unrelated (both in FI and SA) suggests that learners' levels of competence were different in writing and speaking, that is, more fluent speakers or speakers using more grammatically complex language were not necessarily more fluent writers or writers using more grammatically complex structures. In contrast, as regards accuracy, learners producing fewer errors did so both in writing and speaking during FI. After SA, however, more accurate speakers were no longer more accurate writers, possibly owing to a greater impact of SA on oral than on written accuracy. Thirdly, both for oral and written development, those participants who had obtained higher scores at T2 also obtained higher scores at T3, indicating that higher initial level prior to SA resulted in greater benefits. In addition, our findings also suggest that those learners who showed less improvement during FI improved the most during SA. This may be due to the fact that they simply had more room for improvement than those who were at a higher level, something that may indicate a certain ceiling effect in the three-month SA programme analysed in this study.

Finally, the amount of improvement (NGains) was larger during SA than during FI on three of the six written production measures and on four of the six oral production measures (reaching significance in written W/M and GuirIndx and oral W/M), suggesting that the SA period had a positive impact on both written and oral production, although the massive amounts of exposure benefited the oral skills to a greater extent than the written skills, except in the domain of written lexical complexity.

On the basis of such findings, the issue of the differential effects of practice as a consequence of learning context on the development of oral and written skills can be addressed. Our results seem to point in two directions: (a) on the one hand, progress does not take place in a similar way for both modalities, oral and written, in both learning contexts in which learners find themselves, except in the domain of accuracy, where progress is steady – fluency and complexity, in contrast, differ, with oral lexical complexity improving at home and written lexical complexity abroad; (b) on the other hand, this fact notwithstanding, the SA context seems to have a greater impact on both oral and written skills than FI, more specifically for oral fluency and accuracy. In the attempt made in this chapter to try and explore progress in two different skills, and in two different acquisition contexts, different reasons have been given that may account for these findings. At any rate, further research into data collected from different SA programme designs, for example with longer periods spent abroad, should add new dimensions to our findings.

Consequently, we must conclude by stating that, in spite of the differences in the number of opportunities for practising written and oral skills that exist in the two contexts explored in this chapter, development takes place in both written and oral abilities, when learners experience both settings one after the other. This can be attributed to the fact that they complement each other, so that these contexts in combination constitute a great opportunity for enhanced linguistic progress or, along the lines of DeKeyser's (2007) tenet, there can be knowledge transfer from one learning context to another.

Acknowledgements

This research received financial support through HUM2007-66053-C02-01/02, FFI2010-21483-C02-01/02 and ALLENCAM (SGR2005-01086/2009-140) from the Spanish Ministry of Education and the Catalan Government. We would like to sincerely thank Dr Carmen Muñoz for her patience and invaluable comments on an earlier version of this paper. Thanks are due to the research assistants Ann Rebecca Lara and Pilar Avello for their work on the SALA project; their personal investment in collecting and transcribing the data was essential. Finally, we would also like to thank the students who volunteered to participate in the project.

Notes

(1) The *Combination and Complementariness of Contexts Hypothesis* has been proposed, encompassing the contrast between SA, FI and Content-and-Language-Integrated-Learning programmes in Europe, a relatively recent educational approach that will not be discussed in this chapter (Pérez-Vidal, 2011).
(2) Several SALA studies have analysed the mid-term effects of the SA after 15 months with a fourth data collection time.
(3) Measures of writing quality are being calculated in relation to five different components (content, organization, vocabulary, language use and mechanics). These, together with quantifications of lexical sophistication, cohesion, coherence and overlap, should give us further insights for future studies.

References

Celaya, M.L., Torras, R.M. and Pérez-Vidal, C. (2001) Short and mid-term effects of an earlier start: An analysis of EFL written production. In S. Foster-Cohen and A. Nizegorodcew (eds) *Eurosla Yearbook* (pp. 195–209). Amsterdam: John Benjamins.
DeKeyser, R. (2007) Study abroad as foreign language practice. In R. DeKeyser (ed.) *Practicing in a Second Language: Perspectives from Applied Linguistics and Cognitive Psychology* (pp. 208–226). New York: Cambridge University Press.
Díaz-Campos, M. (2004) Context of learning in the acquisition of Spanish second language phonology. *Studies in Second Language Acquisition* 26 (2), 249–273.
Dörnyei, Z. and P. Skehan. (2006) Individual differences in second language learning. In M.H. Long and C. Doughty (eds) *The Handbook of Second Language Acquisition* (pp. 589–631). Malden, MA: Blackwell.
Ellis, R. (1994) *The Study of Second Language Acquisition*. Oxford: Oxford University Press.
Freed, B.F., So, S. and Lazar, N.A. (2003) Language learning abroad: How do gains in written fluency compare with gains in oral fluency in French as a second language? *ADFL Bulletin* 34 (3), 34–40.
Freed, B.F., Segalowitz, N. and Dewey, D. (2004) Context of learning and second language fluency in French: Comparing regular classroom, study abroad and domestic immersion programs. *Studies in Second Language Acquisition* 26 (2), 275–301.
Gass, S. (2006) Input and interaction. In M.H. Long and C. Doughty (eds) *The Handbook of Second Language Acquisition* (pp. 224–256). Malden, MA: Blackwell.
Hokanson, S. (2000) Foreign language immersion homestays: Maximizing the accommodation of cognitive styles. *Applied Language Learning* 11 (2), 239–264.

Hulstijn, J.H. (2006) Incidental and intentional learning. In M.H. Long and C. Doughty (eds) *The Handbook of Second Language Acquisition* (pp. 349–382). Malden, MA: Blackwell.

Isabelli-García, C.L. (2003) Development of oral communication skills abroad. *Frontiers: The Interdisciplinary Journal of Study Abroad* 9, 149–173. http://www.frontiersjournal.com/issues/vol9/vol9-07_isabelligarcia.htm

Kasper, G. and Rose, K. (2002) *Pragmatic Development in a Second Language*. Oxford: Blackwell.

Kinginger, C. (2009) *Language Learning and Study Abroad. A Critical Reading of Research*. New York: Palgrave Macmillan.

Lindseth, M.U. (2010) The development of oral proficiency during a semester in Germany. *Foreign Language Annals* 43 (2), 246–268.

Llanes, M.A. (2010) Children and adults learning English in a study abroad context. PhD dissertation, Universitat de Barcelona.

Llanes, M.A. and Muñoz, C. (2009) A short stay abroad: Does it make a difference? *System* 37 (3), 353–365.

Mora, J.C. (2008) Learning context effects on the acquisition of a second language phonology. In C. Pérez-Vidal, M. Juan-Garau and A. Bel (eds) *A Portrait of the Young in the New Multilingual Spain* (pp. 241–263). Clevedon: Multilingual Matters.

Mora, J.C. and Valls-Ferrer, M. (2012) Oral fluency, accuracy and complexity in formal instruction and study abroad learning contexts. *TESOL Quarterly* (doi: 10.1002/tesq.034).

Pérez-Vidal, C. (2011) Language acquisition in three different contexts of learning: Formal instruction, stay abroad, and semi-immersion (CLIL). In Y. Ruiz de Zarobe, J.M. Sierra and F. Gallardo del Puerto (eds) *Content and Foreign Language Integrated Learning. Contributions to Multilingualism in European Contexts* (pp. 103–127). Bern: Peter Lang.

Pérez-Vidal, C. and Juan-Garau, M. (2009) The effect of study abroad (SA) on written performance. In L. Roberts, D. Véronique, A.C. Nilsol and M. Tellier (eds) *Eurosla Yearbook* (pp. 269–295). Amsterdam: John Benjamins.

Pérez-Vidal, C. and Juan-Garau, M. (2011) The effect of context and input conditions on oral and written development: A study abroad perspective. *International Review of Applied Linguistics in Language Teaching* 49 (2), 157–185.

Pérez-Vidal, C., Juan-Garau, M. and Mora, J.C. (2011) The effects of formal instruction and study abroad contexts on foreign language development: The SALA project. In C. Sanz and R.P. Leow (eds) *Implicit and Explicit Language Learning. Conditions, Processes and Knowledge in SLA and Bilingualism* (pp. 115–128). Washington, DC: Georgetown University Press.

Polio, C.G. (2001) Measures of linguistic accuracy in second language writing research. *Language Learning* 47 (1), 101–143.

Polio, C.G. and Gass, S. (1997) Replication and reporting: A commentary. *Studies in Second Language Acquisition* 19 (4), 499–508.

Sasaki, M. (2004) A multiple-data analysis of the 3.5-year development of EFL student writers. *Language Learning* 54 (3), 525–582.

Sasaki, M. (2007) Effects of study abroad experiences on EFL writers: A multiple-data analysis. *Modern Language Journal* 91 (4), 602–620.

Schmidt, R.W. (1994) Deconstructing consciousness in search of useful definitions for applied linguistics. *AILA Review* 11, 11–26.

Segalowitz, N. and Freed, B.F. (2004) Context, contact and cognition in oral fluency acquisition: Learning Spanish in 'at home' and 'study abroad' contexts. *Studies in Second Language Acquisition* 26 (2), 173–199.

Torras, M.R., Navés, T., Celaya, M.L. and Pérez-Vidal, C. (2006) Age and IL development in writing. In C. Muñoz (ed.) *Age and the Rate of Foreign Language Learning* (pp. 156–182). Clevedon: Multilingual Matters.

Towell, R., Hawkins, R. and Bazergui, N. (1996) The development of fluency in advanced learners of French. *Applied Linguistics* 17, 84–119.

Valls-Ferrer, M. (2011) The development of oral fluency and rhythm during a study abroad period. PhD dissertation, Universitat Pompeu Fabra.

Wolfe-Quintero, K., Kim, H-Y. and Inagaki, S. (1998) *Second Language Development in Writing: Measures of Fluency, Accuracy and Complexity*. Hawai'i: University of Hawai'i Press.

11 Differences in L2 Segmental Perception: The Effects of Age and L2 Learning Experience

Romana Kopečková

Introduction

In today's multilingual world, the everyday experience of hearing various languages spoken by non-natives with foreign accents seems commonplace. This is not surprising, considering the large variety of factors that can affect the way a second language (henceforth L2) is produced, ranging from the learner's native language (henceforth L1) background, to the L2 learning experience, and to motivation to appear native-like when speaking a L2. What may seem more surprising is that L2 learners can also have a 'foreign accent' in the way they perceive L2 speech (Jenkins et al., 1995). The difficulty in perceiving non-native vowels and consonants (or 'sounds' for short) has been systematically related to the learner's ability to hear subtle phonetic differences between L1 and L2 sounds, and between L2 sounds that are not contrastive in their native language (Best, 1995; Best & Strange, 1992; Flege, 1995).

A great deal of research has examined the perception of L2 sounds among learners of diverse backgrounds. In most of this research, it was found that those who began learning their L2 in childhood resembled native speakers in perceiving sounds in the target L2 to a greater extent than those who began their L2 acquisition in adulthood (Baker et al., 2002; Flege & MacKay, 2004; Højen & Flege, 2006). For example, Baker et al. (2002) reported findings from a study with Korean children who outperformed Korean adults in the discrimination of a range of English vowel sounds after about nine years' stay in the USA. The child L2 learners were comparable in their performance to age-matched native English speakers, and were also shown to be more accurate than the Korean adults in perceiving discrepancies between the tested

L1 and L2 vowels. Tsukada *et al.* (2005) reported similar results in a longitudinal study conducted with a comparable population of L2 learners having spent as little as five years in the target language country.

These findings do not necessarily suggest, however, that all early learners perceive an L2 exactly like native speakers; in fact, there is strong evidence indicating that, at the level of subtle phonetic detail, child L2 learners differ from monolingual speakers in their perception of L2 sounds. A body of research with highly proficient Catalan–Spanish bilinguals from Barcelona, focusing on their perception of Catalan mid-vowels, has shown that nonnative sounds that do not contrast phonemically in the L1 are likely to remain perceptually difficult, even if learned in very early childhood (Bosch *et al.*, 2000; Sebastián-Gallés, 2005; Sebastián-Gallés & Soto-Faraco, 1999). These authors interpreted the findings as suggesting that native language shapes the perceptual space of bilinguals at early stages of development in such a way that it irreversibly affects the perception of non-native segments. However, Mora *et al.* (2011) demonstrated that the Catalan–Spanish bilinguals' performance may have been related to other factors, such as lack of robustness in Catalan mid-vowel contrasts and/or amount of L2 exposure, rather than loss of plasticity in L2 speech perception. In addition, Højen and Flege (2006) reported findings from a study with native Spanish speakers, some of whom were able to discriminate difficult English vowel contrasts with native-like accuracy; these learners were dominant in their L2 and were characterized by an extensive exposure to and use of English from the age of three years, especially during their first years of English acquisition. Such findings would, therefore, indicate that, although an early start is an important predictor of a successful outcome in L2 speech perception, it is not sufficient in itself to guarantee complete accuracy.

According to the Speech Learning Model (SLM), age-related changes in L1–L2 interactions and in the quality and quantity of L2 input are among the main sources of child–adult differences observed in L2 speech learning (Flege, 1995, 2002, 2003, 2007; Flege & MacKay, 2011). Specifically, the SLM proposes that, with age, the assimilative power of the L1 phonetic system on the perception of non-native sounds increases, making the establishment of new categories for such sounds more difficult. Child L2 learners, whose L1 sound categories develop slowly into early adolescence (Johnson, 2000) and thus influence the formation of new phonetic categories for L2 sounds less than for adult L2 learners, are therefore predicted in the model to better discriminate between the sounds of their languages. Coupled with L2 input of greater quality and quantity, child L2 learners are expected to perform more accurately in the perception of L2 speech than their adult counterparts (see Jia *et al.*, 2006).

Only a few studies to date have directly compared child and adult L2 learners as they were learning their L2 to investigate the relative effect of cross-language phonetic similarity perception and L2 experience on their non-native phonological acquisition (Baker *et al.*, 2002, 2008). The purpose of the current study, therefore, is to further evaluate the SLM predictions with respect to age and L2 input by examining the discrimination of (Irish) English vowels by two groups of native Polish speakers who had learned English as children, teenagers or adults. The groups of learners differed in their L2 learning experience: some were acquiring English in Ireland, that is, in an immersion setting in the target language country, and otherw were learning the language in Poland in a formal classroom setting. If early starters are indeed less likely than adults to perceive L2 sounds through the lenses of their L1, and if this is a significant predictor of their L2 perception abilities, then its effect should be apparent even in the case of early and late starters who are formal language learners. Also, if L2 sound perception is affected by the stage of development of the L1 sound system at the time of L2 learning, differences between child, teenage and adult L2 learners should also be notable in this regard. Finally, one of the main aims of this study is to examine to what extent the perceptual patterns of the native Polish speakers hearing Irish English vowels vary as a function of their L2 learning experience. Although one might expect there to be an obvious difference between the naturalistic and formal L2 learners in terms of the amount of native-speaker exposure, the specific learning situation of the Polish migrants living in Ireland – characterized by ample opportunities to use their native language and by exposure to English spoken by other non-natives, including compatriots – offers an interesting setting to be explored in the context of L2 speech learning.

Obtaining a better understanding of the role of cross-language phonetic similarity perception and L2 experience in the acquisition of L2 speech by learners of diverse age groups carries both theoretical and practical importance. Theoretically, such an understanding is important in the advancement of adequate models of L2 speech learning; in practical terms, it can help to determine what types of training and encouragement may be most effective for L2 learners differing in age and their L2 learning opportunities.

Learnability of Non-native Sounds

As noted above, one of the determining factors influencing the perception of L2 speech is the native language phonetic system. Depending on the degree of distance between L2 and L1 sounds, some non-native sounds may be especially challenging to perceive, while others may pose no difficulty even for listeners who have never learnt the respective language. According to the Perceptual Assimilation Model (PAM) (Best, 1995; Best & Tyler, 2007), L2 learners go about perceiving L2 sounds on the basis of the phonetic realizations and the phonological organization of their native language when judging the extent to which non-native contrasts are good or poor examples of L1 phonemes.

Accordingly, at least four assimilation patterns are expected to be at play during L2 speech learning (Best, 1995: 194–198). First, both sounds of a non-native contrast can be judged by L2 learners as members of a single native sound category (single-category assimilation), in which case the discrimination is predicted to be very poor. However, if the two contrasting sounds occur in high-frequency words, or come from such phonological contexts that contain many minimally contrasting words, the lexical motivation to learn the distinction may be high (Best & Tyler, 2007), resulting in a scenario in which one sound of the non-native contrast is perceived as a much poorer member of the native language category than is the other (category-goodness assimilation). Discrimination between such non-native sounds is predicted to range from moderate to very good. An example for Polish learners of English might be English /i/ and /ɪ/ (as in *beat* and *bit*, respectively), both of which are likely to be perceived as members of the Polish category /i/, and therefore poorly discriminated initially; however, the need for adequate distinction may encourage the Poles' perceptual learning of the L2 contrast. As their experience with English increases, Polish speakers may come to perceive the English vowel /ɪ/ as a rather poor exemplar of the Polish vowel /i/, and to hear that the vowel approximates yet another Polish high vowel /ɨ/. Discrimination of such a contrast would then fall into a two-category assimilation, a case whereby two non-native sounds are perceived as members of two separate native language categories. This type of contrast is predicted to be discriminated very well. An example of this situation can be English /ɛ/ and /ɪ/ vowels (as in *bet* and *bit*, respectively) compared with Polish /ɛ/ and /i/. The discrimination of these L2 sounds by native speakers of Polish is likely to be very good, since each segment is to be assimilated into a different native category. Finally, when one member of the non-native contrast is perceived as a member of a native language category and one is perceived as uncategorizable (categorized-uncategorized assimilation), the discrimination of such a contrast should also be very good, because it reflects a phonological distinction between an exemplar of a known phoneme and an unknown sound. A possible sound contrast that might fit this pattern is Irish English /ʌ/ and /u/ (as in *but* and *boot*, respectively), since the specific Irish English vowel may be perceived as uncategorizable by Polish speakers.

One of the core questions for PAM has been whether L2 contrasts that are initially difficult to differentiate can eventually be learnt and perceived accurately. Best and Tyler (2007) maintain that L2 learners do continue to refine their perception of speech gestures as their experience with learning an L2 increases, not only thanks to the apparently greater exposure to productions of specific L2 contrasts, but also because of their experience with producing the target contrasts and their increased knowledge of L2 vocabulary (Bundgaard-Nielsen *et al.*, 2011). Previous research examining the effect of L2 experience on L2 segmental perception will therefore be considered in greater detail in the next section of the paper.

Experience Effects in Non-native Speech Perception

Evidence reported in empirical work as to the effects of L2 experience – understood as periods of either varying length of stay in the target language country or formal instruction in the target language – on L2 speech perception has been rather contradictory. For example, Cebrian (2006) found no differences between groups of Catalan–Spanish bilinguals who were undergraduate students of English philology living in Barcelona, and Catalan–Spanish bilinguals residing in Canada for an average of 25 years, in terms of the use of temporal and spectral features in the perception of the English /i/–/ɪ/ vowel pair. However, Bohn and Flege (1990) reported experience effects on German speakers' discrimination of the English /ɛ/–/æ/ contrast after about eight years of life in the USA; these adult L2 learners performed more like native speakers in the perception of this L2 pair than did adults who were recent arrivals. Nevertheless, no such effect was found for the English contrast /i/–/ɪ/. This finding was later corroborated in a comparable population of experienced and inexperienced German, Spanish, Mandarin Chinese and Korean adults living in North America (Flege *et al.*, 1997). In yet another study, Baker *et al.* (2002) found that Korean children benefited from a nine-year-long stay in the USA significantly more than Korean adults did, as their performance was eventually judged to be native-like for all the tested sounds. Again, the Korean adults' perception abilities in the L2 were found to have improved only for those sounds that were initially perceived as non-confusable in respect to their L1.

Such findings seem to suggest that experience effects in naturalistic learning environments are more prominent for some L2 segments and more apparent for child than for adult L2 learners, who might be advantaged in having their L1 sound system still evolving, and as such governing the perception of L2 sounds less, and in being engaged in a qualitatively different L2 learning experience. For instance, Jia and Aaronson (2003) demonstrated that children in immersion learning settings commonly enjoy richer and more intensive L2 learning environments, having ample opportunities to use the target language in a variety of formal and informal domains. Children's intentions towards the L2 and their underlying aspirations for learning it may therefore also be of a different nature than those of adult L2 learners, thus aiding their L2 phonological acquisition to a greater extent (Moyer, 2009).

In the context of classroom learning, which is often characteristic of limited L2 input both in quantitative and qualitative terms (Muñoz, 2008), child–adult differences in L2 phonological acquisition may be expected to be much less apparent. Indeed, the few existing studies conducted in formal learning settings have shown that an early starting age for L2 learning is unlikely to produce any significant long-term benefits in respect to L2 phonology, unless it is associated with extensive exposure to authentic L2 input (Fullana, 2006; Muñoz, 2011) and/or phonetically relevant training (Cebrian, 2006).

The vexing question of the extent to which L2 input matters in the L2 speech perception of diverse learners remains at present unanswered. One of the main aims of the present study, therefore, is to examine whether the specific L2 learning experience of the Polish children, teenagers and adults in Ireland, compared with the L2 learning experience of age-matched formal L2 learners in Poland, might provide greater insights into the role of L2 experience in L2 speech perception by learners of diverse age groups and learning opportunities.

The Present Study

Participants

Two groups of native Polish speakers participated in this study (see Table 11.1). The first group comprised 45 Polish children, teenagers and adults aged between 9 and 27 years of age when they arrived in Ireland (NPI), who had lived in the country for an average of three years. The three age divisions were made to allow for comparisons across the developmental stages

Table 11.1 Participants in the study

Groups	Age	AOE	AOA	LOR	Proficiency	Number of participants
Polish children in IRL (NPI)	12.9 (1.0)	8.0 (1.5)	9.1 (1.1)	3.8 (1.1)	3.9 (1.0)	15
Polish teenagers in IRL (NPI)	14.3 (1.3)	9.0 (2.2)	12.2 (0.9)	2.1 (1.0)	3.1 (1.8)	15
Polish adults in IRL (NPI)	29.9 (7.2)	14.1 (4.6)	26.7 (6.9)	3.2 (1.6)	4.3 (1.1)	15
Polish children in PL (NPP)	11.1 (0.9)	6.2 (1.9)				10
Polish teenagers in PL (NPP)	16.0 (0.0)	8.6 (2.5)				10
Polish adults in PL (NPP)	35.6 (9.9)	14.8 (4.4)				10

Means and standard deviations (in parentheses) are indicated for chronological age (Age), age of first English exposure (AOE), age of arrival (AOA), length of residence (LOR) in years, and for tested proficiency levels, where 1 = beginner, 2 = lower-intermediate, 3 = intermediate, 4 = upper-intermediate; 5 = advanced, and 6 = native-like.

discussed in the literature on L2 phonological acquisition (Bond & Adamescu, 1979; Long, 1990; Scovel, 1988) as well as L1 phonological acquisition (Hazan & Barrett, 2000; Johnson, 2000). Although the majority of the NPI participants had received some formal instruction in the English language in Poland, their exposure to native-sounding English before their arrival in Ireland was minimal. When tested formally using a standardized pen-and-paper placement test (*Anglia Placement Test*, 2009), the NPI participants were evaluated, on average, at an upper-intermediate level in terms of their ability in English vocabulary, structure and reading comprehension. These participants were recruited via advertisements in a Polish newspaper in Dublin in the summer of 2009.

The other group of 30 native Polish children, teenagers and adults lived in Poland (NPP) at the time of the study, that is, they were L2 learners with no English immersion experience, although they all reported having learnt the language in a classroom setting in their home country in the past. Their proficiency levels were self-reported, and ranged from beginner to upper-intermediate levels. Similarly to the participants in Ireland, NPP participants received no English lessons with native English speakers. This group was recruited to represent Polish migrants as they might be on the first day of their arrival in Ireland. The recruitment of this group of Polish speakers took place in average-quality primary and secondary schools in Leszno in the autumn of 2009.

Stimulus material

The stimulus corpus used in the present study was produced by three adult female speakers of Irish English, whose speech was recorded in a soundproof booth in the Phonetics Laboratory at Trinity College Dublin. The use of three speakers, rather than one, was motivated by an interest in eliciting spectral and temporal differences in the acoustical signal that are assumed to be non-problematic for native speakers, but which may be challenging for non-native speakers. Vowel sounds were chosen for investigation in this study because they are more suitable for testing language-specific sound categorization than are consonants, given the fact that they are fewer in number and as such more variable among languages. In addition, the phonological structure of Polish vowels is much simpler relative to Irish English vowels, and thus a number of specific predictions about assimilation of L2 vowels into respective L1 sounds could be tested.

The stimulus material of this study included /i/, /ɪ/, /ɛ/, /æ/, /ɔ/, /əʊ/, /u/ and /ʌ/ vowels, which represent different degrees of learnability for native Polish speakers. While sounds such as /i/ and /ɛ/ occur in both languages, the vowel /ʌ/ is a specific sound of Irish English, with realizations stretching between Polish /a/, /o/ and /u/. This salient vowel sound of Irish English is typically produced as a mid-centralized, back, somewhat rounded vowel, and as such can more precisely be transcribed as /ö/ (Kallen, 1994). The English vowel /ɪ/ is close in articulatory vowel space to Polish /i/, although Polish speakers are known to produce the sound closer to English vowel /i/, and tend to discriminate the /i/–/ɪ/ contrast on the basis of duration differences (Bogacka, 2004). The English vowel /æ/ does not occur in Polish and has been shown to be assimilated to the Polish vowels /a/ or /ɛ/ by Polish learners; it also tends to be distinguished by them from English /ɛ/ on the basis of duration cues (Rojczyk, 2011). The English vowel /ɔ/ and Polish /o/ have similar spectral properties, but because the English /ɔ/ has a longer duration than Polish /o/, the two may not be perceived as highly similar. Finally, the Irish English /u/ and Polish /u/ are spectrally very similar, while the monophthongized /əʊ/ is different from the Polish /o/ in that it is pronounced higher and more frontally in the oral cavity.

The tested vowels were placed in a bVt word context, which is frequent and productive to a comparable extent in both Polish and English, and which embeds real L1 and L2 words that differ minimally in the realization of the mid-vowel. Table 11.2 presents the L2 and L1 stimuli used for the study, phonetically transcribed.

Within the interpretation of PAM, the five tested L2 contrasts fell into the following assimilation patters: the /i/–/ɪ/ pair fell into the single-category assimilation pattern; the pairs /ɛ/–/æ/ and /ɪ/–/ɛ/ fell into the two-category assimilation pattern; the pair /ɔ/–/əʊ/ fell into the category-goodness assimilation pattern; and the last pair, /u/–/əʌ/, fell into the categorized–uncategorized assimilation pattern. Consequently, the predicted order of perceptual difficulty for these contrasts was as follows (from least to most difficult): /ɪ/–/ɛ/, /ɛ/–/æ/, /u/–/ʌ/, /ɔ/–/ʊ/ and /i/–/ɪ/.

Perceptual assimilation task

Similarly to previous studies of cross-language phonetic similarity (Baker et al., 2002, 2008; Cebrian, 2006; Guion et al., 2000), this study used a

Table 11.2 L2 and L1 vowel stimuli used in the study

L2 stimuli	L1 stimuli (English translation)
beat /biːt/	bity /bitɪ/ (beaten)
bit /bɪt/	byty /bɪtɪ/ (entities)
bet /bɛt/	bety /bɛtɪ/ (bedding)
bat /bæt/	baty /batɪ/ (whips)
bought /bɔːt/	boty /bɔtɪ/ (high boots)
boat /bəʊt or boʊt/	buty /butɪ/ (shoes)
boot /buːt/	
but /bʌt or bʊt or böt/	

perceptual assimilation task to test the Polish learners' perception of L1–L2 phonetic distance. The learners heard the eight target vowels in one repetition. First, they listened to an English keyword and matched the vowel in this stimulus to one of six Polish keywords shown on the screen (or, in other words, to the Polish vowel sound) which they believed to be most similar. Second, they made goodness-of-fit judgements regarding the similarity of the English vowel they had just heard and the Polish vowel they had chosen, using a seven-point Lickert scale, with a score of '1' indicating that the sounds were not at all alike and a score of '7' indicating that the sounds were a complete match. Participants were encouraged to use the entire scale and to follow their first impression in completing the task. They could listen to the English words several times if desired, but they were not allowed to change their answers once they were given, in order to maintain the impressionistic element in the task.

Prior to testing, the participants were asked to read aloud the list of Polish keywords from the screen and to concentrate on how 'the middle sound' of the word sounded to them. Then they underwent a brief practice session with two English stimuli from the real task. The participants were encouraged to discuss their first impressions about the stimuli, and they were also given visual prompts on screen with possible answers. They were reminded that it was important to approach this task bearing in mind that there were no 'right' or 'wrong' answers, and accordingly, that basing their answers on spontaneous impression was undoubtedly the best strategy.

A series of t-tests for paired samples showed no significant difference between the means of goodness ratings in the one repetition across participant groups ($t(74) = 0.222, p = 0.825$) or within participant groups (NPI children, $t(14) = -0.979, p = 0.344$; NPI teenagers, $t(14) = -0.371, p = 0.716$; NPI adults, $t(14) = 0.723, p = 0.482$; NPP children, $t(9) = -1.253, p = 0.242$; NPP teenagers, $t(9) = 1.756, p = 0.113$; NPP adults, $t(9) = 0.662, p = 0.525$). An informal analysis of the distribution of the assigned categories for each of the eight vowels, using a cross-tabulation procedure, also revealed no significant differences between the first and second identifications within the groups. Therefore, only the first responses were used for further analyses, as these were understood to be those that were given under the first impression by the participants.

Categorical discrimination task

To test the Polish learners' perceptual abilities, a categorical discrimination task in an oddity format was used, in which the participants were asked to indicate which sound in a triad of stimuli was different from the other two. 'Catch-tokens' were also included, representing a case whereby all three items were the same (but spoken by three different speakers) in order to test the ability to ignore phonetically irrelevant within-category variation. This specific type of a categorical discrimination task was chosen since it had been used successfully in similar L2 speech learning studies conducted with young L2 learners (e.g. Baker *et al.*, 2002).

Each of the five tested vowel pairs was presented in all possible combinations – 38 triad items in total (5 contrasts × 6 change combinations + 8 no-change tokens). The inter-stimulus interval between the members of each pair contrast was set for 1.5 seconds, in order to reduce the possibility that a correct response could be based on information in auditory short-term memory. A brief practice block with five easy trials preceded the test to ensure that the volume of the presentation was adjusted to a comfortable level and that the participants understood the task and were motivated to respond reliably. As in the previous task, the participants were allowed to listen to the stimuli as many times as they desired.

Background questionnaire

All participants completed a background questionnaire, which differed for the NPI and NPP participants, but included a number of overlapping items, such as gender, birth date, age of first English exposure, and current use of and contact with English. The NPI participants, in addition, reported on their use of and contact with Polish in their everyday life in Ireland.

Overall, the NPI participants did not differ in terms of the self-reported amount of L1/L2 use in their everyday life in Ireland, although the NPI adults and NPI teenagers tended to compare more closely on this measure (see Table 11.3), that is, they did not use their L2 in various contexts (e.g. at home, at work/school and at leisure) to the same extent as the NPI children did; in parallel, they used their L1 to a greater extent in those contexts than the NPI children did. The early starters also reported a greater exposure to native-speaker input and a lesser exposure to speech produced by other non-native speakers of English.

It is noteworthy that many more NPI children (87%) and NPI teenagers (80%) than NPI adults (53%) in this study pointed out that the native speakers with whom they maintained contact were their friends, schoolmates, teachers and Irish people in general, that is, native speakers had both formal

Table 11.3 Reported L1/L2 contact by Polish participants in Ireland

Groups	L1 use	L2 use	L2 use with native speakers	L2 use with non-native speakers
NPI children	3.2 (0.6)	3.6 (0.4)	4.6 (0.6)	3.7 (1.2)
NPI teenagers	3.6 (0.6)	3.3 (0.5)	4.4 (0.7)	3.9 (1.0)
NPI adults	3.5 (0.4)	3.3 (0.4)	4.5 (0.6)	4.1 (0.7)

Means and standard deviations (in parentheses) are provided, where: 1 = never, 2 = rarely, 3 = sometimes, 4 = often, and 5 = always.

and informal connections to the young Poles, rather than formal contacts only, as was mostly the case for the NPI adults. The adult Poles often mentioned interactions with their managers and Irish people met in public services as contexts in which they were primarily exposed to native-speaker input. This would indicate that the young migrants in this study were engaged in a variety of English learning contexts, and therefore had increased opportunities for engaging in communications where deeper social and emotional functions were served. In this respect, one could argue, the young Poles in this study were enjoying a richer, albeit not necessarily a more extensive, L2 learning experience during their stay in Ireland.

The NPP participants of this study, in turn, could be considered typical learners of a foreign language in a classroom setting, that is, they reported attending a course of English led by non-native teachers for a limited number of hours per week (NPP children, mean 4.2 hours (N = 10; standard deviation (SD) = 1.0); NPP teenagers, mean = 6.1 hours (N = 10; SD = 0.3); NPP adults, mean 2.8 hours (N = 6; SD = 1.2)), although it is noteworthy that the young learners tended to be exposed to English instruction to a much greater extent than the adults. Four of the 10 NPP adults were not attending any English classes at the time of the study. The NPP participants showed a variety of motivations for learning the language, ranging from compulsory attendance at English classes, as stated by the young learners, to conversational and preparatory courses for Cambridge exams serving their further professional development, as reported by the adult learners. The L2 contact of this group of learners could therefore be characterized as quantitatively and qualitatively limited, and would rarely occur outside the classroom.

Results

Cross-language phonetic similarity perception

Analyses of the cross-language identification judgements revealed that the children, teenagers and adults in this study selected the same Polish vowels as the primary (most frequent) response alternative in their classification of the tested L2 sounds, with the exception of the case of the Irish English vowel /ʌ/. Whereas the majority of NPI adults perceived this vowel to be similar to the Polish vowel /o/, NPI children and NPI teenagers classified it mostly as Polish /u/. A reverse pattern was found for NPP participants, in that the majority of NPP adults and NPP teenagers perceived the Irish English /ʌ/ as Polish /u/, while NPP children heard this vowel as Polish /o/. The classifications of all the English vowels tested in this study are listed in Table 11.4.

The responses to the English stimuli were further evaluated in terms of the participants' judgements of phonetic similarity – a fit of the stimuli to a

Table 11.4 Fit indices derived for the tested Irish English vowels in terms of Polish vowels (1 = poor fit, 7 = very good fit)

Irish English vowel stimuli

		i	ɪ	ɛ	æ	u	ɔ	əʊ	ʌ
NPI child	i	4.07	**2.87 (60%)**						
	y		2.20 (40%)						
	e			4.93					
	a				4.60				
	u					4.07			2.93
	o						5.00	2.87	
NPI teenager	i	4.20	**3.13 (73%)**						
	y		2.27 (27%)						
	e			4.00					
	a				3.87				
	u					3.40			**1.73 (53%)**
	o						4.47	2.73	1.80 (40%)
NPI adult	i	4.20	4.27						
	y								
	e			5.13					
	a				4.73				
	u					3.64			1.00 (36%)
	o						4.73	3.21	**1.86 (57%)**
NPP child	i	5.10	4.30						
	y								
	e			4.40					
	a				3.20				
	u					4.20		1.10 (30%)	1.20 (40%)
	o						4.80	**2.50 (70%)**	**2.30 (60%)**
NPP teenager	i	3.50	3.20						
	y								
	e			4.30					
	a				4.20				
	u					4.20			**1.60 (50%)**
	o						4.50	3.90	2.00 (40%)
NPP adult	i	3.70	2.80						
	y								
	e			3.40					
	a				3.60				
	u					3.20		1.00 (40%)	**2.40 (70%)**
	o						3.40	**1.50 (60%)**	1.10 (30%)

Note: only those identifications common to at least 25% of the participants are included. Primary response alternatives are in bold, where relevant.

Polish category. The similarity ratings (fit indices), also shown in Table 11.4, were calculated by multiplying the proportion of responses receiving the primary identification by the mean goodness rating for that identification. Overall, the non-native vowels /i/, /ɛ/, /æ/ and /ɔ/ were considered to be good perceptual fits with the native Polish counterparts, while the vowels /ʌ/ and /əʊ/ were identified as being poorly related to any Polish vowel category by all the participants. The fit indices ranged from a low value of 1.50 (the fit of English /əʊ/ with Polish /o/, as rated by most NPP adults), to a high value of 5.13 (the fit of English /ɛ/ with Polish /ɛ/, as rated by most NPI adults). What is noteworthy is that NPI children rated the English vowels /i/, /ɪ/, /æ/, /ɛ/ and /əʊ/ as being less similar to the modal Polish response alternatives than NPI adults did, while the NPI teenagers assigned lower similarity ratings on all the eight tested vowels in comparison with the NPI adults. In contrast, NPP children rated all the tested vowels, except for /æ/ and /ʌ/, as being more similar to the Polish counterparts than NPP adults did. The NPP teenagers, in turn, assigned ratings that were intermediate between the NPP adults' and the NPP children's similarity ratings.

Two important trends in the data produced in this task thus emerged (see Figure 11.1). Firstly, NPI children and NPI teenagers tended to be less likely overall than NPI adults to perceive the tested L2 sounds as good instances of L1 categories, and were comparable in their perception of cross-linguistic similarity to NPP children and NPP teenagers in this regard. This finding agrees with the predictions of the SLM model about young learners perceiving L2 segments under a weaker influence of their still-developing L1 sound system. Secondly, NPP adults tended to perceive all the tested L2

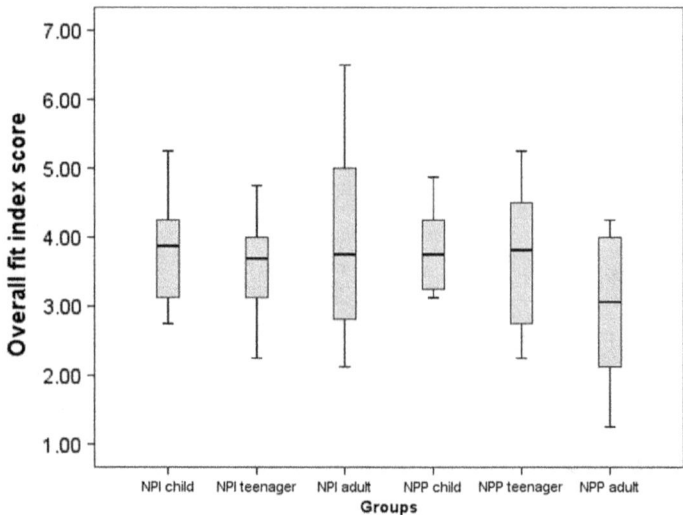

Figure 11.1 Box plots for mean overall fit index scores for the participant groups

sounds as fitting poorly with any of the L1 sounds, showing an overall perceptual bias against similarity between the tested English and Polish vowel sounds.

Categorical discrimination

Perception accuracy in this task was indicated by the percentage of correct responses out of the 38 trials for total discrimination accuracy and the eight trials for each vowel contrast. As shown in Figure 11.2, all NPI groups performed with approximately 65% accuracy for all L2 contrasts, while the NPP groups performed around the chance level, with NPP adults receiving the lowest overall accuracy score of 47.5%. Overall, the NPI adult, teenage and child participant groups performed comparably and more accurately than the age-matched NPP groups. A one-way ANOVA test revealed a main effect of group in this regard ($F(5, 69) = 6.814$, $p = 0.000$), with a *post-hoc* Bonferroni test showing significant differences between the NPI and NPP adults ($p = 0.001$) in terms of their overall L2 vowel discrimination score. However, NPI children did not significantly differ from NPP children ($p = 0.154$); nor did NPI teenagers differ from NPP teenagers in their performance in this perceptual task ($p = 0.078$).

To further examine the group effect for each vowel pair, separate one-way ANOVAs were performed, yielding a significant effect of group for two vowel pairs: /ɪ/–/ɛ/ ($F (5, 69) = 3.342$, $p = 0.009$) and /ɔ/–/əʊ/ ($F(5, 69) = 6.550$, $p = 0.000$). In this case, Bonferroni *post-hoc* tests revealed that the NPI adults

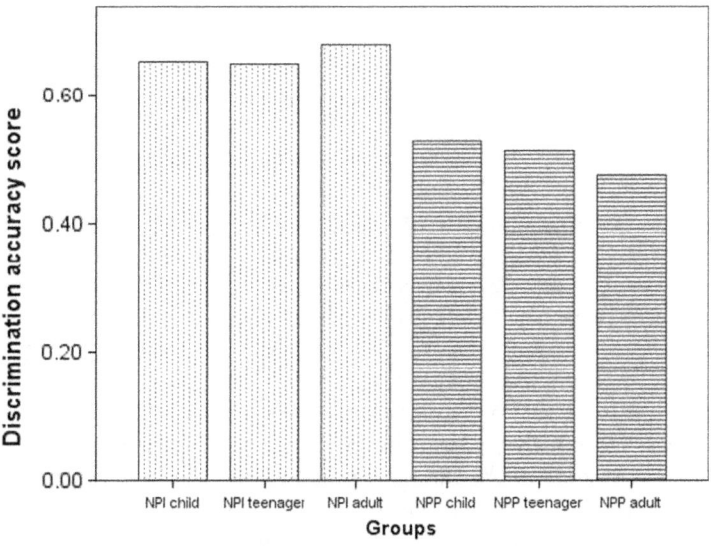

Figure 11.2 Mean discrimination accuracy score for participant groups

Table 11.5 Performance on the five vowel contrasts by participant groups

Vowel pairs	NPI children	NPI teenagers	NPI adults	NPP children	NPP teenagers	NPP adults
/i/–/ɪ/	38.3 (15.3; 25–75)	31.7 (11.4; 13–50)	40.8 (25.2; 13–100)	21.3 (6.0; 13–25)	22.5 (7.9; 13–38)	27.5 (16.5; 0–50)
/ɪ/–/ɛ/	84.1 (11.0; 63–100)	83.3 (16.1; 50–100)	90.0 (9.7; 75–100)	76.3 (21.6; 38–100)	70.0 (24.4; 38–100)	68.8 (13.5; 50–88)
/ɛ/–/æ/	80.8 (22.1; 38–100)	77.5 (23.7; 38–100)	80.8 (26.7; 25–100)	77.5 (26.2; 38–100)	72.5 (33.2; 0–100)	62.5 (33.3; 13–100)
/ʌ/–/u/	65.8 (19.7; 38–88)	72.5 (17.8; 38–100)	73.3 (18.2; 38–100)	61.3 (20.8; 25–88)	62.5 (31.2; 13–100)	48.8 (14.9;8; 25–75)
/ɔ/–/əʊ/	56.7 (20.5; 25–88)	59.2 (26.1; 25–100)	54.2 (27.4; 13–100)	27.5 (11.5; 13–50)	28.8 (14.5; 13–50)	30.0 (10.5; 13–50)
Overall	65.1 (8.6; 50–83)	64.8 (10.0; 48–85)	67.8 (13.8; 40–98)	52.8 (11.0; 35–68)	51.3 (16.1; 23–75)	47.5 (8.4; 38–60)

Note: The score indicates percentage correct discrimination, with standard deviations and range in parentheses.

outperformed the NPP adults in the discrimination of the former vowel pair ($p = 0.028$), whereas the NPI children and NPI teenagers were more accurate than their age-matched NPP counterparts ($p = 0.016$ and $p = 0.010$, respectively) in the discrimination of the latter vowel pair. As shown in Table 11.5, a discrimination of the /i/–/ɪ/ contrast showed low accuracy levels across all the groups, while the /ɪ/–/ɛ/ and /ɛ/–/æ/ pairs posed little difficulty for the participants. The specific Irish–English /ʌ/–/u/ contrast seemed to have been much easier for the NPI adults to discriminate than for the NPP adults.

The pattern of results in this task, that is, comparable discrimination accuracy across the tested age groups, does not fully agree with the traditional notion of early age advantage in L2 speech learning in naturalistic learning environments, although it does confirm the no-long-term-advantage finding for early starters in formal classroom settings. There was a tendency, nevertheless, for Polish children in this study to perform more accurately than Polish teenagers in the discrimination of the non-native contrasts, and for NPP children and NPP teenagers to be more accurate than NPP adults in this perceptual task, suggesting that there was a relationship between an early start and the development of accurate L2 perception abilities for all the participants in this study. Another important point is that the immersion experience benefited all of the NPI participants, although the extent of the benefit depended on the L2 contrast. The L2 immersion learners performed best in the discrimination of those vowel contrasts in which members of the vowel pairs were each identified primarily with a different L1 vowel category, a result confirming the predictions advanced by PAM (1995) about the learnability of specific L2 sounds.

Age-related differences in L2 vowel perception

An important empirical question raised in this study is whether variation in cross-language phonetic similarity perception and L2 learning experience can be linked to the perception of L2 sound contrasts by learners of diverse age groups. We hypothesized that, if young learners are more accurate cross-linguistic perceivers, and if this is an important predictor of their L2 perception abilities, then its influence should be apparent even in the case of formal L2 learners. We also hypothesized that young learners in immersion learning settings will be 'double advantaged' in this respect, since they will also show a qualitatively different L2 learning experience than their older counterparts. Finally, we sought to determine the extent to which L2 input affects the development of L2 speech perception in diverse learners.

The NPP children and NPP teenagers were found to be more sensitive in judging the perceptual similarity between L1 and L2 sounds than were the NPP adults, and these young learners were also more accurate than the adults in their perception of the tested L2 contrasts. It should be noted that the NPP children and NPP teenagers spent at least twice as many hours a week learning English than the NPP adults did. All the NPP learners, however, performed less accurately in the discrimination of the tested vowels than NPI learners did, which points towards the significance of phonetically relevant L2 input in the L2 speech perception of both young and adult learners. Yet, the discrimination of one vowel contrast, the English /i/–/ɪ/, was found to be challenging for all Polish participants, indicating a persistent effect of L1 phonology on the perception of L2 contrasts that are assimilated into a single L1 category. Nevertheless, a substantial number of NPI children and NPI teenagers perceived this contrast on a two-category basis, rather than on a single-category basis, and thus seemed to have been developing an ability to distinguish between the two non-native vowels more accurately than NPI adults. Again, it should be noted that these two groups of learners were also those who reported using English in a variety of contexts. Overall, therefore, the findings of this study agree with the prediction of the SLM (1995), suggesting that the age-related differences in the perception of L1–L2 relationships and in the quantity and quality of L2 input jointly affect the accuracy with which non-native vowels are perceived.

Discussion

One of the main goals of this study was to determine whether judgements of cross-language phonetic similarity differ depending on age of L2 learning. The child and teenage L2 immersion learners in this study were indeed less likely than adult L2 immersion learners to perceptually associate most of the tested L1 and L2 vowel sounds and were more accurate in distinguishing between the relevant vowels. As studies by Baker et al. (2002, 2008) suggested, child and even teenage L2 learners may indeed be more reluctant to assimilate L2 sounds into L1 categories, since their L1 sound system is itself still evolving, guiding their perception of non-native sounds to a lesser extent. In contrast, the adult L2 learners, being 'experienced L1 users', might perceive similarities between the tested L2 and L1 vowel sounds solely with respect to their established L1 sound categories. This tendency towards reliance on stable L1 perceptual representations was clearly apparent in this study in the performance of the adult Poles without any immersion L2 experience, who strictly differentiated between the two sound systems, showing a kind of psychological bias against perception of any phonetic similarities between the two languages.

However, as was also shown in this study, cross-language perception does develop in adult learners as a result of naturalistic experience with learning the L2. After about three years of residence in Ireland, NPI adults were found to be more accurate in their perception of relationships between L1 and L2 vowels than were NPP adults. For their part, NPI children and NPI teenagers performed comparably and similarly to the age-matched groups of NPP participants, suggesting an early age advantage in cross-linguistic perception ability, regardless of L2 experience. In contrast to what was predicted, the child and teenage groups of participants did not significantly differ in this ability, a result that was possibly related to the fact that the differences between the participants' chronological age and/or age of arrival in this study may not have been large enough to allow for any marked effects to be observed as a consequence of stage of development of the learners' L1 sound system. Future studies should include direct measures of L1 sound system development in such learners and systematically examine the relationship between cross-language similarity perception and L2 speech performance.

One possible critical perspective on the findings just described would be that young learners may find it more difficult than adults to perform cross-language perceptual tasks. The use of other methods for measuring perceptual relationships between L1 and L2 sounds might have been more appropriate or might have yielded more significant results. For example, Cebrian et al. (2011) have suggested that a combination of rated discrimination tasks together with perceptual assimilation tasks should be used in reliable assessments of cross-linguistic perception, whereas Baker et al. (2008)

have advocated the use of fine-grained rating scales in experiments in which children and adults provide perceptual goodness ratings.

Nevertheless, an examination of the data reported in this study still suggests that the young L2 learners perceived the discrepancies between L1 and L2 sounds differently and more accurately than the adult L2 learners. First, the NPI and NPP children and teenagers did not provide a higher number of inexplicable or inconsistent answers than the NPI and NPP adults, and therefore their cross-language similarity judgements can be considered valid reflections of their linguistic development. Second, the NPI children and teenagers accentuated differences between pairs of L2 sounds that are acoustically similar to single L1 categories, such as /i/–/ɪ/ and /ɔ/–/əʊ/, to a greater extent than the adults did, further suggesting greater perceptual sensitivity towards degrees of match between L2 and L1 sounds. Finally, the NPP children and teenagers performed more accurately than their adult counterparts at the cross-language perception task, suggesting that child and teenage L2 learners may have a greater capacity for performing such a task, and that – at a more general level – they may be better cross-language perceivers than adult L2 learners.

Another goal of this study was to determine whether age differences found in cross-language perception can be linked to L2 learners' discrimination abilities. The results of the categorical discrimination task revealed that, overall, neither group of Polish young learners discriminated the tested L2 contrasts significantly differently from the Polish adult learners, which may come as a surprise given the oft-reported advantage of early starters in the ability to perceive L2 speech. However, one recalls that early age advantage in L2 speech perception has mainly been reported in long-term immersion studies, whereas this study compared child, teenage and adult L2 learners' performance after about three years of L2 immersion experience, that is, at a specific stage of their L2 phonological acquisition. Perhaps differences in cognitive development played a role in the Polish learners' performance in the categorical discrimination task; the child L2 learners may have reached a learning stage in which they began catching up with the initially advantaged teenage and adult L2 learners (Baker *et al.*, 2008; Snow & Hoefnagel-Höhle, 1977). Also, and similarly to findings reported by Slavoff and Johnson (1995), the child and teenage L2 learners might have been developing their perception of the tested vowels at similar rates during the first three years of L2 immersion, given their comparable levels of exposure to the target language. Furthermore, the Polish immersion learners in this study were all exposed to and used their L1 frequently, which may have affected the development of their L2 speech perception to comparable levels, especially in respect to those L2 sounds that are close in phonological space to L1 sounds (Flege & MacKay, 2004; Højen & Flege, 2006). It may also be possible that the categorical discrimination task was too difficult for the learners to perform at the specific stage of their L2 acquisition, and thus no marked differences could be demonstrated in their performance on the task.

The important finding in this connection was, however, that an age-bound link between cross-language similarity perception and L2 perception abilities was observed in the present study in the case of the formal L2 learners; for instance, the NPP children tended to perceive the Irish English /u/–/ʌ/ vowel pair on a two-category basis, rather than on a single-category basis, and also managed to discriminate the pair more accurately than the NPP adults did. This result suggests that the two abilities may indeed be closely related in child L2 learners and only loosely related in adult L2 learners (cf. Baker *et al.*, 2008), although more research conducted in both learning contexts and with different-aged children compared with adults is clearly needed to examine whether this finding can be replicated and an integrated account of age effects in L2 phonological acquisition offered.

Finally, an examination of the effect of L2 experience on non-native speech perception was at the core of this enquiry. The naturalistic L2 learning experience of three years was found to benefit L2 learners of all age groups in this study. Importantly, the improvement on the part of child and teenage L2 immersion learners was steady and apparent across the range of the tested assimilation patterns, including the challenging single-category case. In turn, adult L2 immersion learners performed significantly more accurately than the adult formal L2 learners, especially in terms of L2 pairs falling within the two-category and categorized–uncategorized assimilation patterns. The results of this study are thus compatible with previous L2 phonological research documenting the importance of L2 input, which is extensive in both quantitative and – perhaps even more importantly – in qualitative terms (see e.g. Moyer, 2009; Muñoz, 2011, for a summary). The reported variety of L2 contact had probable short- and long-term benefits for the child and teenage migrants in this study in terms of their L2 speech learning. This tendency of early learners to engage in qualitatively rich L2 experience during language learning has recently been reported also by Llanes and Muñoz (forthcoming) in a study with child and adult L2 learners in a stay-abroad situation.

Conclusion

The main goal of this study was to further evaluate the role of cross-language phonetic similarity perception and L2 experience on the L2 perception abilities of child, teenage and adult L2 learners. The results of this study indicate that those learners who begin to acquire a L2 in childhood and even adolescence enjoy a greater ability to discern differences between L1 and L2 sounds, suggesting that the interaction between the L1 and L2 sound systems at the time of L2 acquisition may form at least one source of differences in L2 speech learning documented in learners of diverse age groups. A three-year-long naturalistic experience of learning the target language has been shown to benefit all learners in terms of their L2 perceptual abilities, although child and teenage naturalistic L2 learners seem to be advantaged in yet another – qualitatively different – manner in their L2 speech learning. As Flege and MacKay (2011) have pointed out, however, it may not be possible to disentangle the relative strength of the influence of each of these factors on L2 speech learning, as the factor of age is a macro-variable associated with a number of other underlying variables, one of the more prominent ones being phonetically relevant L2 input. Another challenge remains in terms of finding suitable ways to establish adequate measures of L2 phonetic input/learning experience, capturing its qualitative dimensions, and to measure the perception of cross-language phonetic similarity among L2 learners of diverse age groups. The current study hopes to add to this discussion on child/teenage–adult differences in L2 segmental acquisition and to inspire much needed further research in the area.

Acknowledgements

Earlier versions of parts of this work were presented at New Sounds 2010 and appear in the proceedings of that symposium. The research was supported by a grant to the Polish Diaspora Project (2007–2009) awarded by the Irish Research Council for the Humanities and Social Sciences. The author wishes to thank the editor and an anonymous reviewer for their helpful comments on the manuscript.

References

Anglia Placement Test (2009) Anglia Examination Syndicate, Chichester University. Online document, http://www.anglia.org
Baker, W., Trofimovich, P., Mack, M. and Flege, J.E. (2002) The effect of perceived phonetic similarity on non-native sound learning by children and adults. *Proceedings of the Annual Boston University Conference on Language Development* 26 (1), 36–47.
Baker, W., Trofimovich, P., Flege, J.E., Mack, M. and Halter, R. (2008) Child–adult differences in second language phonetic learning: The role of cross-language similarity. *Language and Speech* 51 (4), 317–342.
Best, C.T. (1995) A direct realist view of cross-language speech perception. In W. Strange (ed.) *Speech Perception and Linguistic Experience: Issues in Cross-language Research* (pp. 171–204). Timonium, MD: York Press.
Best, C.T. and Strange, W. (1992) Effects of phonological and phonetic factors on cross-language perception of approximants. *Journal of Phonetics* 20 (3), 305–330.
Best, C.T. and Tyler, M.D. (2007) Non-native and second-language speech perception. Commonalities and complementarities. In O-S. Bohn and M. Munro (eds) *Language Experience in Second Language Speech Learning: In Honour of James Emil Flege* (pp. 13–34). Amsterdam: John Benjamins.
Bogacka, A. (2004) On the perception of English high vowels by Polish learners of English. In E. Daskalaki, N. Katsos, M. Mavrogiorgos and M. Reeve (eds) *CamLing 2004: Proceedings of the University of Cambridge Second Postgraduate Conference in Language Research* (pp. 43–50). Cambridge: Cambridge Institute of Language Research/Cambridge University Press.

Bohn, O-S. and Flege, J.E. (1990) Interlingual identification and the role of foreign language experience in L2 vowel perception. *Applied Psycholinguistics* 11 (3), 303–328.

Bond, Z.S. and Adamescu, L. (1979) Identification of novel phonetic segments by children, adolescents and adults. *Phonetica* 36, 182–186.

Bosch, L., Costa, A. and Sebastián-Gallés, N. (2000) First and second language vowel perception in early bilinguals. *The European Journal of Cognitive Psychology* 12 (2), 189–221.

Bundgaard-Nielsen, R.L., Best, C.T. and Tyler, M.D. (2011) Vocabulary size matters: The assimilation of second-language Australian English vowels to first-language Japanese vowel categories. *Applied Psycholinguistics* 32 (1), 51–67.

Cebrian, J. (2006) Experience and the use of non-native duration in L2 vowel categorization. *Journal of Phonetics* 34 (3), 372–387.

Cebrian, J., Mora, J.C. and Aliaga-Garcia, C. (2011) Assessing crosslinguistic similarity by means of rated discrimination and perceptual assimilation tasks. In M. Wrembel, M. Kul and K. Dziubalska-Kolaczyk (eds) *Achievements and Perspectives in SLA of Speech: New Sounds 2010* (Vol. I, pp. 41–52). Frankfurt am Main: Peter Lang.

Flege, J.E. (1995) Second-language speech learning: Theory, findings, and problems. In W. Strange (ed.) *Speech Perception and Linguistic Experience: Issues in Cross-language Research* (pp. 229–273). Timonium, MD: York Press.

Flege, J.E. (2002) Interactions between the native and second-language phonetic systems. In P. Burmeister, T. Piske and A. Rohde (eds) *An Integrated View of Language Development: Papers in Honor of Henning Wode* (pp. 217–244). Trier: Wissenschaftlicher Verlag.

Flege, J.E. (2003) Assessing constraints on second-language segmental production and perception. In A. Meyer and N. Schiller (eds) *Phonetics and Phonology in Language Comprehension and Production: Differences and Similarities* (pp. 319–355). Berlin: Mouton de Gruyter.

Flege, J.E. (2007) Language contact in bilingualism: Phonetic system interactions. In J. Cole and J.I. Hualde (eds) *Laboratory Phonology 9* (pp. 353–382). Berlin: Mouton de Gruiter.

Flege, J.E., Bohn, O-S. and Jang, S. (1997) Effects of experience on non-native speakers' production and perception of English vowels. *Journal of Phonetics* 25 (4), 437–470.

Flege, J.E. and MacKay, I.R.A. (2004) Perceiving vowels in a second language. *Studies in Second Language Acquisition* 26 (1), 1–34.

Flege, J.E. and MacKay, I.R.A. (2011) What accounts for 'age' effects on overall degree of foreign accent? In M. Wrembel, M. Kul and K. Dziubalska-Kolaczyk (eds) *Achievements and Perspectives in SLA of Speech: New Sounds 2010* (Vol. II, pp. 65–82). Frankfurt am Main: Peter Lang.

Fullana, N. (2006) The development of English (FL) perception and production skills: Starting age and exposure effects. In C. Muñoz (ed.) *Age and the Rate of Foreign Language Learning* (pp. 41–64). Clevedon: Multilingual Matters.

Guion, S., Flege, J.E., Akahane-Yamada, R. and Pruitt, J. (2000) An investigation of current models of second language speech perception: The case of Japanese adults' perception of English consonants. *Journal of the Acoustical Society of America* 107 (5), 2711–2725.

Hazan, V. and Barrett, S. (2000) The development of phonemic categorization in children aged 6–12. *Journal of Phonetics* 28 (4), 377–396.

Højen, A. and Flege, J.E. (2006) Early learners' discrimination of second-language vowels. *Journal of the Acoustical Society of America* 119 (5), 3072–3084.

Jenkins, J.J., Strange, W. and Polka, L. (1995) Not everyone can tell a 'rock' from a 'lock': Assessing individual differences in speech perception. In D.J. Lubinski and R.V. Dawis (eds) *Assessing Individual Differences in Human Behavior: New Concepts, Methods, and Findings* (pp. 297–325). Palo Alto, CA: Davies-Black Publishing.

Jia, G. and Aaronson, D. (2003) A longitudinal study of Chinese children and adolescents learning English in the United States. *Applied Psycholinguistics* 24, 131–161.
Jia, G., Strange, W., Wu, J. and Collado, J. (2006) Perception and production of English vowels by Mandarin speakers: Age-related differences vary with amount of L2 exposure. *The Journal of the Acoustical Society of America* 119 (2), 118–1130.
Johnson, C.A. (2000) Children's phoneme identification in reverberation and noise. *Journal of Speech, Language, and Hearing Research* 43 (1), 144–157.
Kallen, J.N. (1994) English in Ireland. In R. Burchfield (ed.) *The Cambridge History of the English Language* (Vol. 5, pp. 148–196). Cambridge: Cambridge University Press.
Kopečková, R. (2011) Learning vowel sounds in a migrant setting: The case of Polish children and adults in Ireland. In M. Wrembel, M. Kul and K. Dziubalska-Kolaczyk (eds) *Achievements and Perspectives in SLA of Speech: New Sounds 2010* (Vol. II, pp. 137–148). Frankfurt am Main: Peter Lang.
Llanes, À. and Muñoz, C. (forthcoming) Age effects in a study abroad context: Children and adults studying abroad and at home. *Language Learning* 63 (1).
Long, M.H. (1990) Maturational constraints on language development. *Studies in Second Language Acquisition* 12 (3), 251–285.
Mora, J.C., Keidel, J.E. and Flege, J.E. (2011) Why are the Catalan contrasts between /e/–/ɛ/ and /o/–/ɔ/ so difficult for even early Spanish–Catalan bilinguals to perceive? In M. Wrembel, M. Kul and K. Dziubalska-Kolaczyk (eds) *Achievements and Perspectives in SLA of Speech: New Sounds 2010* (Vol. II, pp. 183–194). Frankfurt am Main: Peter Lang.
Moyer, A. (2009) Input as a critical means to an end: Quantity and quality of experience in L2 phonological attainment. In T. Piske and M. Young-Scholten (eds) *Input Matters in SLA* (pp. 159–174). Bristol: Multilingual Matters.
Muñoz, C. (2008) Symmetries and asymmetries of age effects in naturalistic and instructed L2 learning. *Applied Linguistics* 29 (4), 578–596.
Muñoz, C. (2011) Input and long-term effects of starting age in foreign language learning. *International Review of Applied Linguistics in Language Teaching (IRAL)* 49 (2), 113–133.
Rojczyk, A. (2011) Production and perception of vowel /æ/ by Polish learners of English. In M. Wrembel, M. Kul and K. Dziubalska-Kolaczyk (eds) *Achievements and Perspectives in SLA of Speech: New Sounds 2010* (Vol. II, pp. 239–250). Frankfurt am Main: Peter Lang.
Scovel, T. (1988) *A Time to Speak: A Psycholinguistic Inquiry into the Critical Period for Human Speech.* New York: Newbury House Publishers.
Sebastián-Gallés, N. (2005) Cross-language speech perception. In D.B. Pisoni and R.E. Remez (eds) *The Handbook of Speech Perception* (pp. 546–566). Oxford: Blackwell Publishing.
Sebastián-Gallés, N. and Soto-Faraco, S. (1999) Online processing of native and non-native phonemic contrasts in early bilinguals. *Cognition* 72, 111–123.
Slavoff, G. and Johnson, J. (1995) The effects of age on the rate of learning a second language. *Studies in Second Language Acquisition* 17 (1), 1–16.
Snow, C. E. and Hoefnagel-Höhle, M. (1977) Age differences in the pronunciation of foreign sounds. *Language and Speech* 20 (4), 357–365.
Tsukada, K., Birdsong, D., Bialystok, E., Mack, M., Sung, H. and Flege, J.E. (2005) A developmental study of English vowel production and perception by native Korean adults and children. *Journal of Phonetics* 33 (3), 263–290.

Index

abroad 60–61, 141–142, 146–147, 151–156, 161–176, 193–207, 213–231, 239, 252
  stay 146–147, 151–156, 161, 164–165, 169, 175
  study 60–61, 141–142, 155, 161–176, 193–207, 213–231
  term 218–219, 231, 239, 252
accuracy 119–120, 125, 127–129, 195, 197, 219, 228, 230
  grammatical 119–120, 125, 127–129, 219
  oral 195, 197, 228
  written 197, 230
age 37, 141–142, 143–144, 193–207, 235–236, 238, 250
  starting 37, 141, 143–144, 238
agency 147–157
AH *see* at home
aptitude 46–49, 60–61, 145, 170
assimilation 147, 153–156, 236–237, 240–242, 250–252,
at home (AH) 25, 119, 142, 146, 153–154, 174, 200–204, 211–212, 216–228, 230
attitudes 13, 28, 38, 61, 161, 164, 166–168, 171, 174–176, 188–189
Audio-Pal 13, 92–93, 95–98, 106
automatization 11, 156, 206, 215

beliefs 155, 161–162, 165–170, 174–176, 187–188
bilingualism 28–29, 31, 39–40, 113, 131, 204

complexity 119–120, 125–128, 197, 205, 219, 223–224, 228
  grammatical 119–120, 125–128, 197, 205, 219, 223–224, 228
  lexical 205, 219, 224
concentrated form 47–48

development 3, 15, 48, 59, 88, 130, 134, 156, 165, 166–167, 171–172, 174–175, 215–216, 219, 222, 223, 226, 226–227, 229, 230, 251, *see also* language, linguistic, oral, written
distributed 5, 10–14, 17–18
  conditions 11, 18
  schedules 5, 11
  sequences 10
distributions 7, 10, 14, 49
  spaced 7
drip-feed 12, 16, 45, 48, 58–60, 89, 142, 166
  approach 166
  courses 12
  instruction 142
  programs 16

Erasmus 162, 165–167, 217
  experience 166–167, 172
  program 166, 168, 175
  scheme 218
  students 162, 165–166, 169, 175, 198–199
errors 29, 70, 117, 122, 125, 195–206, 220, 223, 230
ESL (English as a second language) 31, 33–38, 41, 66, 70, 88–93, 101, 105–108, 111
European Schools 111–134
exposure 10–11, 16, 45–50, 58–60, 67–68, 70, 79, 81–84, 119–124, 141–144, 161, 169, 196–197, 213–218, 230

fluency 74–75, 80, 94, 96–101, 104–106, 117–118, 120, 122–123, 197, 205, 216, 224
  oral 120, 193, 197, 216, 219, 229–230

pause 74–75, 80, 94, 96–101, 104–106, 117–118, 122–123, 216
  repair 118
  speed 104–105, 118
  written 197, 205, 216, 224

immersion 13, 25, 25–41, 111, 113, 115, 130–133, 142, 154, 156, 193, 238, 249–252
  dual 31, 38–40
  French 13, 27–34, 37, 39–40, 115
implicit 142–143, 205–207, 215
Info-Gap 13, 92–96, 101, 104–106, 109
input 66–67, 70–71, 76, 82–83, 125
  classroom 67, 82, 125,
  instructional 66, 70–71, 76, 83
  teacher 27, 34–35, 59–60, 67, 71, 74, 76–78, 81–82, 125
intensive 12–19, 23, 32–34, 36–38, 40–41, 46–50, 52, 55–56, 58–62, 66–67, 83, 88–109, 142–144, 142, 153–154, 207, 213–218
  context 48, 83, 146, 153–154
  course 12, 15–16, 18, 47
  English 12–15, 34, 66
  experience 46, 48, 50, 52, 55–56, 58, 60, 67
  exposure 142–144, 207, 213–218
  French 13, 32–33, 37–38, 40
  instruction 13, 15–18, 23, 36, 41, 47–48, 92, 106
  program 13–19, 46–50, 58–62, 88–109
  students 83, 98–101, 103–104
intervals 4–7, 9–11, 15, 18
  retention 4–6, 9–10, 15, 18
  spaced 7
items 4, 6–10
  massed 4, 8–10
  spaced 4, 6–8, 10

L2 *see* second language
language development 3, 15, 48, 59, 130, 156, 165
le bain linguistique 32, 43
learners 143, 235, 252
  early 143, 235, 252
  late 143
learning 41, 60, 91, 116, 119–121, 124–125, 143–144, 146–147, 153–155, 162, 165, 193–207, 213–230, 234, 236, 238–239, 244, 249, 252–253

context 119–121, 124, 146, 153–154, 162, 193–207, 213–230
experience 41, 60, 91, 125, 146–147, 162, 165, 195, 234, 236, 238–239, 244, 249, 252–253
histories 143–144, 154–155
mechanisms 116, 205–207
linguistic 15, 125, 161–162, 165, 171–172, 174, 213, 215–217, 220, 230
  development 134, 166–167, 171–172, 174–175, 216, 223, 251
  gains 15, 161–162, 165, 171–172, 220
  progress 125, 172, 174, 213, 215–217, 230
literacy 27–28, 30, 36, 38, 41, 112, 114, 216
  skills 38, 41

majority language 30, 38, 40
  children 30
  groups 32, 39
massed 4–12, 14, 18
  condition 11
  presentations 4, 8, 10
  programme 14, 18
  sequences 6–7, 10
mini-intensives 13–14, 16
minority language 25, 30–32, 34, 39–40
  children 30, 39
  groups 32
  students 31, 40
mixed methods design 89–90

oral 13, 59, 88–96, 108, 175, 194–195, 220–230
  competence 219–220
  development 88, 216, 226–227, 229
  production 13, 59, 108, 175, 194–195, 220, 222–230
  skills 59, 88, 113, 149, 172, 194, 205, 215–216, 227, 229–230
orientations 143, 145, 165–167, 171, 174, 176, 189

past tense 11, 68, 72–76, 78–81, 83,
PDs (possessive determiners) 69–84
perception 236, 238, 248–250, 252
  abilities 236, 238, 248–250, 252
perceptions 139, 147, 156, 161, 164–171, 174–175, 195
Perceptual Assimilation Model (PAM) 236–237, 241, 249
possessive determiners 67–72, 78, 80, 82

practice 4–5, 16, 18, 107, 147, 151, 154–156, 204–207, 213, 215–217, 219, 227
proceduralization 215
production 13, 59, 83, 108, 168, 175, 194–195, 204, 220–230
programs 3, 14, 12–19, 26–42, 47–49, 58–61, 88–109, 111–117, 121–123, 129–134, 137–138, 142, 154, 194, 198, 213–214, 218–219, 230
   concentrated 3, 12, 14–16, 18, 47–48, 142
   distributed 14, 16–18, 142

recency effects 9, 18
retention 4–6, 8–10, 12, 15–16, 18–19 *see also* intervals

SA (study abroad) *see* abroad
salience 68, 70, 74–85
school 12, 26–42, 66–67, 70, 88–93, 101, 105, 107–108, 111–134, 166, 240
   primary 34, 112–113, 123–124, 126, 129–131, 166, 240
   secondary 12, 29, 36, 112–115, 124, 128–131, 166, 240
second language (L2)
   acquisition 4, 9–12, 84, 90, 133, 141, 164, 193, 196, 234, 251–252

learning 3, 13, 15–19, 47–49, 66, 11–112, 116, 118–125, 128–133, 195–196, 234, 236, 238–239
perception 236, 248–249, 252
stay abroad *see* abroad
study abroad *see* abroad
production 204
spaced 11, 18
   conditions 11
   sequences 18
spacing effect 3–19
speech learning 235–237, 243, 248, 252–253,
Speech Learning Model (SLM) 235–236, 246, 249
Story-Retell 92–98, 101, 106
strategies 99, 101, 104–106, 164

teacher 27, 34–35, 59–60, 67, 71, 74, 76–79, 81–82, 91, 107–108, 113, 125
talk 76, 79, 82 (*see* input)
time distribution 3–4, 7–8, 10–19

written 59, 205–206, 215–216, 219, 222–223, 225, 227–230
   development 215–216, 219, 222, 226, 230
   production 59, 222–223, 225, 227–230
   skills 205–206, 215–216, 219, 230

For Product Safety Concerns and Information please contact our EU Authorised Representative:

Easy Access System Europe

Mustamäe tee 50

10621 Tallinn

Estonia

gpsr.requests@easproject.com

www.ingramcontent.com/pod-product-compliance
Lightning Source LLC
Chambersburg PA
CBHW070556300426
44113CB00010B/1278